The 65 Best Bicycle Park & Rail Trails in Ontario*

* till the next edition

Second Edition, 2019

ISBN 978-1-9991353-2-4

No government funding or support was provided for this project.

All photos and maps by Dan Roitner, unless otherwise noted - photo credit page 144, 146 public domain, 8, 147 Shutterstock, 151 B.Bieri

Terms of Use

We hope you enjoy using this guide and have a great bike ride.

By using this guidebook, you agree to take on all risks and responsibilities.

This book is for informational purposes only. The author takes no responsibility for, nor guarantees the accuracy of, the content of this book. Efforts were made to be up-to-date, but trails and conditions do change frequently so do not assume the information and maps to be accurate.

By using this published information, you agree we cannot be held liable for any injury, inconvenience, or financial loss that may occur while visiting any area mentioned or when dealing with any club, organization, or business listed in this book or on the website.

Ride safely, and within your own skill level. Always wear a helmet, be sure you can be seen, and have lights at night.
Bike riding can be dangerous,
so
RIDE AT YOUR OWN RISK
but have FUN too!

Table of Contents

Introduction

Welcome, bike riders, to the **second edition** of my **Trail Guide**. It's bigger and better, with updates and more polish!

This book is meant to act as a starting point for you to dream about and plan future bicycle outings. The weekend is here, the sun is out... where to go?

My goal has always been to limit the time wasted trying to find new riding locations. You want to head out, not sit around and do research!

Therefore, I've kept the listings and reviews short, with maps and a few photos to either pique your interest or help you move on to the next page.

Once you understand how I rate trails, I'm confident this guide has enough detail for you to quickly assess which spots are worth trying.

This guide contains the **best cycling trails** and **paths in Ontario** that I know of, and have visited. I assure you I have ridden each at least once, if not many times in the last few decades.

Not everything out there is in here yet; I hope to keep adding content in future editions. Still, this guide will keep you busy riding your bicycle for a good long while.

My idea was to list trails long enough for the average cyclist to enjoy as an outing. Locations needed to be worth the drive, with at least **10 km** of potential riding trail, for a **minimum of two hours** of enjoyment.

This amount will vary with a bicyclist's abilities and fitness level, as well as weather conditions. I also added a few shorter rides that are either so popular or so scenic/interesting that they warrant mentioning.

My goal was to **rate trails consistently** so you have a **reliable comparison** and reference. I find this is preferable over many websites, which often have incomplete, user-submitted info that varies greatly.

Another reason I wanted to publish this guide is due to the lack of current data on the trails. Some locations have next to no public information to compile a listing, but I do my best to provide what details I can. It is impossible to be 100% accurate or complete, but I sure do try!

Every bicycle **trail** is 85 to 100% **off-road, car-free cycling**. Even when I mention access roads, I've never seen any vehicles.

Some Rail Trails allow ATV or snowmobile traffic on certain sections or even the entire length of the route, yet most have little traffic—except for summer weekends. Even then, my experience is that most ATV drivers will slow down and are friendly folk.

Finally, some routes may have detours that use public roads to connect, but thankfully most stick to quiet side streets.

Also, remember that all Park and Rail paths are wide enough for **two-way traffic**. Keep to the right and hope others do when riding around blind corners.

Trail maps and signposts are not all placed where I feel it makes good sense. There is a science to informing and directing travellers!

Methods vary widely, so this book tries to fix that; but when in doubt print a map or use a GPS app while you ride. I will point you in the right direction, and even offer suggestions for parking and amenities, but I leave it up to you to tailor your trip from there.

About **80%** of the rides highlighted in this book are suitable for anyone who can stand up on a bike. All city Park paths are designed to offer everyone, from kids to seniors, access to safe and relaxing recreational bike rides.

These paths and many of the Rail Trails are very effortless to travel, but I leave it to you to judge how far your friends and family can go and still keep smiling.

Above all, be conservative about your riding abilities. If you only get out a few times a year, nothing is worse than overdoing it on the first ride of spring. Bad experiences can lead to your bicycle hanging, oh so lonely, in the garage long after that.

Some trails are classified as both a **Park trail** and a **Rail trail**. These are situated in a park setting, and use an old railway line as the path.

Trails listed in **forest areas** are known primarily for mountain biking. Yet, when I MTB at these places, I see other easier paths perfect for a Park rider to enjoy. Therefore, you will find not only city Park paths in this guide, but also more **Intermediate**-skilled forest routes.

Who knows? When riding a Park path in the forest, you may be tempted to transition to beginner Mountain Bike (MTB) trails that loop off these main routes. You might like it and advance into that sport too!

Still, this guide focuses on Park and Rail-type trails at these locations. I will be publishing a separate **Mountain Bike Trail Guide** eventually, which will cover those trails specifically.

You may see a few comments about MTB loops or trail lines on a map, but I do not attempt to add them all. I also do not mention "unofficial" locations or trails, as I want landowners and riders to stay on good terms.

In this edition, I interchange the words **trail** and **path** at times—they generally mean the same thing. However, I consider a path wider than a trail.

The province of Ontario is a big place, it's immense! Though there are a few trails up in Northern Ontario and beyond Lake Superior, my focus is here in **Southern Ontario** where the population is. My apologies to fellow Northerners, perhaps in the next edition...

Finally, I'd like to mention that all trails listed are suitable for any type of **hybrid bicycle** in good working order. A bike that is well-maintained and has wide tires with some tread will fare well.

Race bikes with skinny road tires can be used on most city paths; it gets too rough for these bikes on forest Park trails and Rail Trails. A safer, more enjoyable and comfortable ride, can be found using a hybrid bike or MTB with shocks.

So as not to be too repetitive here, refer to the back of this guide to learn the finer points of what a Park and Rail Trail experience is.

eBikes, or electric-powered bicycles, are a new form of bike riding. I confess I am waiting for the status of these zippy two wheelers to get established. Right now, there is some confusion and backlash seeing them on our paths.

Even the definition between an electric scooter and a smaller bicycle with a motor are thought of as the same thing. Yet are they? Regardless, I am starting to see new signage appear to keep them off the trails. If you own one, be sure to check into this yourself.

I do question the wisdom here, as these powered bicycles can help elderly or disabled riders enjoy the outdoors, and go farther as we do. Perhaps one day we shall have to employ the same to keep our cycling pastime going.

Did we not have a similar shake down when those evil mountain bikes and snowboards came on the scene years ago?

I've done my best to include most of Ontario's top trails, but there are a few more still to scout and even some I do not know of!

If you can recommend any good ones I've missed, send me, Dan Roitner, a note at staff@ontariobiketrails.com. I welcome any feedback to improve this guide and inform the bicycling community we belong to.

Remember you can certainly post **your own Ride Review** at the bottom of any trails page on the OBT website. We all want to know how your ride went!

A portable **PDF version of this edition** is also included for **free** with the purchase of a printed hardcopy of this book. Download instructions for the **eBook** file are found at the back of this book.

Use the **eBook** as a handy guide on your phone, tablet, or desktop computer. Some details will change with time, so refer to the links provided within the eBook to bring you up-to-date.

Finally, working on this **book project** took more hours than I can count. This included many revisions, proofreading, map-making, photo-editing, and page-layout skills to get it to where you can enjoy this edition. (Add the time and expense to ride these locations and you know I don't do it for the money!)

With that, I would like to **thank you for buying this book** to support me, my Ontario Bike Trails (OBT) website, and the world of cycling. I thank you for caring and making it happen!

I hope you enjoy reading, (and dreaming), about these trail locations, and then go out and actually ride them! Promise?

Happy Trails, Dan Roitner

Using This Guide

Definition of Trail Listings:

Here is a list of the headings found on each trail review, with descriptions to help you understand and use this guide.

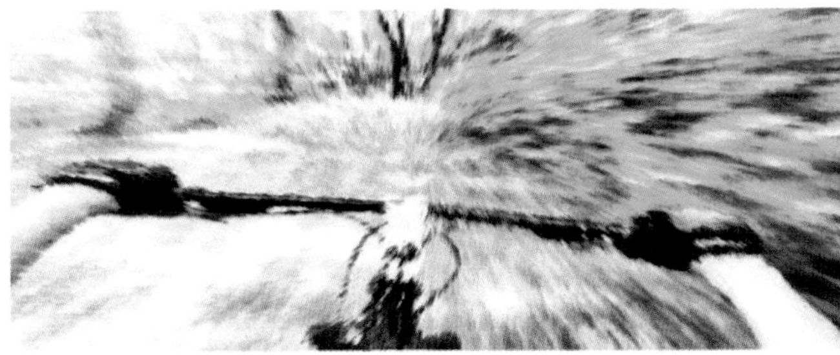

Length: All trail lengths are marked in kilometres and rounded up; they indicate the length of the ride going **one way**. Double the mileage for a return trip on the same path.

(I estimate the **% percentage** of the type of trail/path/road you may encounter or expect at that location.)

Park path: These are as wide as a car, and are most often paved asphalt; they wind through parkland over gentle hills, if any.

Hiking trail: These are narrow and single person in width; mostly rather straight lines hikers have made. Some hills may get steep.

Double-track access road: Wide as a car with perhaps two worn grooves made by wheels (although vehicles are seldom seen). Many are cross-country ski trails in the winter, with gradual, sloping hills.

Mountain Bike (MTB) single-track trail: These paths are narrow, similar to a hiking trail. They meander, have steep hills, are cut for less erosion, and contain difficult challenges like rocks, logs, drops, and wooden structures.

Rail trail path: These are flat, old rail-track beds repurposed for recreational traffic. They are as wide as a train, but likely grown over through the years to some degree.

Roads, crossings, and detours: These refer to roads or road crossings where regular vehicle traffic is to be expected. Usually, these roads are quiet neighbourhood streets and country side roads. Stairs may be encountered on these paths, and some have a handy wheel track to roll your bike along as you walk up the steps.

Detours take you off the regular path due to temporary trail repairs or permanent obstructions like private land and missing bridges.

Elevation: Basically, this warns you of any hills you may need to power up along the way. Most city Park trails are easy on the hill climbs, and a few short, gradual ups-and-downs through underpasses or over bridges may be all you encounter.

Since most trails tend to follow running water, like creeks and rivers, you may find there is a slight slope.

Note that a Park ride through a **forest tract** is different and harder, and thus rated as an **Intermediate** ride for you city cruisers. I mention any sizable, gradual hills the naturally landscaped paths may have.

As for **Rail Trails**, they have no hills at all; trains don't do hills—at least none that are noticeable. There may be a slight incline of only a few degrees over the course of many kilometres.

Terrain: This refers to the ground you ride over. Most city Park paths are smooth, with paved asphalt and wide dual lanes; a few turn to crushed-stone dust or soil at the outer ends.

With **Park trails in the woods**, paths can get a little rough with a mix of smooth soil, fine stone, gravel, sand, or even wood chips. There may also be mud, puddles, holes made by animals, and rocks to navigate around.

The more popular and well-maintained **Rail Trails** typically have crushed stone dust as a base, as well as sections of paved asphalt.

Lesser used, more remote routes can get rather rough and weedy with tall grasses, gravel, sand patches, large puddles (ponds) and even gopher holes to contend with. (To some this gets to be too much effort or risk, but for others who love the challenge and adventure—bring it on! A mountain bike is a better choice at this point.)

Skill: I use a simple, three-level rating system: **Easy, Intermediate, Advanced**.

Trails are rated at the **minimum skill level** a bike rider needs to enjoy the trail and be safe. This is determined by how easy or hard the **elevation** and **terrain** is for a rider in that **category**, be it a Park or Rail Trail.

(Note: **I do not base it on the distance one could travel.** I leave that to you to judge how far you can cycle there and back.)

Maps: To guide you, most locations have a map at the trailhead and signs on the routes. I have made note of the few locations that have nothing; no maps or signs. (In this case, printing a map beforehand or using a map phone app may be wise.)

City trails are usually well marked, although a route may suddenly fork and leave you to wonder which one to take. (Typically, the straighter, more level, and well-used path is the right one to pick! Often, trails that veer off and go up, end by exiting onto a neighbourhood street.)

On forest trails you are likely to come across signs stating their difficulty by rating the skill level required to take that loop.

A green circle is **Easy**, a blue square is **Intermediate**, black diamond is **Advanced,** and a double black diamond is **Expert** —just as you would see on a ski hill. (I have seen these ratings vary from accurate to humorous, and none even compare to the killer stuff in Utah or BC!)

Traffic: On Park paths in the city, it is a given you may be sharing the route with **walkers (and their dogs), joggers, people rollerblading, strollers, eBikers, skateboarders, little kids**, and other **cyclists.**

Not to say the trails are a constant traffic jam by any means, but on nice, sunny warm days you and everyone else may have the same idea....

Rail Trails and forest paths have a greater variety of users you may encounter. This ranges from **cyclists, hikers, joggers, horseback riders,** and even **Nordic skiers** in the winter. Some routes allow **ATVs, dirt bikes** and **snowmobile** users on some or all of the length. Posted trail signage will let you know what is permitted.

Traffic on **Rail Trails** in the country is always very light. Some are seldom used.

Facilities: I listed those services and amenities useful to cyclists, located either along the trail or close by: **public parking,** areas to find **food/drink** (variety stores to restaurants), **toilets, lodging** and **camping sites, swimming areas, bike shops** and **rentals.** Some of these key locations I have added to the maps.

Highlights: Included is a short list of what you might see and experience as **scenic, interesting, or unique.**

Trail Fee: Most locations are **free**, but some carry a small cost for a trail pass. (A big thanks to all the volunteers who keep these trails going!)

Phone: Some locations have a phone number for general information; most do not.

Website: Search this name of government or landowner related websites, if one exists.

Similar Trails: These other locations would be similar in **difficulty, features** and **terrain**. Find other trails in this book or on the ontariobiketrails.com (OBT) website to try!

Local Clubs: Regional bicycle clubs that may ride at this location. These are typically **MTB and road-riding clubs** that may incorporate off-road trails in their group ride schedules.

(Check them out! It is always good to try new rides, go farther, and make new friends.)

Access: This lists the location of the trail, as well as a few tips on how to get to a **parking lot** and find the **trailhead**. Some locations have an exact address, others have none.

Routes that are long, with no definitive starting location and many entry points, will have no set address but I have noted popular parking areas on the maps.

I also may mention basic directions to get to the trailhead, but a better, more convenient and accurate way is to use a map phone app or your car's navigational system.

Also on the OBT website, on any trail review site page, you will find the **TAB - Map & Directions** linked to **Google Maps** to help get you there.

History: Many **Rail Trails** have a history to them, and I find a little history is a good thing to reflect on as you "ride the rails". Not every old rail line has a colourful history, but if I find some interesting points, I do add them. (notated in blue text)

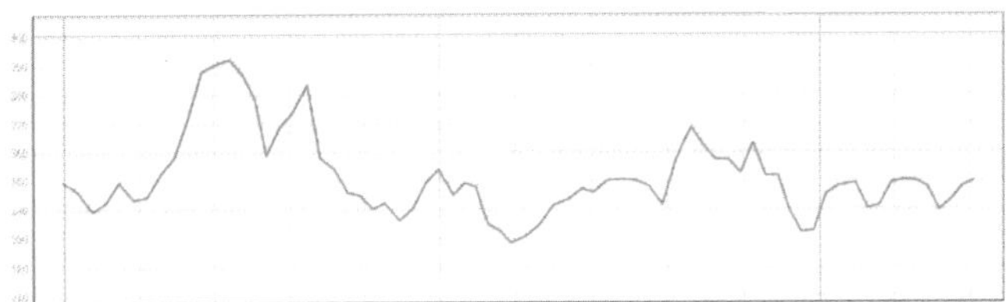

Elevation Graph: A new addition exclusive to this edition, is elevation graphs of the terrain. All diagrams show a span of **100 metres of height** unless otherwise noted. The trails on the charts **run left to right,** starting either at the beginning on the **west end** or **south side** of the route.

Where the location has numerous trails looping around, a **general cross-section** of the elevation is illustrated.

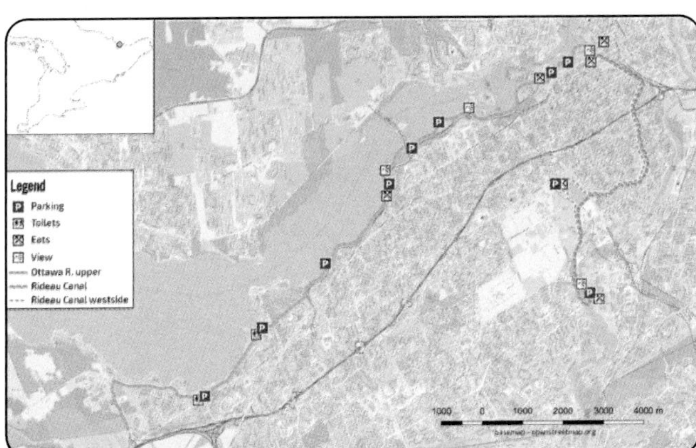

Route Map: I made these maps, just for this book. They show the general layout of the trails and paths for **Park** or **Rail Trail** routes.

There may be other, lesser roads or MTB routes included as aids, but not necessarily all. I encourage you to use these maps as a general guide when planning your ride; but they are still basic so don't rely on them solely for survival!

There are **4 key points** riders want to know: where to **park the car, are there toilets, where to get food** and **drink,** and any **interesting views?** They are marked accordingly:

 - the location of suggested public car parking (usually free)

 - the location of a toilet or outhouse on a route

 - the location of nearby food stores or restaurants (which have toilets, so I do not mention this twice)

 - the location of a key lookout, significant feature, place of interest

(At times I did not place every known item, as it would clutter the map with too many square markers.)

Review: After riding each location, I write a general description of the experience and summarize the key points: what is the **topography** like, the **condition** of the paths, and any **interesting sights** or hazards to watch for. I may suggest a few sections of the trail you should **favour,** or alternate side loops back to keep the cycling fresh and varied. (noted in brown text)

Some reviews are short, with little on the ride to note, but are included as they still make for a good outing. Others have so much more to mention and I cannot fit it all in!

Photos: Unless noted, all images have been taken by me. I have picked a few choice pictures to include with the reviews, hoping to illustrate what the path looks like or show any significant highlight on the route.

But showing photos of endless trails winding through the woods with no cyclists as reference gets boring; therefore, you may see my son, Trevor, and wife, Teresa, or even me in a few shots.

Ajax Waterfront – Park Trail

Pickering to Ajax

Length – 13+ km (one way)

95% park path
5% road, detours

Elevation – Flat sections with rolling, gentle hills on a coastline hillier than expected, due to small bluffs.

Terrain – Wide with paved asphalt; very little sand or gravel.

Skill – Easy

Maps – Well-marked by large map boards at entrance; follow the white centre line.

Traffic – This is a popular trail on sunny weekends, so expect other bikes, walkers, kids, strollers, dogs, joggers—it's busy.

Facilities – Street parking, washrooms, playgrounds, and park benches.

Highlights – Enjoy waterfront views, biking over bridges, past marsh wildlife and beaches; note the nuclear plant and wind turbine.

Trail Fee – Free

Phone – 416 943 8080

Website – Waterfront Trail, Town of Ajax

Similar Trails – Rouge Waterfront, Beaches Boardwalk, Hamilton Beach

Local Clubs – Durham Cycling Club, Oshawa Cycling Club

Access – Start your journey at one of the many parking lots along the path. **Lake Driveway W. Ajax** is in the middle of the route. The **Pickering GO Train station** is close by, just north of where you can start, for those who do not want to drive.

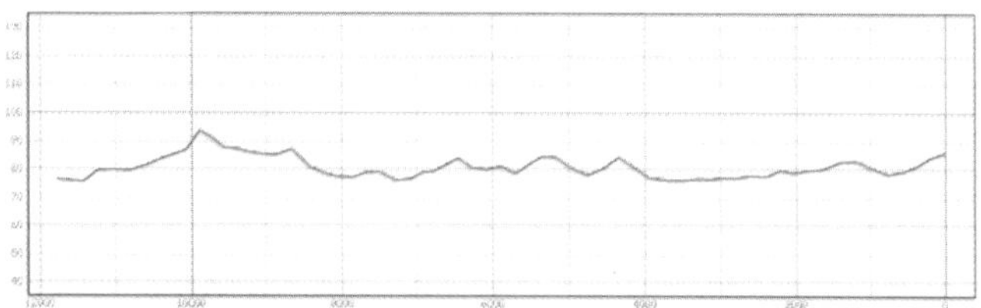

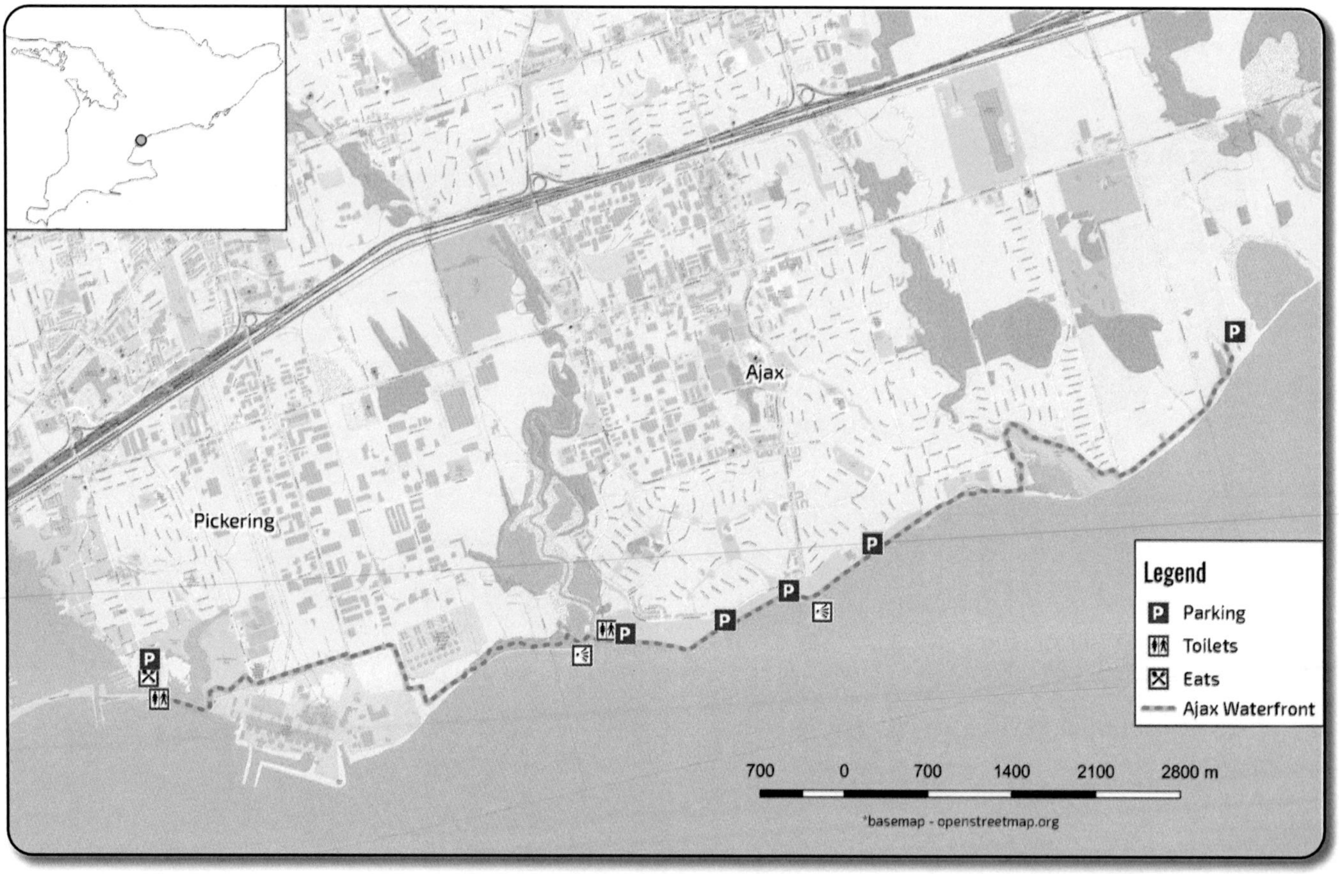

Ajax
Pickering
Legend
Parking
Toilets
Eats
Ajax Waterfront
700 0 700 1400 2100 2800 m
*basemap - openstreetmap.org

Review:

The **13 km Ajax Waterfront trail**, on the east side of **Toronto**, has some of the **best waterfront Park** trail along **Lake Ontario**.

I recommend this section as it is **very scenic**, paved, and free of cars. The views of the lake are almost continuous; something, unfortunately, lacking on the **west side of Toronto.**

Surprisingly, there are a few rolling hills along the route and it winds nicely so as not to make things boring. Most of the trail follows the tops of the **low cliffs** along the lake.

Cruising along here provides many opportunities to stop and go to the **water's edge**. Expect a **cooler ride** with that **lake breeze**, which is welcome on a hot day.

Along the route are enough comfort stations and benches to sit on and **gaze out over the water.**

I suggest starting this section of the trail at **Frenchman's Bay Marina** in **Pickering,** located at the bottom of **Liverpool Rd.** From here, one can ride east to the **Lynde Shores Conservation Area**.

Continuing east, the first part takes you around the **ominous nuclear plant** and past a giant **wind turbine**.

Then, you are back by the lake and will cross **Duffins Creek** via a long metal bridge that is an excellent viewpoint.

Beyond this is open parkland and small beaches. You can turn back at **Shoal Point Rd.,** or go up and around a small, marshy bay through **Lakeside Park** and back to the waterfront, then east to the next marsh at **Halls Rd. - Lynde Shores.**

Here you would head back ... or, beyond either end of this **13 km path**, the trail takes you away from the lake and up around the large bays, which you can certainly ride if you wish.

The **Waterfront Trail** does continue on for hours either way, in a similar patchwork.

There is one tricky intersection which can have traffic: behind the power plant, cross at the lights at the bottom of **Brock Rd.**

The rest of the route is **all paved park trail** and is in great shape. I noted little gravel and sand, and it was not hard to ride. (Code for mellow hills, no potholes, or tight turns.)

Come out with the family this summer and roll along for good times and cool breezes. Enjoy!

Albion Hills – MTB/Park Trail

16500 Hwy 50, N. of Bolton

Length – 50 km

40% MTB single track
30% hiking trail
30% double track access roads

Elevation – Rolling medium hills, with open grass fields, some steep climbs, nice switchbacks, gnarly bits.

Terrain – The smooth soil can be very muddy, also sandy spots, a few rocks, wooden bridges, ramps.

Skill – All levels; best for Intermediate MTB riders or **Park path** riders.

Maps – Paper map at gatehouse; numbered signposts.

Facilities – Parking, bike wash, washrooms, showers, snacks, pool, camping, and Fatbikes for rent.

Highlights – Well maintained, black race trail, lots of variety, chalet, plenty of camping.

Trail Pass – $6.50

Hours – 9 am – 4 pm, weekends to 5 pm

Phone – 905 880 0227

Website – Albion Hill Conservation Area

Similar Trails – Durham Forest, Palgrave, Hardwood

Local Clubs – HAFTA , Caledon Cycling Club, Milton Bicycle Club

Access – Enter the main gate at **16500** on **Hwy 50**, north of **Bolton**. Drive to the parking lot by the chalet; most trails start south up around the bend.

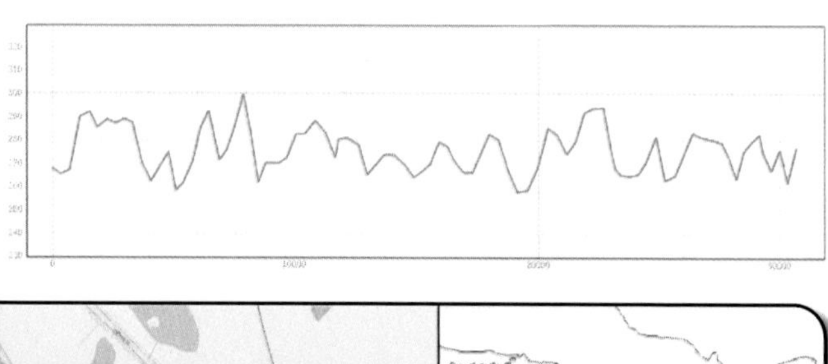

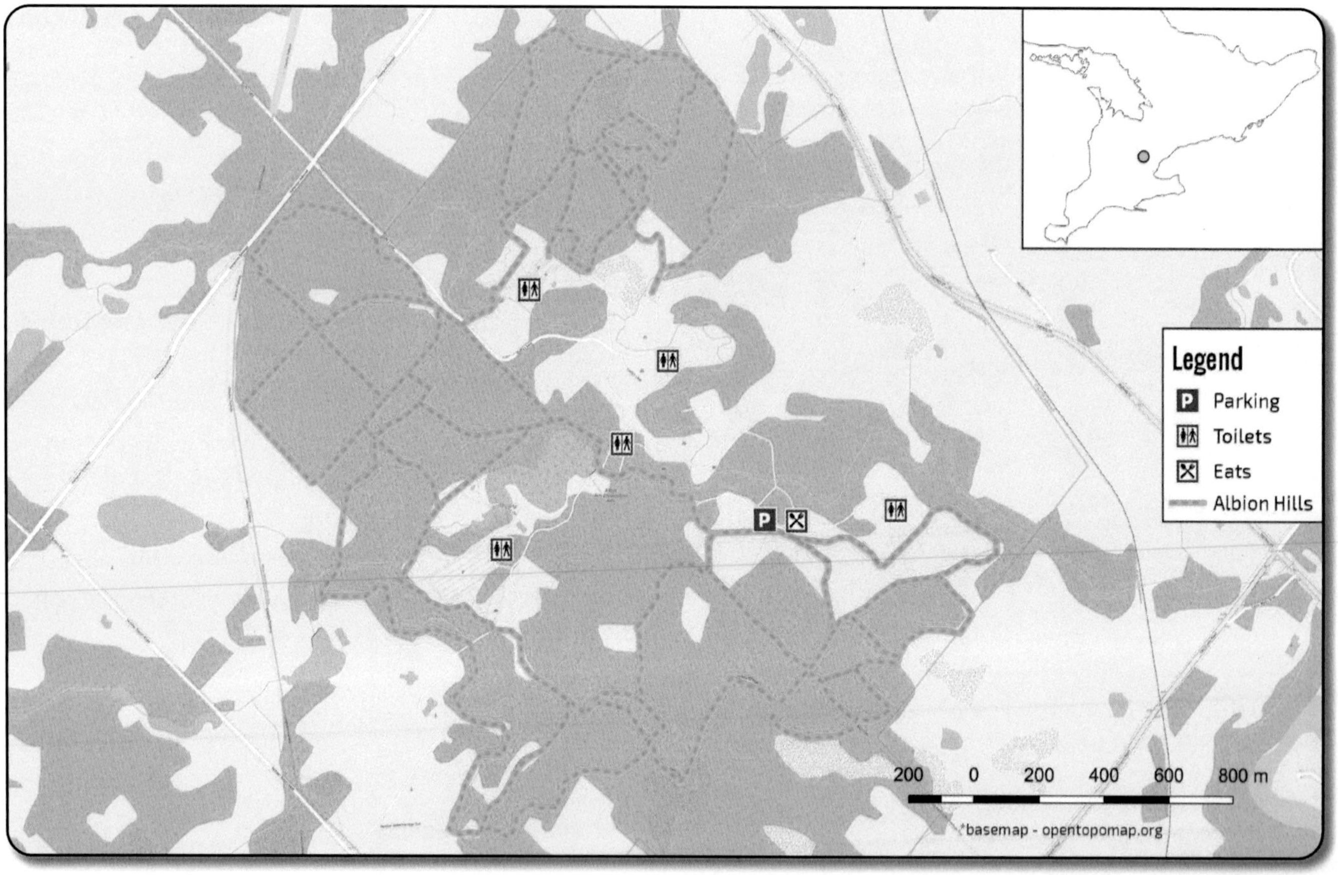

Review:

Albion Hills Conservation Area is a **top MTB destination** on the NW side of **Toronto**.

It offers a **well-cut variety of trails** through a forested area of cross-country ski trails, with lots of single track loops added.

The terrain has a **little of everything** and as the name implies, it has **hills!**

Most of this course flows well, with **bridges, steep climbs, twisty tracks,** open areas, and a scenic cliff view onto the pond (which is now drained!?).

It has some nice, well-cut **switchbacks** that are a blast to ride and a few new **log rollovers, rock drops,** and **rock gardens** added (with optional easy bypasses for the timid).

Recently, a **few route changes have made it even better.** As with any popular area, it has races, so the trail is getting wider, and roots are starting to get exposed, making it now a bumpy ride in sections.

You can work up a good sweat doing the **20 km race course,** which pro MTB riders will love.

In the spring, it can have **bugs** around the wetlands, so keep that bike moving.

As a **Park Trail** type of ride, stay on the easier cross-country ski paths, which are wide on rolling medium-sized hills.

There is **lots of variety** for the family, with various loop lengths you can pick, as you ride in the shade of the woods.

Full amenities make the **trail fee** worth it. As a park, it has **camping** right at the trailhead and decent services to change, shower, swim, wash your bike, and have a snack by the chalet.

Take the **paper map** provided at the **gatehouse** because there are not enough posted maps, except at the chalet. Sure the trails are well-marked with numbers, but without a **map for reference,** you might get lost.

This top spot on warm weekends **gets busy.** Get out of the city, make your way there for the exercise, the challenge or just a recreational ride that you will certainly enjoy.

Awenda – Park Trail

670 Concession 18, E. Penetanguishene

Length – 19 km

80% hiking trail
10% single-track
10% road

Elevation – Rather flat with a few quick dips; pretty mellow overall.

Terrain – Wide, smooth dirt path with some sandy spots, but it can be muddy as not much is paved.

Skill – Easy. Family friendly, with a few hidden harder tracks.

Traffic – Varies, as these trails cut through, and around, a few campgrounds. On a summer weekend it can be busy with family riders and walkers with dogs.

Maps – The main loop has some signs, but it is hard to get lost.

Facilities – Parking, toilets, showers, group and single campsites, and swimming.

Highlights – Georgian Bay and side trails.

Trail Fee – Park day pass is approx. $ 11.00 and up, and a camping pass is approx. $ 33.00 and up.

Phone – 705 549 2231

Website – Ontario Parks

Similar Trails – Bendor, Bracebridge, Fanshawe

Local Clubs – Midland MTB Club

Access – Drive north of **Penetanguishene**, on **Lafontaine Rd. E.** to **Concession Road 16 E**, then turn west to **Awenda Park Rd.**; up the park road a few kilometres is the gate. (670 Concession 18, E.)

There are numerous entry points to the park trails from campgrounds and parking lots.

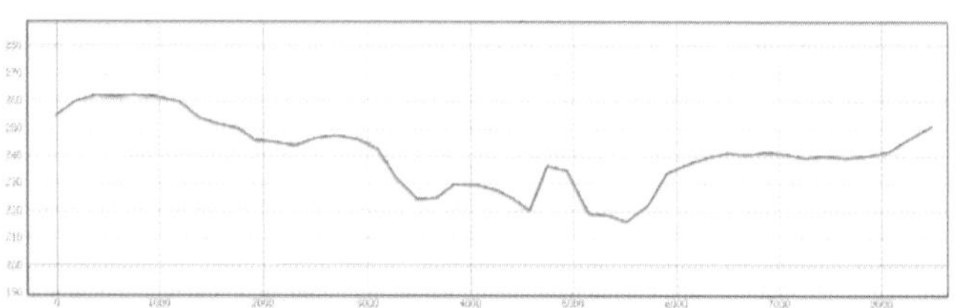

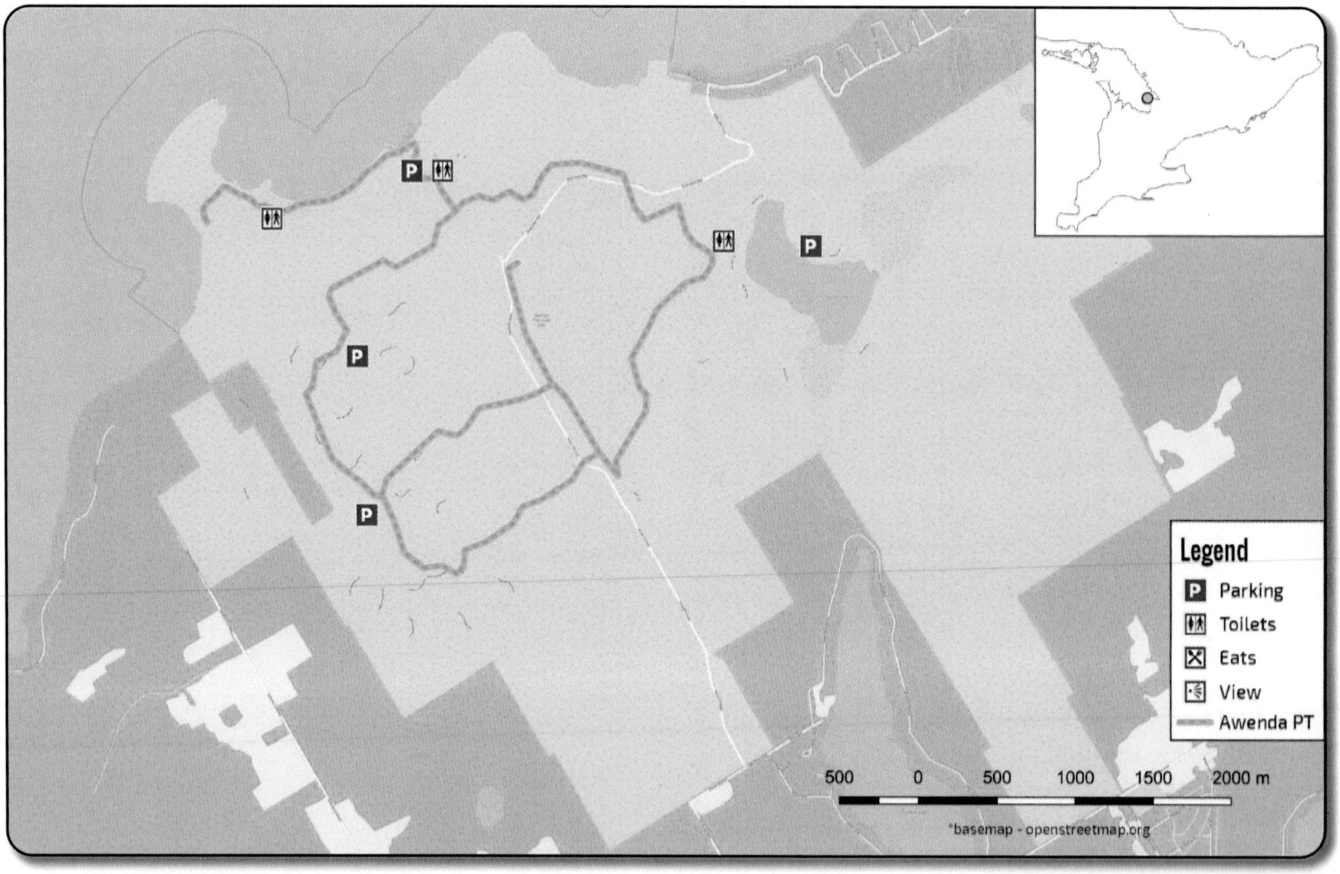

Review:

Awenda Provincial Park is a medium-sized park on the shores of **Georgian Bay,** north of the cities of **Penetanguishene** and **Midland**—also intriguing places to visit.

At **Awenda** there are **three trail options**, plus side trails and park roads.

The **main circular loop** is the **13 km Bluff Trail,** going around the interior of the park. It has a few hills and is good for a morning cycling exercise.

You will travel through a mix of forest and open campgrounds, with views of the **bay** and **the beach** from the **high bluffs** once you get close to the water.

The short, **4 km Brûlé Trail** runs on straighter paths across the main loop and through the forest.

Down at the water, the flat, sandy **4 km Beach Trail** goes west along the Georgian Bay shoreline. Pleasant, open **views of the bay**, with opportunities to soak your feet, make this a suitable endpoint in your riding plans.

At the park, the terrain is flat with gentle hills—except when you head down the bluffs to the beach.

Here, expect a mix of **smooth soil paths** comprised of old forest trails and access roads, with some paved sections.

I do not recall many if any, **rocks or roots** to watch for along these routes. Therefore, it can be a long yet **easygoing pedal,** with enough **shortcuts** to suit any rider and little ones in tow.

Since these trails are inside a **Provincial Park,** you can make plans to **camp** and **swim** while visiting.

Definitely a great destination for a summer weekend outing, and in the fall the colours are really showy.

Beaches Boardwalk – Park Trail

Beaches, Toronto

Length – 9 km (one way)

97% park path
3% road, detours

Elevation – Mostly level, with small, rolling hills on the peninsula.

Terrain – A wide asphalt path with centre line, some sand blown in from beach and gravel spots.

Skill – Easy. Great for cruising.

Traffic – It can get busy, especially around the above ground pool at Woodbine Ave. Watch out for dogs, kids, and meandering tourists that stray onto the bike path—and give people rollerblading lots of space, too!

Maps – Map boards can be found on the trail; follow the blue-green centre line.

Facilities – There are washrooms at four change stations, as well as fast food and rain shelters; limited parking.

Highlights – Take in the beach, lake, city skyline, and parks. Tour Queen St., and see the Leuty Lifeguard Station, RC Harris Water Treatment Plant.

Phone – 311

Website – City of Toronto, The Beaches Wikipedia page.

Similar Trails – Taylor Creek, Toronto Island, Ajax Waterfront

Local Clubs – Toronto Bicycling Network

Access – You can cycle in along the **Martin Goodman Trail**. Parking is a challenge in this area, especially during summer weekends, but try the **Woodbine Park** parking lot. If you can cycle there, then all the better.

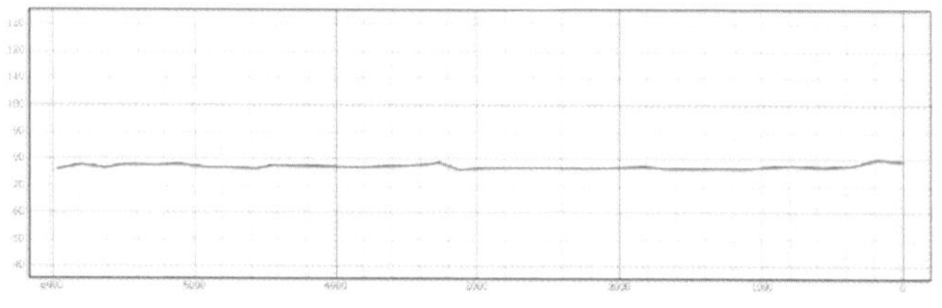

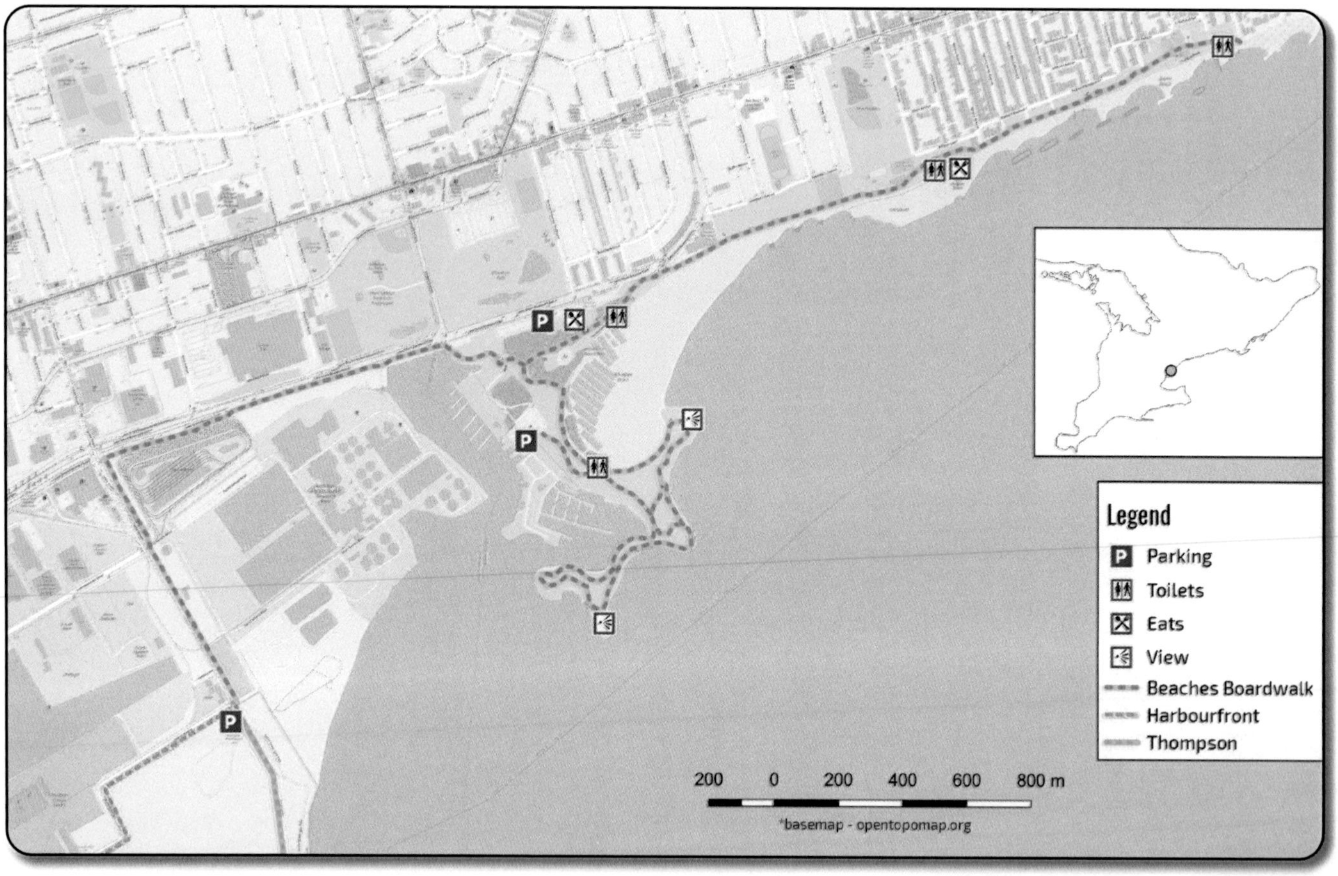

Legend
Parking
Toilets
Eats
View
Beaches Boardwalk
Harbourfront
Thompson

200 0 200 400 600 800 m

*basemap - opentopomap.org

Review:

This **very scenic** bike path is along the **Toronto Beaches**, which runs parallel to the **wooden boardwalk** then around the peninsula and into town.

The eastern starting point of the **20 km Martin Goodman Trail** system can take you cycling for hours through town and to the **Humber River** in the west end—all off-road.

However, the focus for this review is the **Beaches** section, from the bottom of **Leslie Street,** for a short but satisfying **9 km ride** (18 km return trip).

This **Beaches** ride consists of **Woodbine Beach, Kew Beach,** and **Balmy Beach,** plus the **Ashbridges Bay Park** peninsula. On the way there are short side paths to discover, which wind around **Woodbine Park** and **Kew Beach Park**. All are enjoyable spots for a picnic or a nap under a tree.

This paved path starts where **Silver Birch Ave.** meets the lake, and follows the **Lake Ontario** shoreline west. It is naturally a level route with no hills.

Plenty of map boards along the way help plan your route, or you can follow the painted centerline and see where it goes!

As much as you may like to, the wooden boardwalk is for pedestrians only, so please stick to the asphalt bike path.

The view of the lake, and the breeze coming off it, is a pleasure for cyclists on hot summer days. However, it can also get cooler if you go on a spring or autumn spin, so be sure to carry a jacket.

A pleasant side trail can take out to loop around the **Ashbridge's peninsula** for spectacular views of the Beaches area and the marina in the bay.

When you get to **Coxwell Ave**. the path straightens out as it passes **Ashbridges Bay** and parallels **Lakeshore Rd.** This stretch down to **Leslie Ave**., then south, is newly landscaped (but I find dull). It does, however, take you west to **Cherry Beach** or, for another easy ride, onto the **Tommy Thompson Park** peninsula.

North of the path is a chance to visit **Queen St. East,** which bustles with activity and retains a **quaint feel of old Toronto.** Lots of hip shops and eateries are to be found as you stroll. This neighbourhood was, at first, cottage country for the well-off in what was a much smaller **Toronto** in the 1800s.

On the far-east end, beyond the boardwalk, is the water filtration plant, designed in a striking **Art Deco** style.

So, there you have it, my local favourite escape! A short ride mixed with an invitation to check out the neighbourhood and be lazy at **Toronto's best beach area.**

Beltline – Rail Trail

Caledonia Rd. to Bayview Ave., Toronto

Length – 9 km (one way)

75% rail trail path
25% cemetery roads, road crossings, detours

Elevation – Level and flat, with gradual yet long descent after cemetery to the bottom of the east side of Don Valley.

Terrain – A wide path of crushed stone, as well as some gravel, asphalt, dirt sections.

Skill – Easy; Intermediate if you do the valley hill. (Alternate route is at times not well-maintained, Balfour Park, and you might opt to walk.)

Traffic – Bicyclists, joggers, dogs, kids, and a few cars in the cemetery. Will be busy on summer weekends.

Maps – Maps and signage can be found at key points on the route.

Facilities – Nearby stores, pubs on Yonge St.,at Brickworks with toilets.

Highlights – See the subway stockyards at Yonge St., and visit the historic cemetery, the Brick Works gardens, and the ravines.

Phone – 311

Website – None

Similar Trails – Speed River, Greenway

Local Clubs – Toronto Bicycle Network

Access – There are many entry points to this trail. Parking can only be found on side streets, but a large (expensive) lot is located at the **Brick Works.**

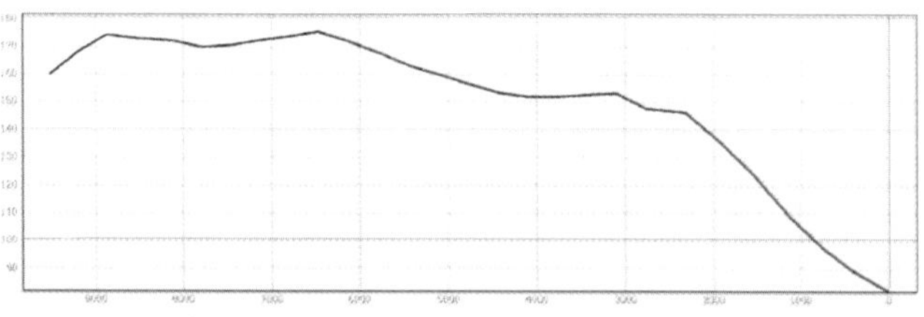

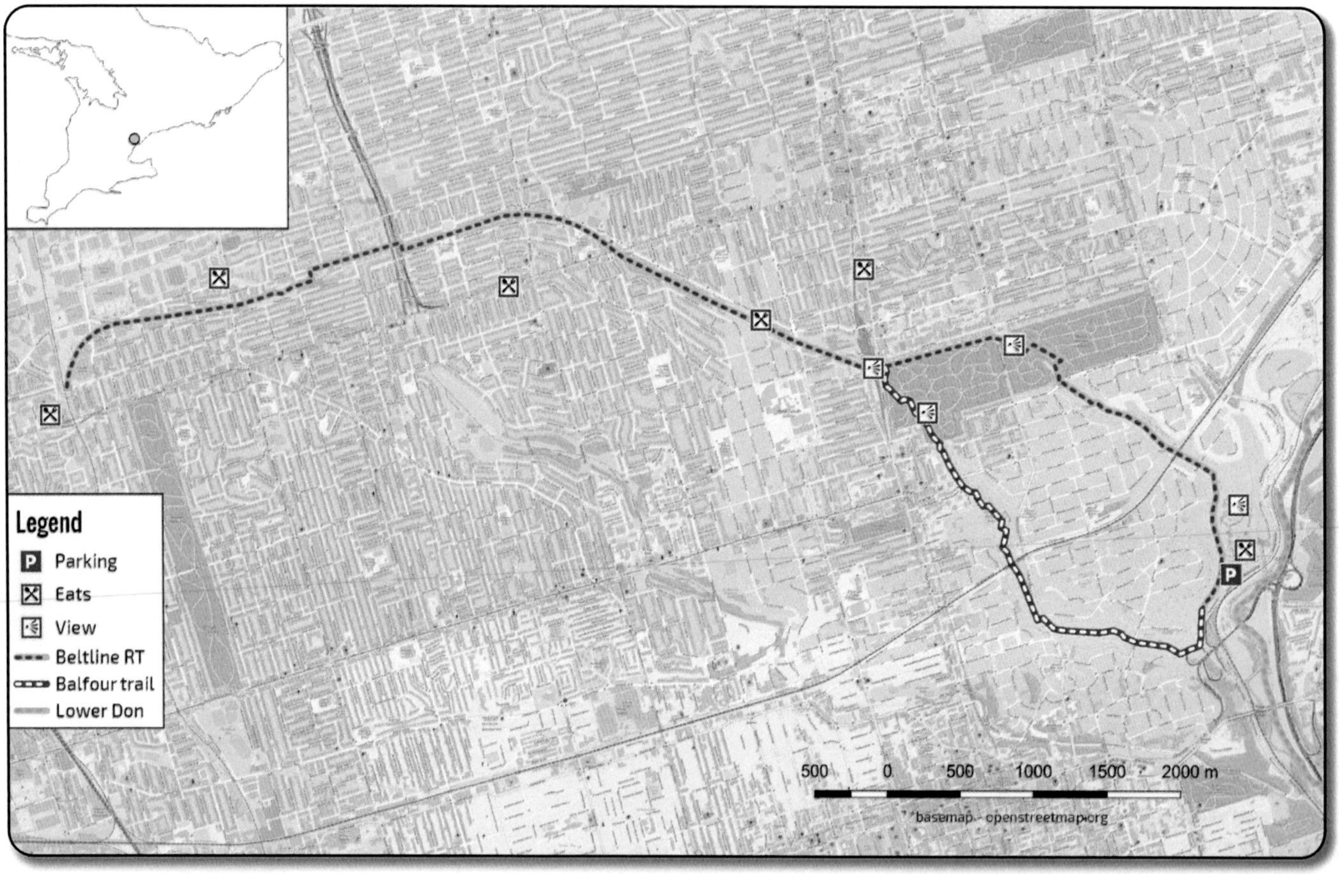

Legend
P Parking
Eats
View
Beltline RT
Balfour trail
Lower Don

500 0 500 1000 1500 2000 m
basemap - openstreetmap.org

Review:

The **Kay Gardner Beltline** and **York Beltline** was once a rail loop that circled the city of **Toronto** in the 1890s. Now, it sits in the **middle of the city**, and you can ride **9 km** of this very popular Rail Trail along the back of homes, as well as past ravines and through a cemetery.

Busy on weekends, it is **a favourite for many bike cruisers** looking for a bit of solitude and fewer cars. Most of the trail is well **treed, shady,** and is a **fun,** flat cycle path. It does have (I've counted) **10 main roads** to get across. Take care at these busy street crossings, and perhaps use the lights to be safe!

From the **east side**, this Rail Trail starts behind the **Brick Works** at the bottom of the **Don Valley.** Up behind the trees you need to follow the **old rail bed** the trains took to get out of the valley. (This has a 4% grade of elevation.) As with any grade found on old rails, it is gradual and anyone in good health will make it up this wide, forested route. (Trains, not so easily!)

Once out of the valley, cross the road and travel through **Mount Pleasant Cemetery.** Here you can find where many famous and well-off people are buried. Head northwest, where there is an underpass to avoid the busy traffic of **Mt. Pleasant Rd.**

On the other side of this underpass, you can connect to the straight **Beltline** trail that crosses **Yonge Street.** I prefer to stay on the cemetery roads and meander westward while checking out the old epitaphs.

As you cycle over the old train bridge, stop for a moment to watch the **TTC subway trains** pass underneath. Here is the main and busiest section of the Rail Trail, full of cyclists, joggers, dog-walkers, and kids.

After a few kilometres of riding under the shady trees and looking in on people's backyards, you reach the wall of the **Allen Expressway.**

To continue, detour north to the next bridge, cross, and follow **Roselawn Ave.** until you see **Beograd Gardens** two blocks away. Take this south to again connect with the path between the buildings. This brief extension of the old rail bed goes another **2 km** to **Bowie Ave.**

Being in the heart of the city, this path has many opportunities to **explore the side streets** lined with **grand homes** in this well-to-do area. Many **local cafes** are nearby to sit awhile, or you can head to the parks or cemetery to relax and read a book.

You can also take a side trail behind the **Brickworks** to explore the ponds created by the big pits which were dug out by the city, many years ago, to make bricks.

ALTERNATE LOOP – On your return, you can take an alternate, **3.5 km,** loop down through **Mount Pleasant Cemetery** again. This time, there will be an entrance to a ravine that follows the **Yellow Creek** past **Balfour Park.** It takes you through a valley, across **Mount Pleasant Rd.,** and on to **Bayview,** on a variety of trail surfaces, and back to the **Brickworks.**

This ravine trail may still be rough and under repair.

History – The **Toronto Beltline Railway** has a short history as the route was used only briefly. Built in **1892** as a **40 km** commuter steam-railway line, trains circled the city, looping from **Union Station** up through **North Toronto** and back.

Over the years, parts of the rail loop were used by other railways as spur lines. Eventually, all rail traffic petered out when the city bought out the land from **CN Rail** in **1972** and is in use today as a public trail.

Bendor – Park Trail

Kennedy Rd., north of Davis Dr, GTA

Length – 7 km

100% park path

Elevation – Small hills with gentle slopes.

Terrain – Wide, treed paths with smooth, packed soil covered (at times) with mulch and leaves. Some sand and open fields on the east side.

Skill – Intermediate for Park riders; Beginner MTBs.

Traffic – Occasional bike, hiker, Nordic skier in winter. Dog-walkers favour this place, so watch for them and poop (especially at the entrances!).

Maps – Map at trailhead; no signposts.

Facilities – Parking only

Highlights – Well treed; close to Toronto but not well-known, so nice and quiet.

Trail Fee – Free

Phone – 877 464 9675

Website – York Regional Forest

Similar Trails – Eldrid King, Whitchurch, Awenda

Local Clubs – Toronto Bicycle Club

Access – Use entrance at the dead end on **Kennedy Rd**. and **Davis Dr.** There is also access from **McCowan Rd.,** which also has a parking lot.

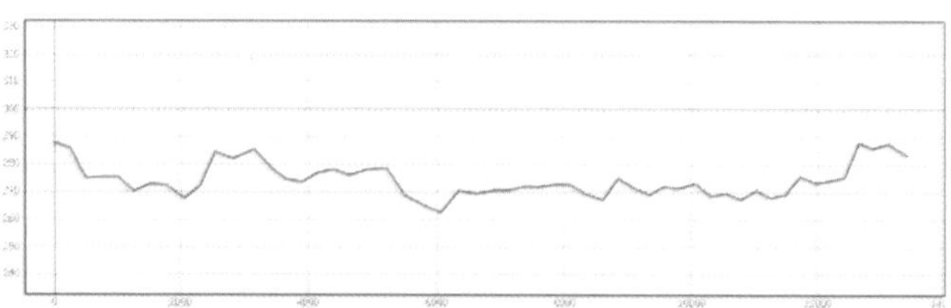

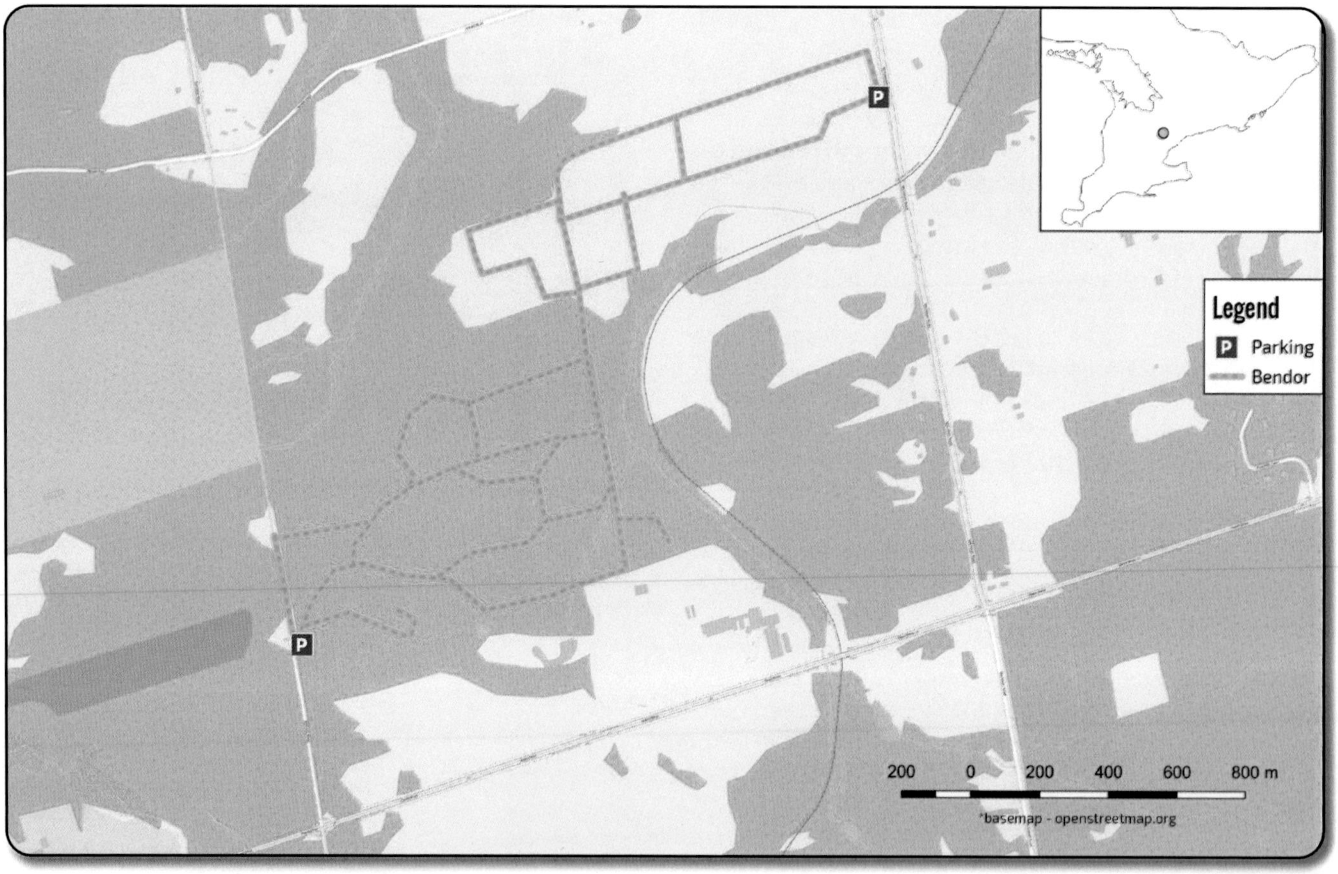

Legend
P Parking
Bendor

200 0 200 400 600 800 m

*basemap - openstreetmap.org

Review:

The **Bendor & Graves Tract** is rated as an **Intermediate Park** type bike ride because it is **not paved**. Beyond that, it is an easy ride for any fit person with a decent hybrid bike.

At **7 km** this is a **short ride**. (It almost didn't make my list, but **being so close to Toronto**, quiet, and ideal to take family or friends out for a quick spin, well, here it is!)

Paths can be described as wide, dirt access roads. No gravel to be found, but there is some muddy and mushy ground, covered in leaf matter, in the low areas.

The trails are pretty straight and **easy to navigate**, with no surprises. Although, being a forest, there are some hills that gently slope up or down.

Use the trailhead at the dead end on **Kennedy Rd.,** just above **Davis Dr.,** where you will also find parking.

As you ride northeast from here, the path splits into alternate routes which eventually reach an open field of newly planted trees.

One can cycle further, but expect a **boring, straight path through the field** to the **McCowan Rd**. dog pen and parking lot.

The **beginner MTB** crowd could find this a fun and safe ride too. I spotted a few short, single-track trails you could explore.

That's it! Another spot to ride if you're curious and need to get out of town for a quick one.

Caledon – Rail Trail

Terra Cotta to Tottenham

Length – 39 km (one way)

90% rail trail path
10% road, detours

Elevation – A flat path with some slopes to the west and a large bridge to ride over Hwy 10.

Terrain – Crushed, hard-packed limestone, with gravel, soil, and tall grass. The east end gets rather rough.

Skill – Easy

Maps – There are many directional and interpretive signs,

Traffic – Bicyclists and hikers, as well as the occasional horse and cross-country skiers in the winter.

Facilities – Services in most towns are listed, with picnic benches and portable toilets on the trail in Inglewood and Caledon East.

Highlights – The charming towns of Terra Cotta, Caledon East, Palgrave, and Tottenham.

Phone – None

Website – Town of Caledon

Similar Trails – Kissing Bridge, Omemee, Oro Medonte

Local Clubs – Caledon Cycling Club

Access – There is parking on cross streets for a few cars, on side streets, as well as a large lot aton **Hwy 10** at the **Ken Whillans Resource Management Area,**

Towns; the towns of **Tottenham, Palgrave**, and **Caledon East** are also good startstarting points.

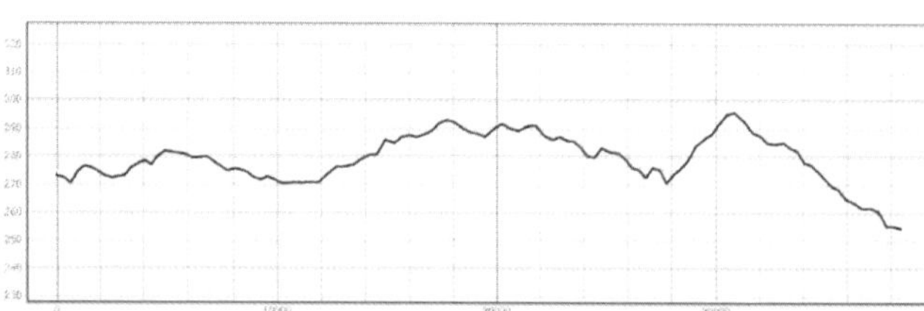

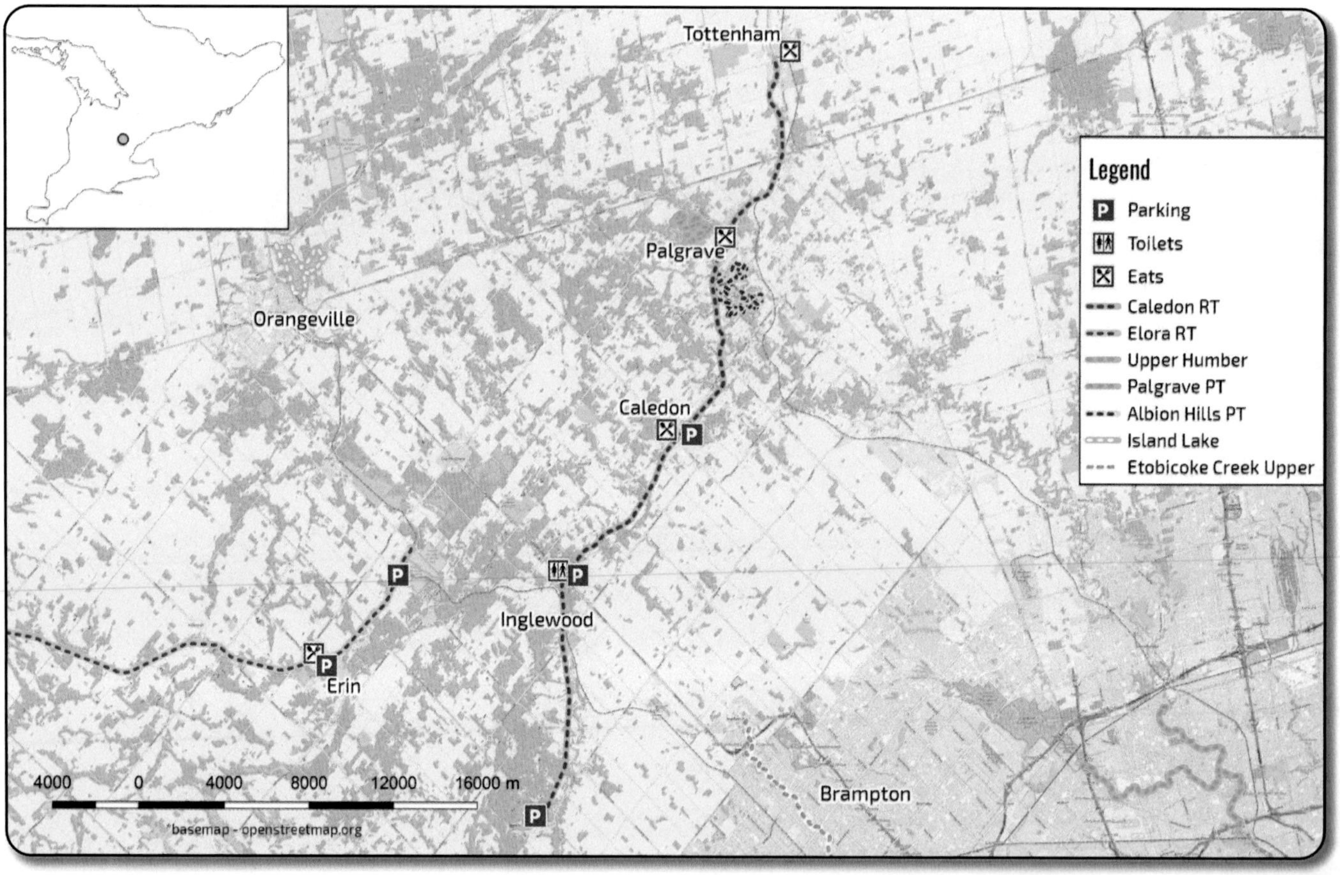

Tottenham
Palgrave
Orangeville
Caledon
Inglewood
Erin
Brampton

Legend
Parking
Toilets
Eats
Caledon RT
Elora RT
Upper Humber
Palgrave PT
Albion Hills PT
Island Lake
Etobicoke Creek Upper

4000 0 4000 8000 12000 16000 m

*basemap - openstreetmap.org

Review:

As one of the **most popular Rail Trails** in Ontario, the **39 km Caledon Rail Trail** takes cyclists along a pleasant route through farm country and small towns.

Its popularity is due to the fact it was one of the first, and it is the **closest Rail Trail outside of Toronto**. As a result, the paths are **well-maintained,** have ample signage, and are never too busy. (But what Rail trail is?)

This route has a mix of terrain; mostly graded, crushed limestone, and while only some is double-track the entire trail is a wide and established path.

There are also quiet **tree-lined stretches** that cut through typical **Ontario farm country,** with many vistas to take in including **fields, farms, wetlands, country homes,** and **neighbourhood backyards.** You may even see some wildlife or a beaver den.

Along the way, riders climb very gradually up and down the **Niagara Escarpment,** although you will likely not notice these subtle inclines.

The path travels over the **Oak Ridge Moraine** and across many established **hiking trails**, as well as a few rivers and valleys. The lower third of this trail runs along the bottom of the escarpment, with the **Credit River** on the other side ending at the base of **Terra Cotta Conservation Area.**

Some good starting points are the colourful towns of **Caledon East** or **Palgrave**. Little parks with **picnic benches** and **shelters exist**. Or, start at the north end in **Tottenham** and take up the offer of a steam train excursion by the **South Simcoe Railway.**

Along the path, look for **interpretive displays** of the history and nature of the area.

There is some **poison ivy** on the shoulders, and even a few **turtles may cross**. Both, I think, you can easily dodge as they move slowly!

Watch while crossing some of the busier roads. **Highway 10** now has a long trail **bridge** to avoid any hazards, and is also a popular starting point at the **Ken Whillans RMA** park.

An easy and **close ride** for anyone in the **Greater Toronto Area** (GTA) who wants to avoid cars and hills and enjoy a nice cycle with friends or family. Make it a favourite too!

History – The **Hamilton & Northern Railway** started running in **1877**, carrying passengers and goods from **Hamilton** to **Barrie.** A few years later the line was extended to **Collingwood** and **Midland.**

With competition from other rail lines and the changing times, service dwindled and the line was decommissioned in the late **1980s.** From **1994**, local governments took ownership and redeveloped the path.

It has since become part of the **Trans Canada Trail.** Other sections of this route have disappeared into subdivisions or farm fields, yet there are fragments you can ride near **Hwy 27** and beyond **Barrie**.

Dundas Valley – Park Trail

650 Governors Rd., Dundas

Length – 40 km

60% park path
20% dirt, single-track
20% road

Elevation – Flat along the valley with a few quick hills, some quite steep.

Terrain – A mix of old roads and paths of asphalt, gravel, and crushed stone.

Skill – All levels; some MTB trails.

Traffic – A popular ride, but not too crowded. Expect to see not only bikers but hikers, dogs, and even horses.

Maps – There is a map at the trailhead and signs on the trail. (Note: Some are missing.)

Facilities – A large parking lot with outhouses, as well as snacks, water, and washrooms at the train station.

Highlights – Plenty of bridges, sulphur springs, water falls, ruins of a stone mansion, and an old train station.

Trail Fee – Free if you ride there, or $10.00, per car, to park.

Phone – Weekends: 905 627 1233;
weekdays: 905 525 2181

Website – Hamilton Conservation Authority

Similar Trails – Morrison Valley, Taylor Creek, Eldred King

Local Clubs – Hamilton Cycling Club

Access – There are many access points, but the parking lot in the **Dundas Valley Conservation Area** is a good central starting point. Enter from the side road into the park at **650 Governors Rd.** near **Ridgewood.**

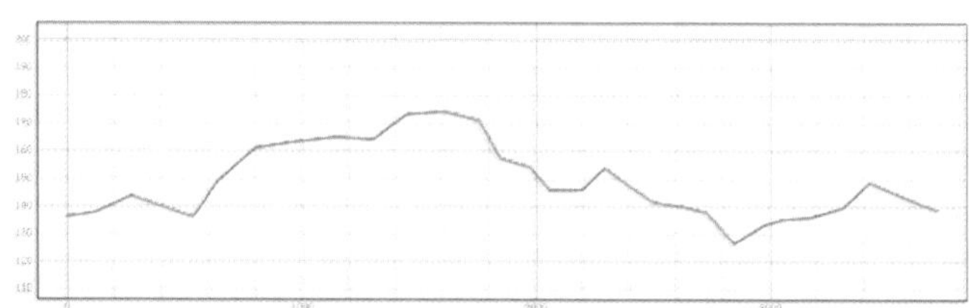

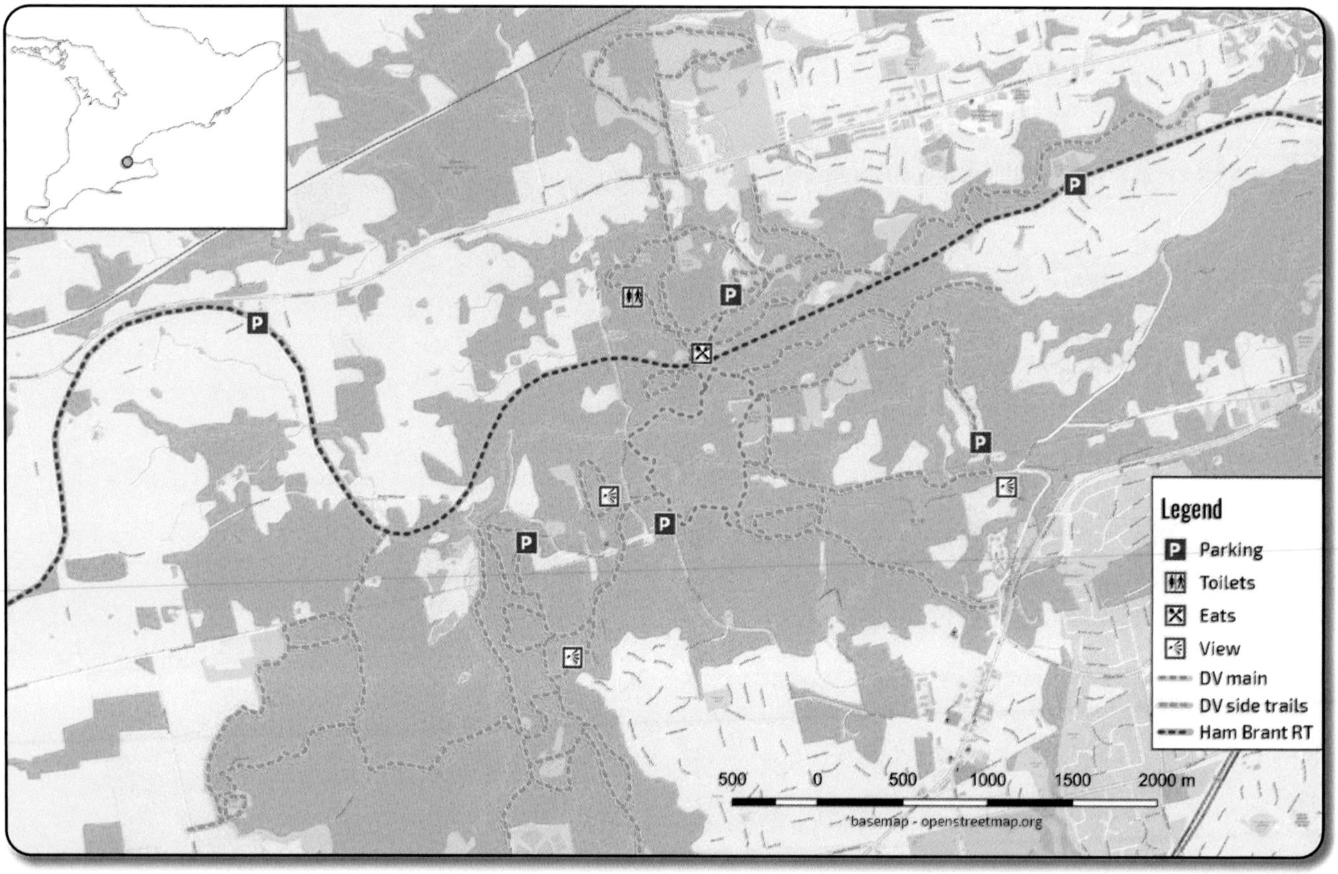

Legend
Parking
Toilets
Eats
View
DV main
DV side trails
Ham Brant RT
500 0 500 1000 1500 2000 m
basemap - openstreetmap.org

Review:

The **Dundas Valley Conservation Area**, right at the west end of the Lake Ontario, beside **Hamilton,** is a beautiful park with **40 km** of well-treed bike loops and trails.

Here, you will find many paths and even a **Rail Trail** that runs through this large forested area.

The bicycle paths are wide, consisting mainly of **crushed gravel** with a few **hilly sections**. Some hills are short yet steep, and you may opt to walk up them.

The **Main 3 km loop** also passes the **train station** and a large, **abandoned stone farmstead** known as **The Hermitage.** A very odd sight to come upon, indeed. Covered in ivy, the shell of this **once-stately home** has a fascinating history you can read about at the gate.

Signs will keep you on the right track, with trail branches leading out in all directions. There is a lot to ride here besides the Main loop.

Find time to explore a few side trails. Some paths loop around, others end at side roads or go into neighbourhoods.

However, not all side trails are suitable for the causal **Park rider.** I found some routes thinning out, more for mountain bikers who would appreciate the efforts needed.

That said if you have a good hybrid bicycle, good legs and enough steam, do try the more **Intermediate Park** trails offered.

In the centre of the park is a replica of a **Victorian train station**, which is owned by the **Hamilton Rail Trail** that runs to **Brantford,** or east into **Hamilton.**

This trail has **washrooms, maps,** and places to **eat.** This forest area has been designated a **World Biosphere Reserve by UNESCO** for its unique plant life and post-glacial terrain.

Look for moss-covered **limestone boulders** as you cycle; they are part of the **Niagara Escarpment** and very **photogenic**. There are a few scenic **waterfalls** on the hillsides. You may have to walk your bike to get to them.

The **Bruce Trail** comes through this valley, and these routes are designated for **hikers only**.

The **Main loop** is a great start for a **day outing** with family or friends, or simply to explore this **forest valley.**

Durham Forest – MTB/Park Trail

3613 Concession Rd. 7 & Hwy 21

Length – 40 km

50% MTB single track
50% double-track access roads

Elevation – Rather large hills and valleys (by Ontario standards) at the north and south end; more level in the middle.

Terrain – Smooth soil, a few rocks and roots, some gravel; sandy on north end, drains well after a rain.

Skill – All levels, but best for Intermediate, Advanced MTB, and Intermediate Park-style riders.

Facilities – Parking lot, outhouse, no food or water close by; can get busy on weekends.

Highlights – Has lots of variety for all levels; fast, gnarly, and hilly track, new MTB trail cut and ramps built.

Maps – At trailhead and a few in the interior at junctions and MTB loops.

Trail Pass – Free

Phone – 905 895 1281

Website – Lake Simcoe Region

Similar Trails – Glen Major, Dagmar, Albion Hills

Local Clubs – Durham Mountain Biking Association (DMBA) does a great job maintaining and developing new trails, plus scheduling rides.

Access – Drive up **Brock Rd.** from the **401**, go east on **Hwy 21** to **Concession 7** for the paved route.

Park on the side of the access road. Past the large map at the gate, most riders head south or east to start a ride. Go north to start the grand MTB tour.

An **alternate gravel road** route leads from the south coming up **Concession 7** from **Hwy 5.** This passes the **Glen Major** and **Dagmar** trailheads on the way.

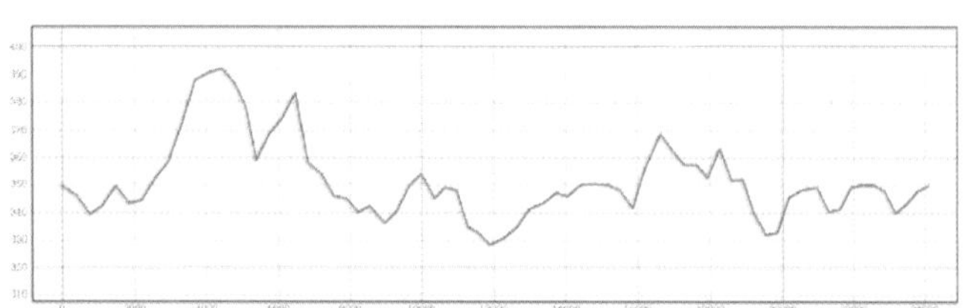

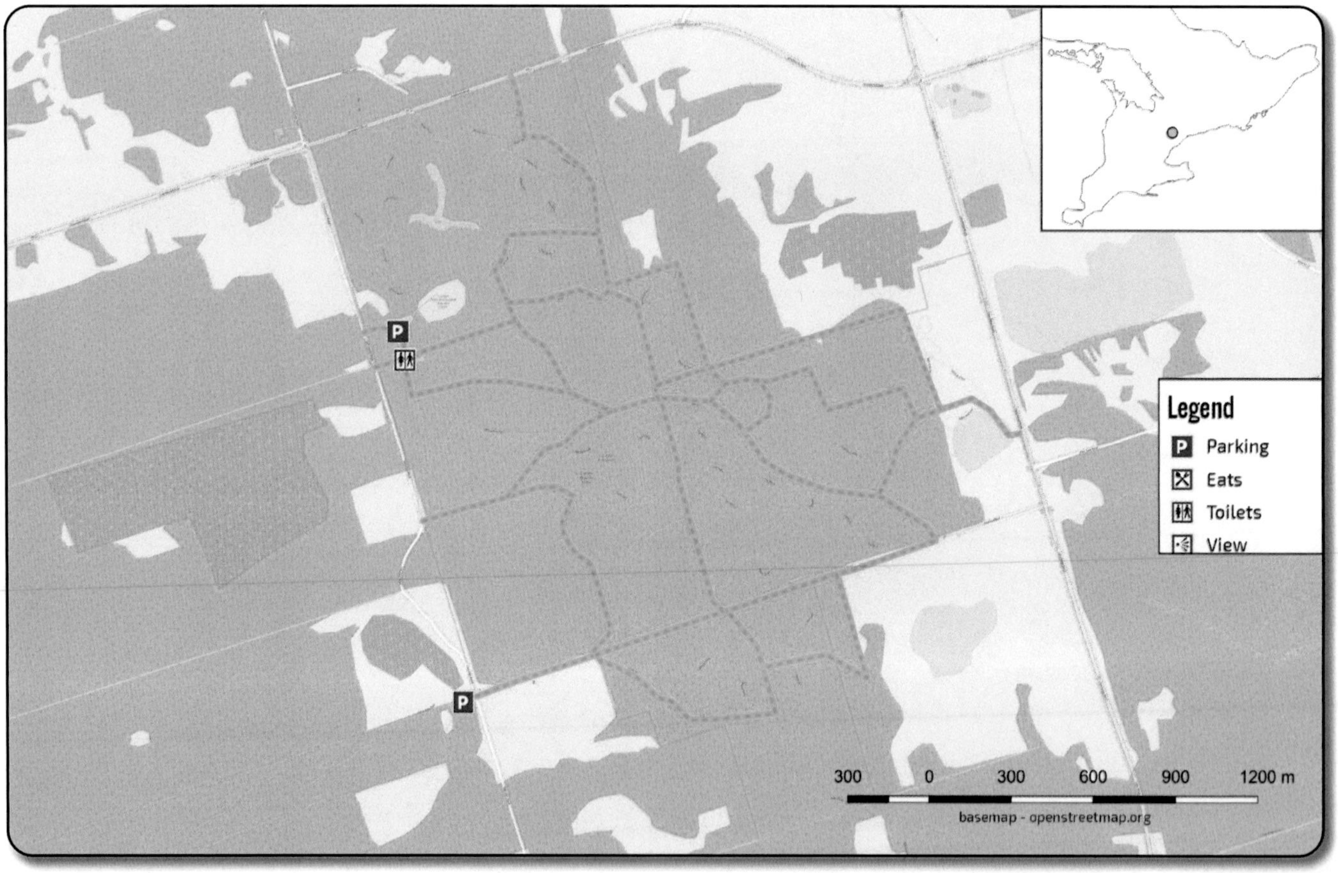

Legend
Parking
Eats
Toilets
View

300 0 300 600 900 1200 m
basemap - openstreetmap.org

Review:

One of the **top rides** on the east side of **Toronto, the Durham Forest** has 40 km of **bike trails for all skill levels.** This large, popular forest brings out many MTB riders and for good reason: the challenges, variety and cardio does it.

Durham Forest has everything from easy wide-access roads, to hard uphill cranks and **fast, twisty** descents.

The terrain here is hillier at the south end and north side, which also has patches of sand. The land flattens out more in the middle, where the easier trails reside.

While riding, **not everything flows together well**, and you might repeat a loop or get a bit lost. Does it sound like your typical MTB haunt? It is, but isn't that part of the fun? No worries, within minutes that will get sorted out as you cannot truly get lost here.

Personally, I find it hard to pick my favourite MTB runs as they all have different qualities. But staying to the **backside** of the forest is where all the sweet stuff tends to be.

For the grand tour, head north to the **Burnt Toast** trail to start your adventure. For a good workout, try the Advanced **Little Butter** and **Missing Link** trails. For some easier **boardwalk** action, head further south to find **Ogre and Out**. Or, fill your need for speed and get to the top of **Tower Hill** for a long bomb down.

There is plenty to like in **Durham Forest**—you just have to find it. A few map boards at junctures and trail signs at the entrances help, but I find there are not enough so you may want to carry your own map.

The most **challenging track** is on the **south end,** where the **most significant hills** are. If you reach ski chair lifts you have definitely gone too far south!

For **Park-style cyclist,** there is **20 km** of main double-track access roads that cut straight across throughout the forest.

Smooth soil and gravel are all you have to contend with, but you'll need to know there are a **few gradual hills** to conquer. These routes are wide and marked by posts with **Maple, White Pine, Red Oak,** or **Spruce** symbols.

Watch for hikers and dog walkers and, in August, for those delicious raspberries near the **Bell Tower** in the open areas that have been logged.

A very **active MTB club** maintains and updates trails in this area. New ramps and a single track were cut last year for thrills. (But no spills please!)

Durham Forest is an excellent place for **Fatbikes** in the winter. Volunteers **groom 15 km of trail,** with even more you can try if the snow base is firm. Just stay off the cross-country ski tracks, please.

Not too buggy in the summer, the trails at Durham Forest drain well—but please **avoid when muddy** or **slushy** to lessen erosion.

Set your sights for **Durham Forest**. I am sure it will become a favourite for you too.

Need more riding? This area has tons. Simply head across the street, as a ride in **Glen Major,** and **Dagmar** can keep you crank'n for the whole weekend.

Eldred King – MTB/Park Trail

16232 Hwy 48, Ballantrae

Length – 20 km (approx.)
30% MTB, single-track
30% hiking trail
40% double-track access roads

Elevation – While the trail has small to medium hills, the access roads are mostly flat; the single track can also be hilly.

Terrain – The access roads are gravel, the soil smooth with some muddy spots and some very sandy stretches—watch out for horse patties!

Skill – Easy to Intermediate; recommended for MTB or Park-style riders.

Traffic – Bikes, hikers, dogs, horses, Nordic skiing in winter.

Maps – A basic map can be found at the trailhead, but there is no other signage; the MTB track can be hard to find.

Facilities – There is a large parking lot, and an outhouse.

Highlights – A lovely pond and dam that is fun to explore; plenty of sand for Fatbikes.

Trail Fee – Free

Phone – 905 895 1281

Website – Oak Ridge Trail Association

Similar Trails – Ganaraska, Northumberland, Palgrave

Local Clubs - Durahm MTB Association

Access – Take **Aurora Rd.**, going north on **Hwy 48** to **Markham Rd.** to marker **#16232** marked by an **Eldred King Forest Tract** sign go down the gravel road and find parking on the west end.

The trail can be accessed in any direction west from the parking lot. For most of the good ride in a southwest direction.

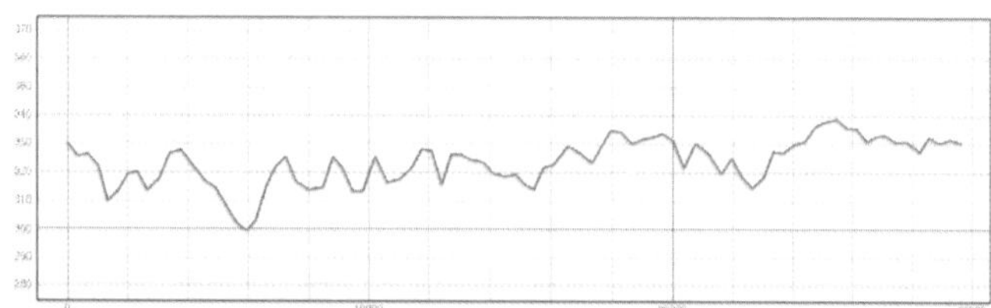

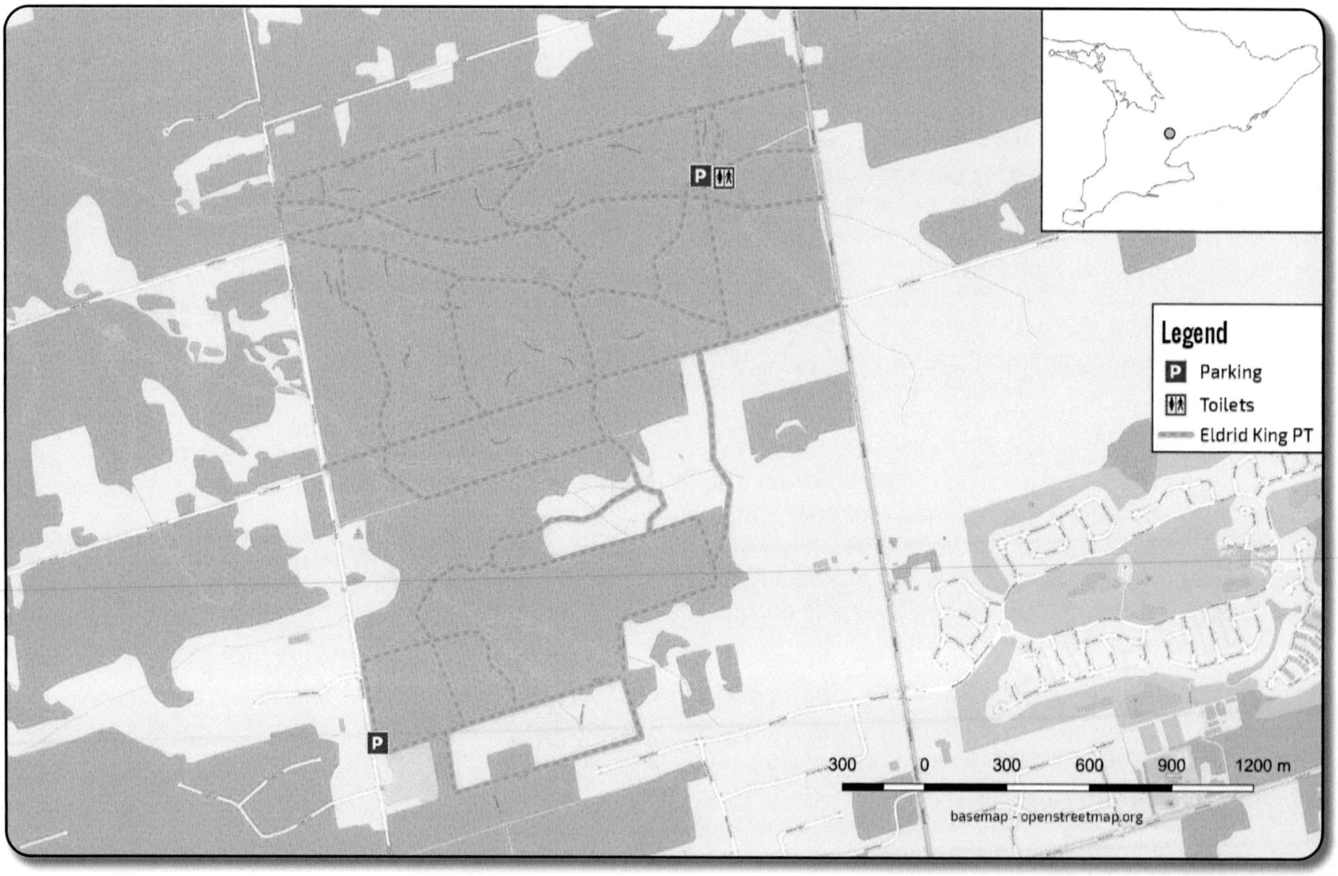

Legend
Parking
Toilets
Eldrid King PT

300 0 300 600 900 1200 m

basemap - openstreetmap.org

Review:

Eldred King Forest Tract, north of **Markham**, is a little-known, medium-sized ride MTB riders need to **try at least once.** It's also an excellent spot for **beginners!**

Intermediate Park-style cyclists can find plenty of access roads to ride if they have **wide tires** capable of handling gravel and sand.

The only map is found at the trailhead, so I recommend a GPS app or printing one out. The roads and tracks have **no signposts** and run every which way—a great place to explore and find your own adventure.

The tricky part is getting to the **single-track** trail among the access roads, as there are **no signs** and **few entry points.** But once you get in and ride around, you'll be delighted at the length of trail which **flows well**.

Most of the **MTB runs** are located at the **south end,** with a few hilly spots that will keep it fun and just challenging enough. Every time I go, I find more twisty MTB trail.

Some of the side trails have been carved out by **local horse riders.** You will know them when you come to them, as these trails are **straighter** and **lumpier,** with annoying hoof marks left behind.

Unlike other ride spots, you may likely meet a horse (and their **poop) on the trail,** which in itself is **technically a trail obstacle!**

Note: When you see a horse, stop ahead and ask the rider how the horse may react. Some horses have never seen an alien mountain biker; they may get spooked, and throw the rider/kick you.

Also, expect to see **dog walkers** near the parking lot and pond.

This mixed pine and hardwood forest is logged at times in the winter. A few areas have **large swaths of sand** that are next to impossible to ride (unless it has just rained).

The **sand** found here is likely why it is not an all-around popular MTB ride. Though a perfect spot for **unstoppable Fatbikes!**

I have not checked out all corners of this forest tract.

Southewest of the parking lot, it goes for a good stretch in many directions. At one point I came across an archery range.

Plenty of **trails you could explore.** Some of these routes are **straight dirt roads,** others **sand traps** or **dead ends.**

Yet you may find something special on **your adventure** if the trail calls you to try them.

Ganaraska Forest – MTB/Park Trail

10585 Cold Springs Camp Rd.

Length – 60+ km

40% single-track MTB trail
20% hiking trail
40% double-track access roads

Elevation – Gradual incline northward, with large rolling hills.

Terrain – Smooth soil/sand, with some roots, rocks and gravel; watch for poison ivy on the shoulders.

Skill – All MTB levels; Intermediate Park ride.

Traffic – This area is so vast it never feels congested; bicyclists, hikers, ATV and dirt-bike riders, as well as snowmobiles all have their own areas in which to play.

Maps – There are a few maps at the trailhead; it has mainly double-track access roads for Nordic-style skiing, and the single-track trails have a few signs. (Look for the IMBA Epic trail.!)

Facilities – Parking lot, as well as outhouse, bike wash, and showers.

Highlights – Tons of trails to explore and wilderness to experience; flows well.

Trail Pass – $12.00 Adult, Youth $6.00. (The season pass is the best deal.)

Phone – 905 797 2721

Website – Ganaraska Forest Centre

Similar Trails – Northumberland, Dufferin, Palgrave

Local Clubs – Peterborough Cycling Club, Cobourg Cycling Club

Access – Drive north 3 km from **Hwy 9 (Ganaraska Rd.)** to **10585 Cold Springs Camp Road**, and then on to the gatehouse for **The Ganaraska Forest Centre**. The trailhead is across the field from the parking lot, on the north side by the map board.

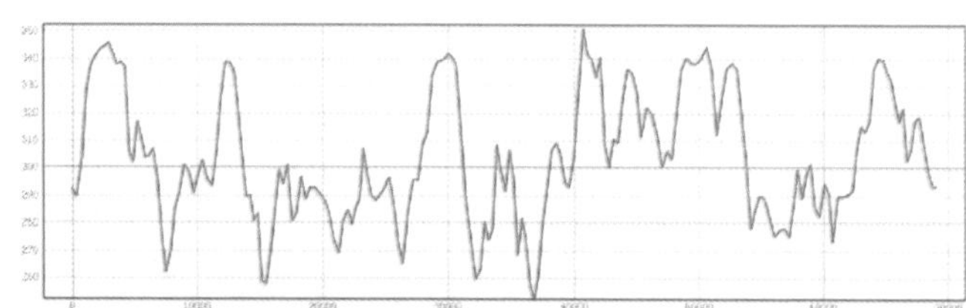

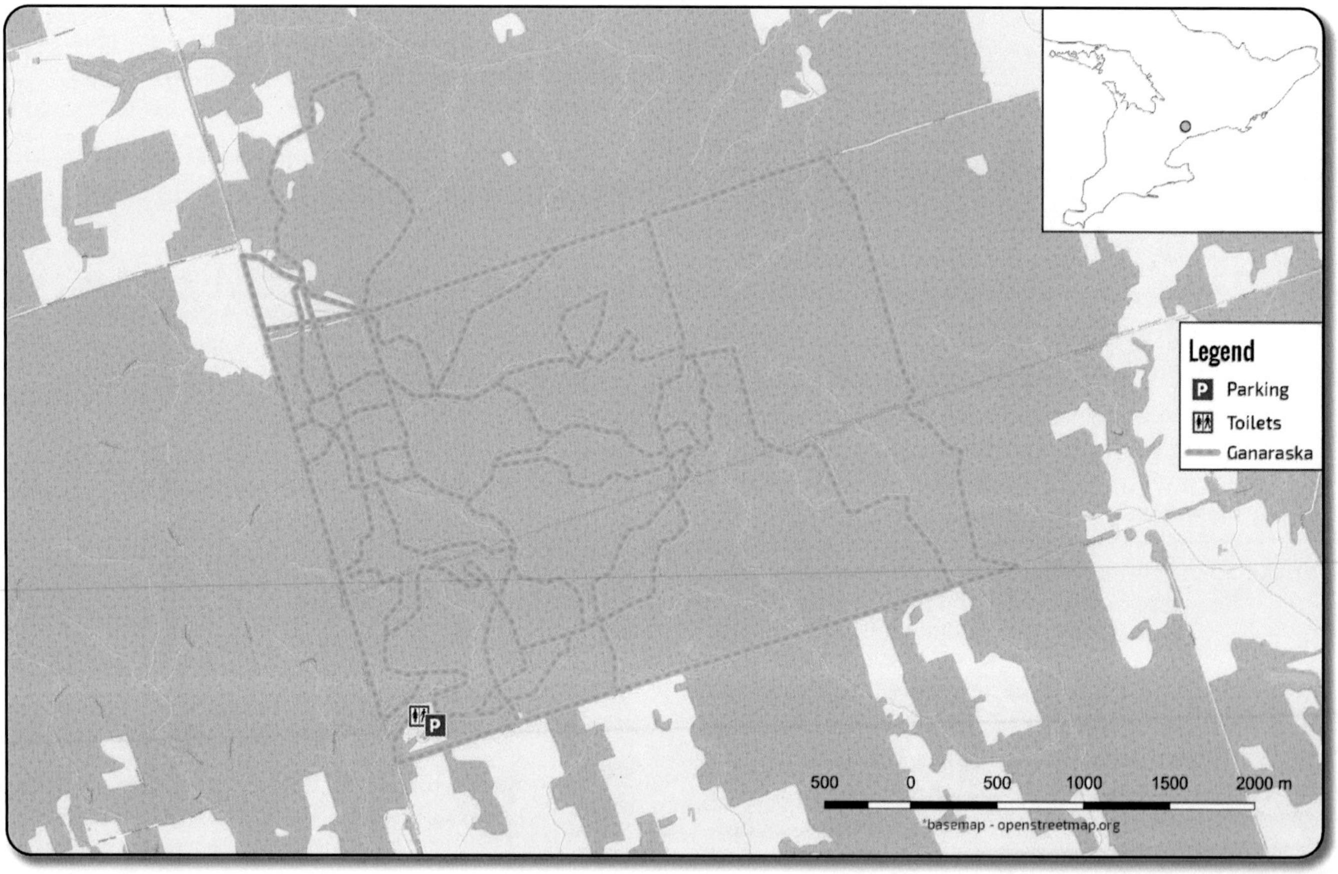

Legend
Parking
Toilets
Ganaraska

500 0 500 1000 1500 2000 m
°basemap - openstreetmap.org

Review:

Ganaraska Region Conservation Area (aka "Big G", "The Ganny") is likely **Ontario's largest bike trail** area with **60+ kilometres** to explore. A huge, multi-use trail system covers a wooded, northward-sloping incline with large, rolling hills.

If you want to **ride forever**, deep into the woods, this is the place to be! **Cross-country distance cyclists** will love it.

The main paths are wide access roads, some straight, taking you over **large hills** with **gentle inclines,** as well as **long descents** with some **sandy stretches** that slow you down. There are a few **technical challenges**, but nothing too nasty. For MTBs, this is a **fast ride** if you want it to be.

Or, if you are out for a **Park** style ride through the forest, feel free to meander along. There is plenty of space to do it! Wider tires are preferred with the soft ground.

Plenty of fun MTB loops can be found, but are spread over some distance. They flow well if the sand does not bog riders down. Here and there are some twisty, gnarly sections to keep it interesting.

The International Mountain Bike Association (IMBA) lists Ganaraska as one of the **top rides in North America**, and you will find 3 trails they designed at **15 km, 30 km,** and **60+ km.** Indeed, it is an *epic* ride by **Ontario standards**, but nothing compared to the insanity of British Columbia MTB runs.

The main access roads, used for cross-country skiing, have colour-coded signage. As for the smaller MTB loops that cut in and out of these paths, not so much. You can get rather lost as **this forest is extensive,** with few distinguishing features.

The gatehouse hands out maps when you pay, so be sure to take one or use **GPS** if you wish to venture far. Cell coverage is spotty, but GPS seems fine.

Ganaraska Forest is divided into three sections: **bike riding** in the **centre part**, with motorized **ATV,** and **dirt bikes in the west.** (You may want to explore that area, too!)

There are endless, fun **berms** and **jumps** cut by the motocross crowd, but these areas can be very sandy and tiring using only leg power.

Be careful of vehicles, and since hunting is allowed in April, May, and November, **wear bright colours**.
The **east side** has **horse riding** and even more trails … which I have not yet ridden.

Watch for **raspberry bushes** and **poison ivy** by mid-summer. They can close in on the trail, making it a challenge not to get winged.

I should add, that as far as MTB trail fees in Ontario go, at $12 Ganaraska is a tad pricey for what there are by way of services, so you may want to stay a while….

For **beginner mountain bikers,** this is a safe spot to ride and to not worry about getting wounded or having to walk the steep hill climbs all day.

Book the whole day off and make your way out; there is plenty to like and trails to ride for all!

Hamilton Beach – Park Trail

Lakeshore Rd., Hamilton

Length – 12 km (one way)

100% park path

Elevation – A somewhat flat ride with a few quick ups-and-downs, some of which are over an old rail bed.

Terrain – A wide, asphalt path with a few spots of crushed stone and sand along the beach.

Skill – Easy

Traffic – A popular route with cyclists, it is also enjoyed by joggers, dog walkers, and families; summer weekends are busy.

Maps – There are plenty of signs and maps along the trail.

Facilities – Ample places to park, with washrooms, snack bars, beaches, and places to eat close by.

Highlights – The beautiful Lake Ontario shoreline, long piers, and massive bridges, as well as beaches that offer plenty of swimming.

Trail Fee – Free

Phone – None

Website – Great Lakes Waterfront Trail

Similar Trails – Ajax Waterfront, Beaches Boardwalk, Toronto Island

Local Clubs – Hamilton Cycling Club

Access – There are many parking lots and entry points along the route, on **Lakeshore Rd.** in **Burlington** and **Beach Blvd.** in **Hamilton.**

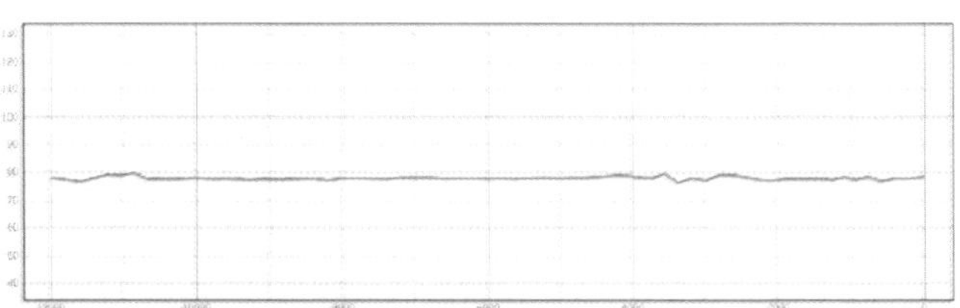

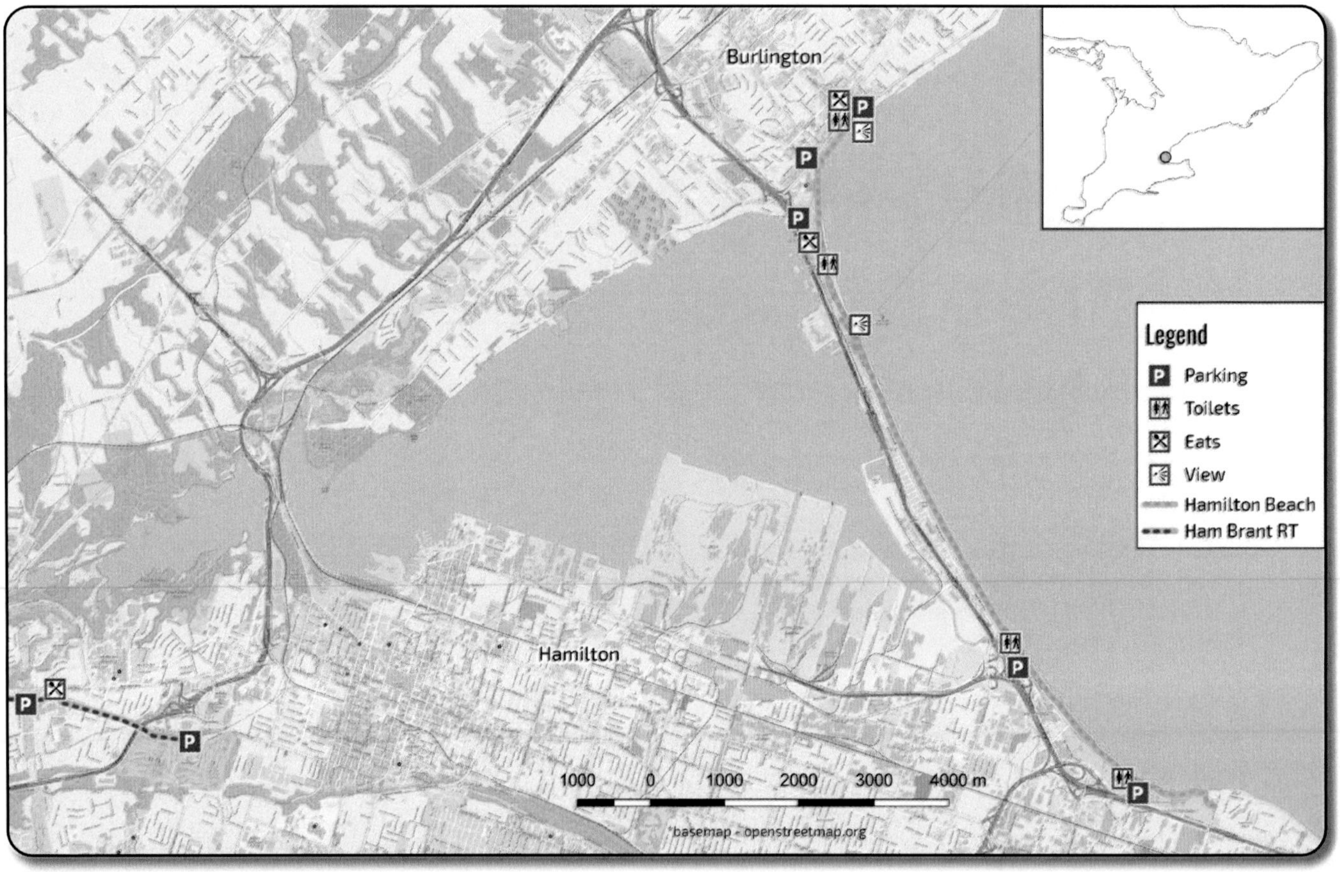

Review:

The **12 km Hamilton Beach Park Trail** is a very scenic, comfortable, and relaxing bike path along the edge of **Lake Ontario.** With the trail hugging the shoreline, you get **great views of the lake** and a **cool breeze** on a **hot day.**

The route is rather flat but does wind and change enough to keep riders interested. Trees supply little shade on this ride, which makes for frequent views of the water, but could be too much sun and wind for some people's liking. Remember, in the **spring** and **fall** it will be **cooler** by the water so pack a jacket.

The **path flows well,** with no need to cross roads or stop pedalling! One minor detour is to take the lift bridge access path up and around to **cross the canal**.

The path loops around the base of the lift bridge and takes you across on the sidewalk. Time your arrival, since this bridge may be up to let pass tall ships that enter Hamilton Harbour.

After the lift bridge, the trail passes the backyards of many old cottages and homes along **Beach Blvd.** This section of straight pavement offers no shelter from the sun or wind.

Further along, you will ride by numerous theme parks. This allows you to add to your outing some other entertainment. Various waterparks and pools, mini putt, go-karts, batting cages, rock climbing, ziplines...

This off road route ends at Grays Rd. were you meet a row of homes at a suburb.

This ride is **well-marked** and **mostly paved.** I recommend the **12 km** section that leads southwest from the waterfront in **downtown Burlington** along to **Confederation Park** in **Stoney Creek.**

This is part of the larger **Waterfront Trail** system, which continues in both directions but will lead into city streets. (Since this site is for off-roading, I ended there.) Unfortunately, west and beyond to Toronto provides little off-road waterfront trail until you get closer to the **Humber River**; eastside **Toronto** has so much more!

If you have a chance, do ride out to the **two long piers** for a great view of the shoreline (and take pictures!). The first is the rather funky and modern **Brant St. Pier**, located in **Burlington,** and the second spans a canal with a nearby **lighthouse** for the large lift bridges.

On the **Burlington** side of the trail are many fine eateries, as well as **fast food** and **snack bars** on the beach.

If all that flat, level trail riding leaves you wanting more exercise, then try the **Red Hill Valley** trail. This **8 km** path takes you to the top of the escarpment so you know that will be a major climb! The cut off is were Van Wagners Beach Rd. turns inland and there are signs posted.

The **Hamilton Beach** ride is sure to please everyone with its waterfront views, relaxing cruise, and laid-back, endless summer vibe.

Hamilton Brantford – Rail Trail

Hamilton to Brantford

Length – 32 km

95% rail trail
5% roads, crossings, detours

Elevation – The east side offers a slow, easy climb from about 13 km, starting from the lake in Hamilton through farm country where the path levels off.

Terrain – A wide, well-maintained path, consisting of crushed stone, some gravel and asphalt, and a few road crossings.

Skill – Easy

Traffic – Bicyclists, hikers, and horseback riders; cross-country skiers in the winter.

Maps – Signs are located at the gate, and the path is well-signed along the way with map boards.

Facilities – Parking, with washrooms and a store nearby; benches along the trail.

Highlights – The picturesque Dundas Valley Conservation Area and train station, as well as stunning views of Hamilton farms and the quarry.

Phones – 1 866 900 4722

Website – Grand River Conservation Authority

Similar Trails – Caledon, Uxbridge, Kissing Bridge

Local Clubs – Hamilton Cycling Club

Access – In **Hamilton**, parking can be found at the **Dundas Valley Conservation Area**, and in **Brantford** at **Jerseyville.**

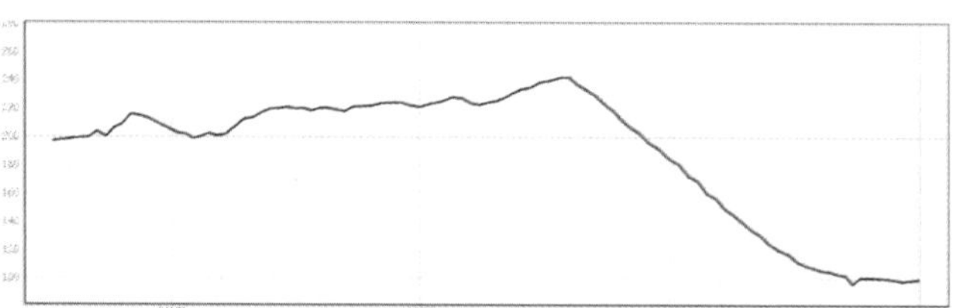

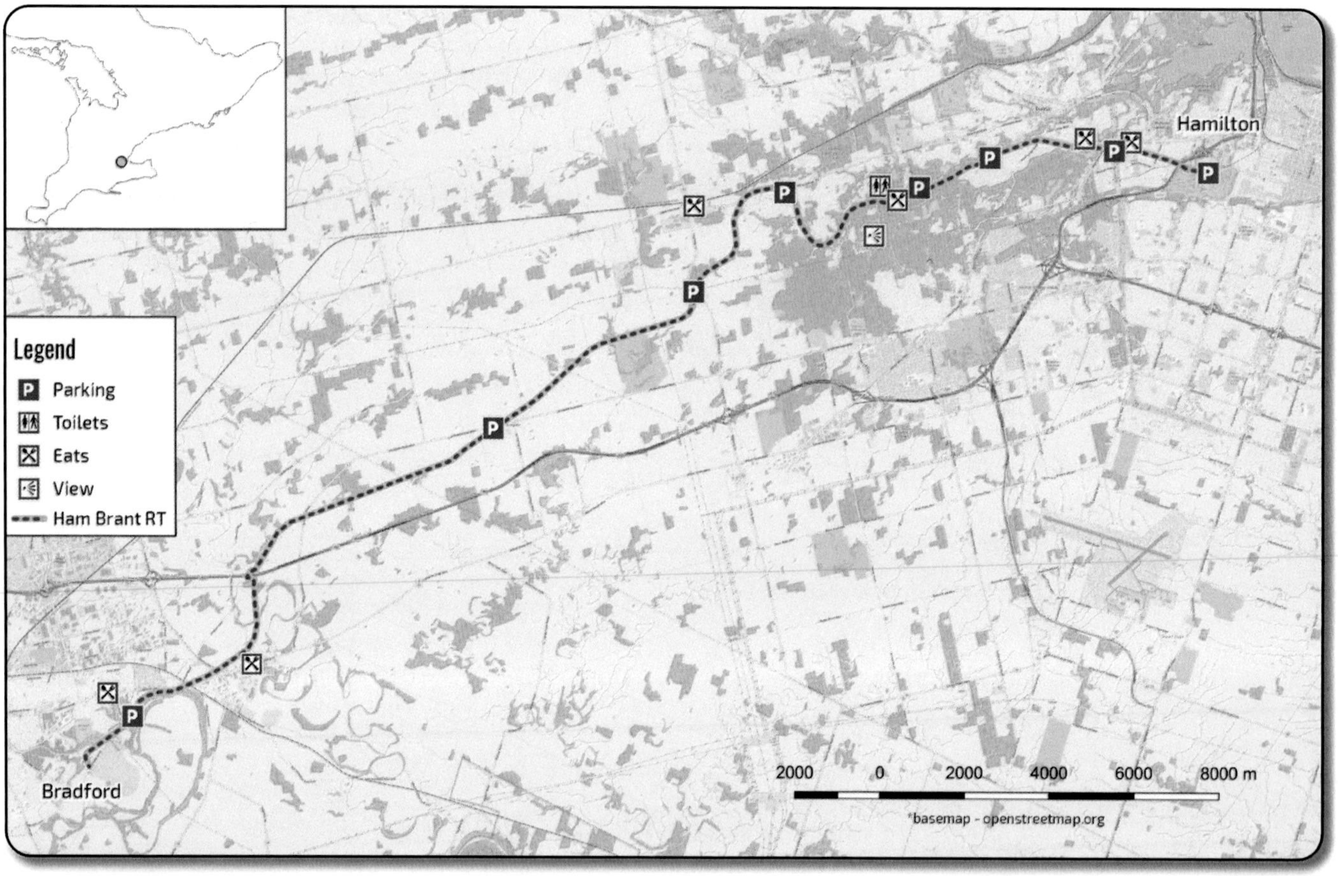

Hamilton
Bradford
Legend
Parking
Toilets
Eats
View
Ham Brant RT
2000 0 2000 4000 6000 8000 m
*basemap - openstreetmap.org

Review:

The **Hamilton to Brantford Bicycle Rail Trail** is one-third of the full length of this popular route, which continues to **Cambridge.** Overall, it is a total of **80 km** and part of the **Trans-Canada Trail.**

Starting in **Hamilton,** enjoy a **long, gradual climb** through the treed **Dundas Valley Conservation Area** and up into the farmlands of Southern Ontario. After **18 km** you pass the small village of **Jerseyville** before reaching **Brantford.**

Riders setting out from **Hamilton** may want to begin at the **old starting point** at **Ewen Rd.** From here, the trail is more **naturalized** and has a firm, crushed-stone base.

The trail continues as a flat path before it becomes even more treed, **slowly climbing 9 km** up the valley and into the **Dundas Park** forest.

Here, riders can stop at the **replica of the old train station** to refresh with a bathroom break, get water or buy a snack. From here, continue on or **take a side trail into the park**.

Heading west up the valley will take cyclists around a large S-curve. This longer route originally was to give locomotives a gentler slope to negotiate.

The Rail Trail peaks at the ruins of **Summit Station.** Congratulations – that was a **240 metre climb,** and I'm sure it will be much easier for you than for a train pulling freight!

The trail now gradually descends for **20 km** through farmland and into the village of **Jerseyville** before going on to **Brantford** in what is now a more linear and open path.

Once out of the forested area, this tree-lined route has sunny spots and provides glimpses of country homes and farms, with their fields and livestock. You may even see a golf course and a greenhouse on the route, depending on how far you ride.

There are plenty of signs along the way to keep you going. A nice touch was the posting of old railroad-crossing signage.

A few bridges remain, but expect a fair share of **road crossings** on this journey; none are too tricky to manage, yet you should always be cautious.

The line has been extended at the east end, by just a few extra kilometres. This is a paved **urban** route, and is a good connection for those coming in from the **Hamilton** city core. To start at the very beginning, you can park by the rail stockyards (How appropriate) near the end of **Studholme Rd.**

There are few conveniences to be found on the route beyond the old station, so carry your own provisions. Of course, at either end in Hamilton or Brantford, you will find whatever you need.

Rated as one of the **best Rail Trails in Ontario** for being well-maintained and scenic, be sure to ride it one day soon!

History – Part of the **Toronto, Hamilton, and Buffalo Railway** (**TH&B**), this route was first used in **1894** and was jointly owned by **CP Rail** and **New York Central**. The line was abandoned in **1988** because of the cost to repair a landslide.

After, it was converted into one of Canada's first multi-use trails in **1996.** The rail line still runs trains through **Hamilton**, beyond where this Rail Trail ends.

Harbourfront – Park Trail

Queens Quay, Toronto

Length – 9 km (one way)

95% park path
5% road, detours

Elevation – Flat, following the Lake Ontario shore.

Terrain – All designated bicycle path, this route is lined, paved asphalt with a few road crossings.

Skill – Easy

Traffic – Watch for meandering tourists, stop lights, other bikes. Crazy busy on nice days.

Maps – Map boards, painted lines show you the way.

Facilities – Plenty of restaurants and pubs, boat tours, bike rentals, and shopping. The TTC and washrooms can be found nearby (at **Cherry Beach** and **Coronation Park**).

Highlights – The gorgeous Toronto waterfront and boardwalk**, Cherry** and **Sugar Beaches**, as well as the **Wavedecks**, the **Toronto Music Gardens**, the **Harbourfront Centre**, and the **Power Plant Art Gallery**.

Trail Fee – Free

Phone – 416 973 4000 or 311 Toronto info line

Website – Harbourfront Centre, Waterfront Trail

Similar Trails – Beaches Boardwalk, Toronto Islands, Ajax Waterfront

Local Clubs – Toronto Bicycle Network, Toronto Bicycle Club

Access – I would suggest biking here if you can, as it is a rather congested place to drive through and expensive to park.

You may consider parking at either end of this trail. Try the **Ontario Place** parking lot ($15.00 daily max.) or, on the eastside, park along **Leslie St**. or in the lot at **Thompson Park** and **Cherry Beach**

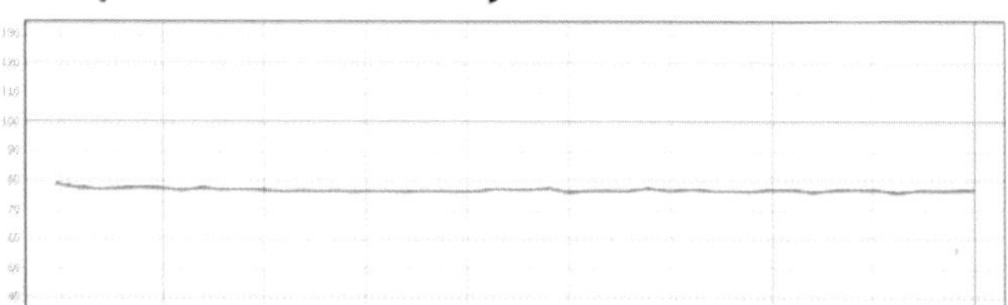

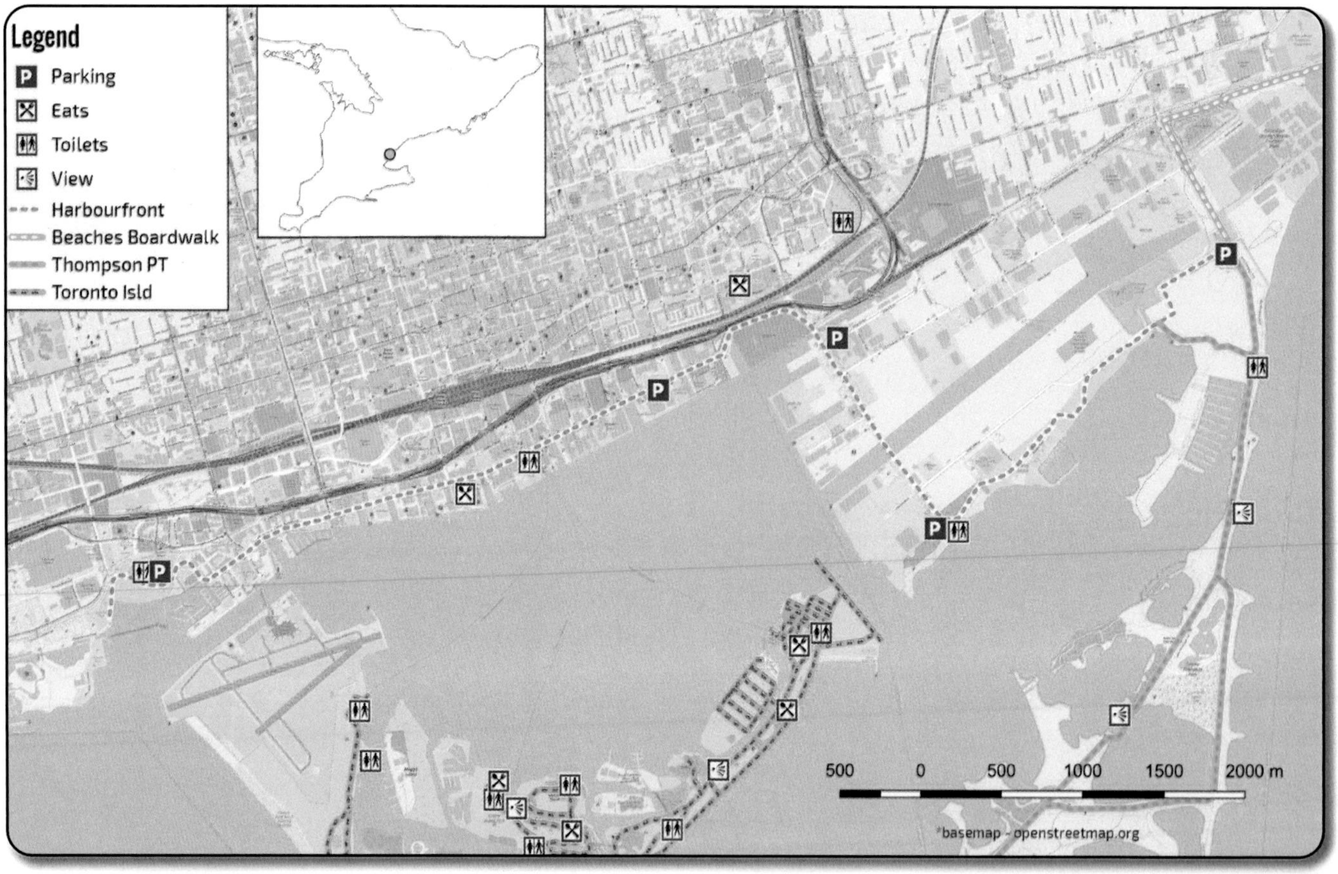

Legend
Parking
Eats
Toilets
View
Harbourfront
Beaches Boardwalk
Thompson PT
Toronto Isld

500 0 500 1000 1500 2000 m

°basemap - openstreetmap.org

Review:

This **9-km** section of the **Martin Goodman Trail** winding along **Lake Ontario's** shoreline is likely the **most popular ride in the city,** and for good reason.

Riding through the centre of **Toronto's** continually evolving waterfront offers many sights and things to do for both locals and tourists.

Plan to stop a lot, as there are numerous places to walk along the boardwalk, have lunch, hear live music, or see artisans and buy their crafts. There are also a few **galleries,** as well as **gardens** to enjoy, or just sit on a bench and watch the sailboats.

Having ridden this path for many years, I have waited until now to say **it's fully ready to ride!** After much redesign, upgrades, and construction, it is finally finished.

The result is **a joy to cycle,** and a lot **safer** to navigate through the centre of Toronto's tourist-filled **Harbourfront** district than before. Riders can now enjoy **designated bike lanes** of their own, which are not shared with cars.

This Park ride is unlike most listed in this guide. There is less park landscaping and more concrete, as well as the general bustle of the city as it cuts across downtown, but it sure is fun to do.

Starting from either **Ontario Place** on the west side or at the entrance of **Tommy Thompson Park** on the east side, this route makes for an easy going bike ride for the whole family.

The route can be divided into **two zones:** the busy and vibrant central harbour, or the calmer beach/industrial setting in the east.

Riding in from the east and heading west along the path, the **Unwin Ave.** bridge brings you to **Cherry Beach.** Enjoy a calm stretch of paved, winding pathway through treed sections that open up to a quiet beach and excellent swimming spot.

Heading north on **Cherry St.** leads riders into old dockland industries; the path runs parallel to the road on the east side and over the lift bridge to **Commissioner St.,** where it switches to the other side of the road.

Once over the second bridge, you can ride west around the raised expressway area and along a short, still-undeveloped (aka ugly) part back down to **Queens Quay E.** Here, recent improvements to the path can be seen; the city has widened the lanes and laid a painted bike path right through town. There are even dedicated stop lights to control the flow of bicyclists.

Through the neighbourhood at the end of **Queens Quay W.**, the path meets up with a marina. Here, take a quick right around **Coronation Park** to end at **Ontario Place.**

Ontario Place is now open again, and has a **tiny new path** in a newly landscaped area, which I recommend checking out. Named the **William Davis Trail,** it makes for a good place to stop and snack while taking in a **great view** of the city across the water.

This route makes for a pleasant outing for anyone and is an opportunity to get out, see the sights, and play the tourist.

Heber Down – Park Trail

500 Lyndebrook Rd., Whitby

Length – 10 km

90% park path
10% road

Elevation – Mainly flat, with a few hilly parts and one tough switchback.

Terrain – A little of everything: asphalt, gravel, sand, and smooth soil.

Skill – Intermediate

Traffic – Bikes, hikers or dog walkers visit, and it can be busy on nice days.

Maps – A map is found at the trailhead, with signs on the trails.

Facilities – Plenty of parking, outhouses, and picnic tables.

Highlights – A bridge, pond, creek, and old railway line.

Trail Fee – Parking is $3.00/hr or $6.00 per day

Phone – 905 579 0411

Website – Central Lake Ontario Conservation

Similar Trails – Long Sault, Stephen's Gulch, Ganaraska Forest

Local Clubs – Uxbridge Cycling Club, DMBA, Cobourg Cycling Club

Access – Drive in from **500 Lyndebrook Rd**. where it meets **Country Lane**, just north of **Whitby**.

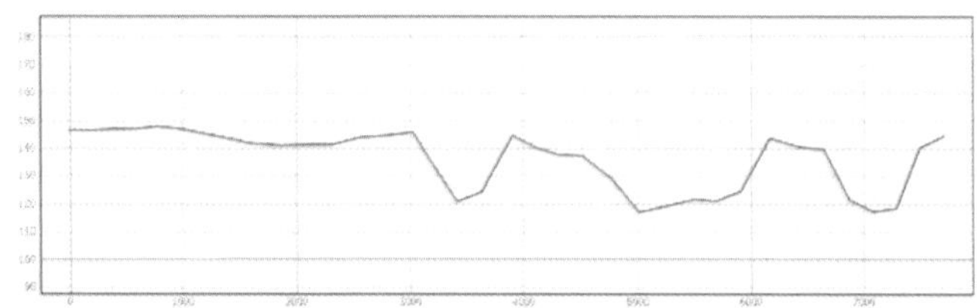

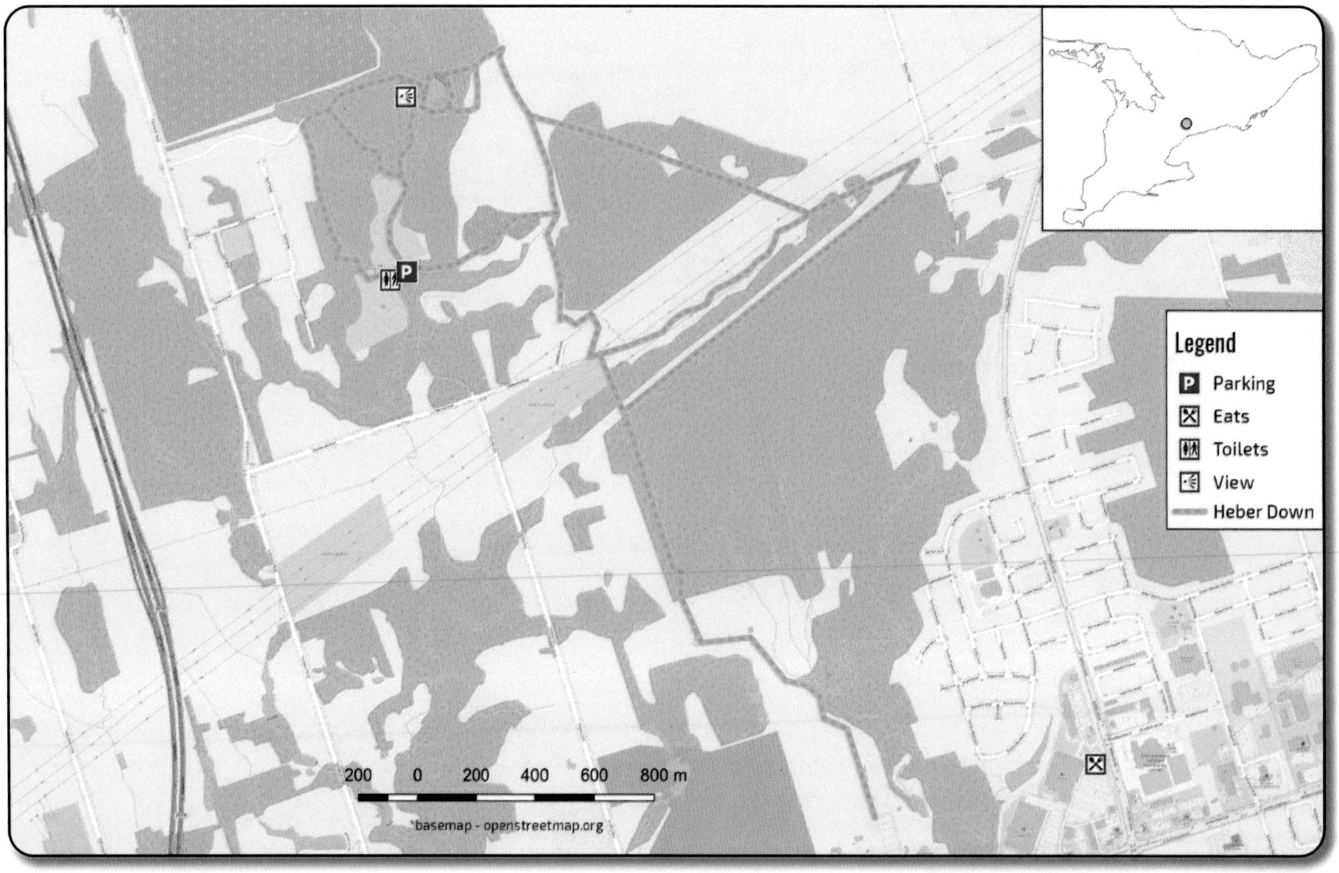

Legend
Parking
Eats
Toilets
View
Heber Down

200 0 200 400 600 800 m

*basemap - openstreetmap.org

Review:

With **10 km** of trails to discover, the **Heber Down Conservation Area** is a local wooded area **north of Whitby** that will suit the typical **Intermediate Park rider.**

Most of the trail is **wide** and **flat,** with trees to shade you from the sun. Other corners of this property offer a completely different landscape not found elsewhere.

I came across open swaths of sand and brush, then fields with towering power lines.

What also varies as one cycles about is the path's terrain; it **changes constantly.** Pay close attention as you go to one kind of surface than another and back again.

Most of the trail is not paved, so this is rated as an **Intermediate Park** ride. I did come across a few hills, but no overly tricky parts to master (and no MTB action).

By the pond, at **Devil's Den** you will find a **small dam** and **bridge.** Take this across to a picturesque spot to stop. (I actually saw a **deer** here, how rare to see on my rides!)

Along the trail, there is a **switchback hill** to climb to a **lookout** over the pond. Unfortunately, over the years the trees have grown taller and there is no longer much to look at.

The other side of the pond has a **hilly, gravel** path that may be **hard to climb** for most, so you may opt to walk.

As an alternate route, try the **switchback trail** located on the west side instead. Going down will be fun!

At **Heber Down**, on one of the **four trails** is a short ride along an old, abandoned **railway bed**. The ride is what's to be expected: flat, wide, and straight.

Here you can also pick up the **2-km Iroquois Trail** and head south out of the conservation area into **Cullen Central Park.** (Some of this area is under development.)

For **2.2 km**, the **Springbanks Trail** roams around a natural, high flat section through the trees.

At **10 km** this is not a lengthy ride, yet enough for most **casual riders** out for a little exercise and meandering.

Part of its draw is being so close to **Whitby,** and the terrain and vegetation will keep you riding pleasantly along.

(Note: I am slightly confused why the official website does not mention cycling as an activity here, although the signs on the trails allow it.)

Highland Creek – Park Trail

Scarborough, Toronto

Length – 7 km (one way)

90% park path
10% roads, crossings, parking lots

Elevation – Ride the hill down to get to the bottom of the valley; then a flat path with a slight slope down to the lake.

Terrain – A wide asphalt path with some sections of gravel and sand, as well as crossings at both metal and wooden bridges.

Skill – Easy

Traffic – Cyclists, walkers, dogs, strollers; never too busy.

Maps – There is a map at the trailhead, as well as signs on the trail. (Note that some were missing.)

Facilities – Plenty of parking lots and a few washrooms, as well as park benches and picnic tables. There are no food stores close by.

Highlights – Views of Lake Ontario, beaches, bridges, and a quiet ravine valley; Morningside Park and University of Toronto, Scarborough campus.

Trail Fee – Free

Phone – Toronto 311

Website – Toronto Conservation

Similar Trails – Humber River, Taylor Creek

Local Clubs – Toronto Bicycle Network

Access – Find parking on the west side end of **Greenvale Terrace**, central **Morningside Park**, or on the east side at **Old Kingston Rd.** and **Highland Creek Dr.**; also access from the **Waterfront Trail** at the lake, or park in the east at the other side of the treatment plant.

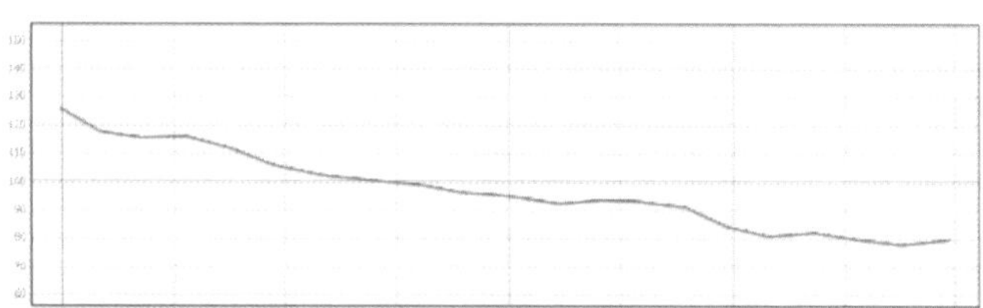

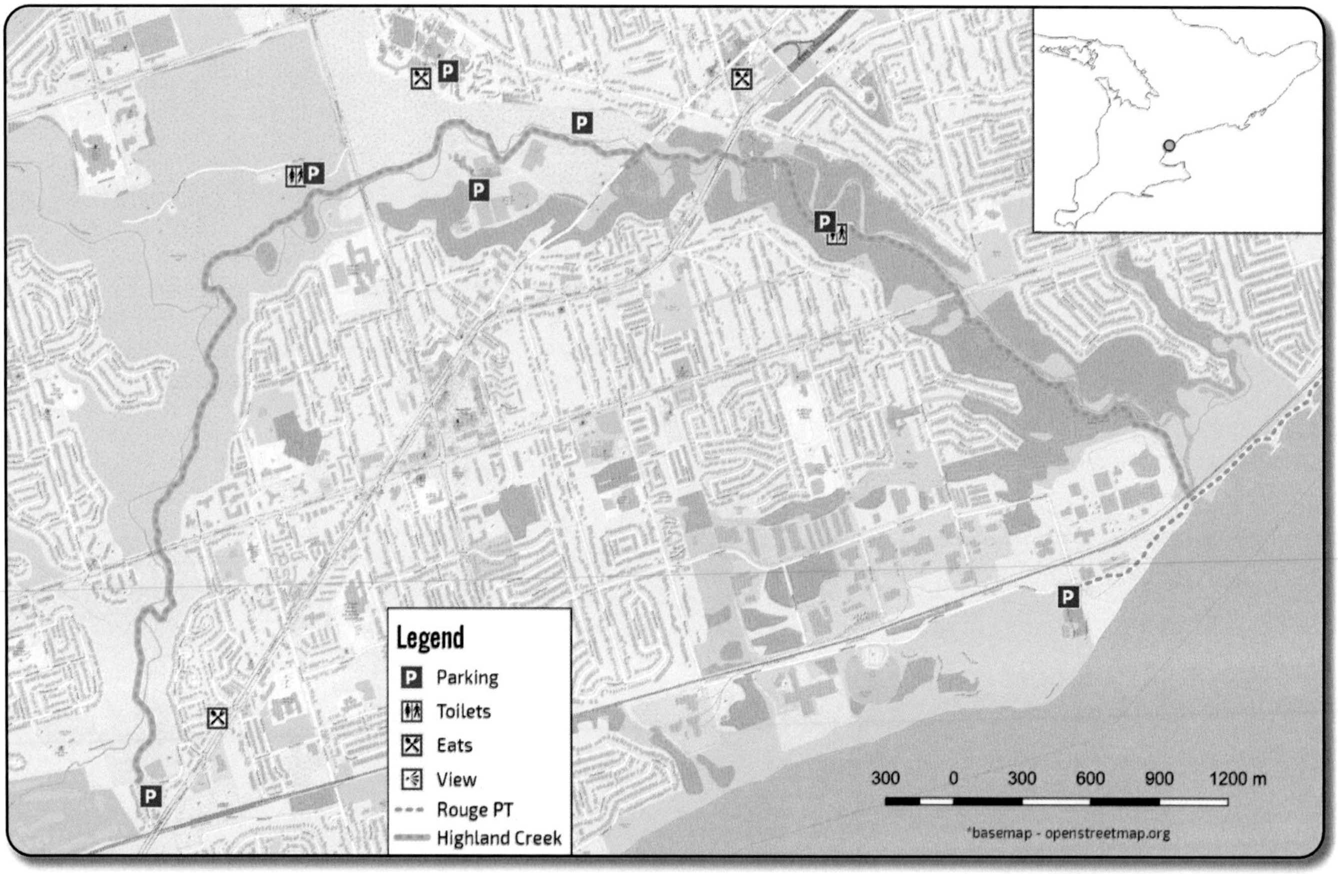

Review:

Highland Creek Park is a **favourite local** getaway. Explore the ever-changing landscape as you ride this **7 km** trail, especially when the **fall colours** are out.

This bike path curves up and around **Kingston Rd.** to **Morningside Park** then back down to **Lake Ontario**.

I recall the path as **smooth** and **paved,** flowing back and forth over the creek via bridges and on to the lake.

The route never seems too busy, and **feels as though you are riding out of the city.** Looking up from the path at the treeline it's not hard to imagine you are in the country, as the houses are just out of sight.

The park has a **half-manicured parkland, half-wild ravine feel.** Two creeks meet in the valley, and flash floods seem to damage the path every year. There may be detours set up, as the city is always working on the problem.

Once down in the valley, there are no monstrous hills—until you need to get out. The signage keeps you on track, but a few more markers would be nice.

In the middle of the route is **Morningside Park,** a large woodland that can be a starting point or the perfect picnic stop. With families coming here for BBQs, it has plenty of picnic tables and washrooms.

East, and up the north bank of the valley, sits the **University of Toronto's Scarborough campus.** These modern, architectural builds are worth a look, but the path there starts as a gradual climb and soon ends at a flight of stairs. (Hmm, not so bike friendly. Time to hike-a-bike....)

Watch for the **two large road bridges** you pass under, as you ride farther down. Growing on the flood plains at the mouth of the creek are some lovely **fields of ferns** under the tree canopy.

When you reach the lake, **three metal bridges** greet riders at the mouth of the creek. Wait fifteen minutes and I am sure a train will roar by.

Down at the water's edge, find a place on the beach to stop and dream away the day, or read a book.

Take in the view of **Lake Ontario** and decide which way to go: head back or find much more path to ride, heading east along the **Rouge Valley** part of the **Waterfront Trail.**

MTB riders will only find the odd short trail, surprisingly not much here worth trying.

For those coming from farther away, the **Guildwood GO station** is close to the west end of the trail.

This is the **best bike trail in Scarborough,** and a top ride in the city. I am not sure everyone knows this, but now you do!

Hilton Falls – MTB/Park Trail

4000 Campbellville Rd, Milton

Length – 18 km MTB + 17 km Park trail = 35 km

35% single-track MTB trail
35% hiking trail
30% double-track access roads

Elevation – Level around the falls, with some small rolling hills.

Terrain – Smooth soil that can be muddy in spots, as well as gravel, rocky roads, rock gardens, limestone outcrops, boardwalks, and bridges.

Skill – Intermediate; Advanced for experienced MTB or Park riders.

Traffic – Cyclists, hikers, Nordic skiing in winter; busy near the falls.

Maps – Maps at trailhead and at some intersections, although does not list all trails; going too far could briefly get you lost.

Facilities – A parking lot, toilets, snack bar, and picnic tables.

Highlights – Crazy, gnarly rocks; the reservoir; and Hilton Falls, with ruins of an old mill. See the tree colours in the fall.

Trail Fee – $6.75 for Adults, $5.00 for kids; pay at the gate.

Phone – 905 854 0262

Website – Hilton Conservation Area

Similar Trails – Agreement Forest, Kelso, 3 Stage

Local Clubs – Halton Agreement Forest Trail Association (HAFTA)

Access – 4000 Campbellville Rd, Milton From the large parking lot, head past the gate and up the gravel road on the left. (Give it some speed, the first climb is a good one!)

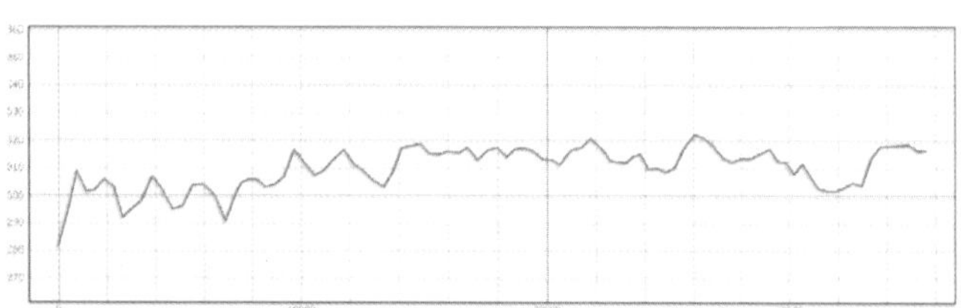

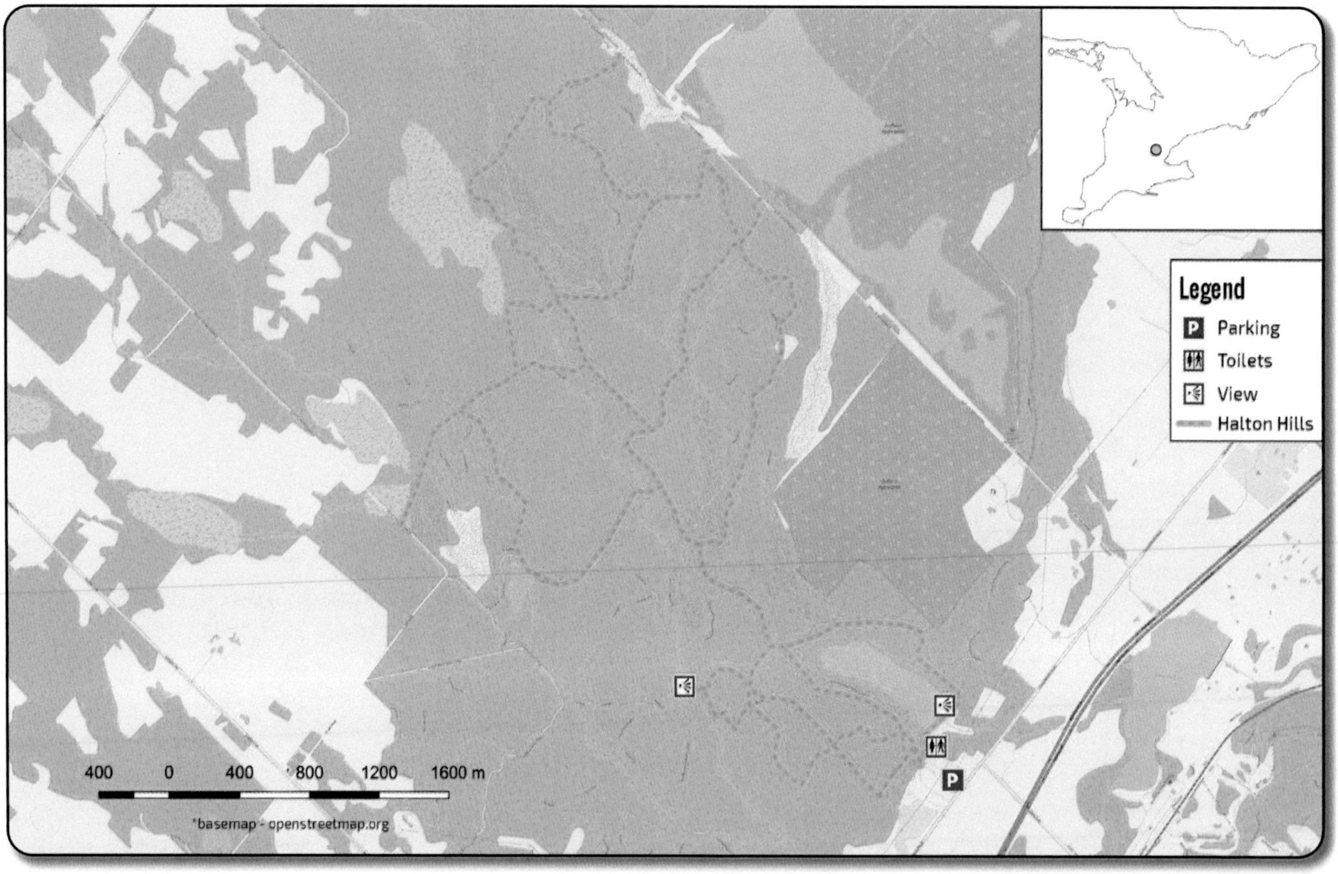

Legend
Parking
Toilets
View
Halton Hills

400 0 400 800 1200 1600 m

*basemap - openstreetmap.org

Review:

Near **Milton**, the **Hilton Falls Conservation Area** has diverse terrain for the **Intermediate Park** rider to **hard-core mountain bikers** who love the challenge of rocks.

Find **gravel roads** that take you in and around the reservoir, and on to **intense rocky sections** only **experienced riders** with **dual suspension bikes** should attempt.

I would consider this a **harder ride** than Kelso, located across the valley. Riders may wish to wear padding or other armour if they are an aggressive MTB rider.

Still, there is some good fun to be had. The **blue loops** on the park map, as well as the **Five Bridges** trail and the **Wally and the Beaver** are local favourites. Beyond, the brown **Lynx trails** are also a great ride.

Expect plenty of **rocky limestone outcrops** to navigate, **wooden bridges** to cross, and **log hops** and **trees roots** a-plenty. Yet the pace and easy gaps make it enjoyable to ride.

Less enjoyable is the **aptly named and infamous Bent Rim Trail.** Even with a **full suspension bike**, the long rock gardens are **ridiculously hard** to clear. Too much walking and cursing.

This I would perhaps attempt with more substantial wheels on a **29er rim.** But remember I warned you, ride at your own peril! (Naturally, you will have to check it out. lol)

As a **Park ride**, this route consists of **Intermediate** to **Advanced** terrain, and I suggest sticking to the main dirt roads on the map. Expect lots of **rocks** and **ridges** on the access roads, and the roads by the reservoir have some **sizable hills** to conquer.

Consider riding around the **dam,** packing a lunch to enjoy at the falls. Here are also **ruins of an old mill,** which are the highlight of the park and is located on the **easiest route**. It's a **beautiful area** in the fall when the colours are out.

When starting out, take the **right trail** from the parking lot to avoid an **even steeper climb** the other way.

Beyond the official riding area, the hiking trails and roads extend northward along the **6th line** and are part of the **Bruce Trail** or head west past the **Lynx trail** system.

Yes! There is more **rock mayhem** beyond to please ... in the Agreement Forest trail network.

Humber River – Park Trail

Lake Ontario to Weston Rd., Toronto

Length – 13 km (one way)

90% park path
10% road, crossings, detours

Terrain – Mostly flat path, some river bridges, a few gentle slopes; detours, one road crossing at lights.

Surface – It is all paved asphalt, with some sand and crushed stone.

Skill – Easy

Facilities – Includes parking, three washrooms, fountains, benches.

Highlights – Bridges, small waterfalls, James Gardens, the lake waterfront, Oculus Pavilion.

Maps – Found at the trailhead; signs on the trail.

Trail Fee – Free

Phone – 311

Website – City of Toronto

Similar Trails – Upper Humber, Highland Creek, Nokiidaa, Upper Etobicoke

Local Clubs – Toronto Bicycling Network, Toronto Bicycle Club

Access – You can connect from the south by bike from the waterfront trails, or from the many side streets and parks on the route.

Car parking can be found at **Riverwood Pkwy** entrance, **Etienne Brule Park, James Gardens** (scarce on weekends), **Edenbridge Dr., Raymore Park**, or **Weston Lions Park** on **Hickory Tree Rd.**

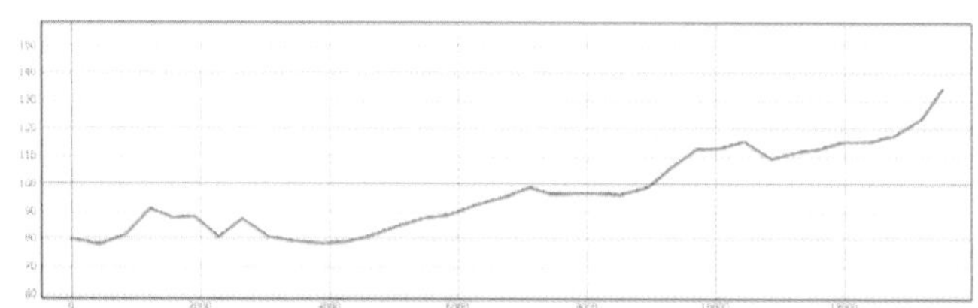

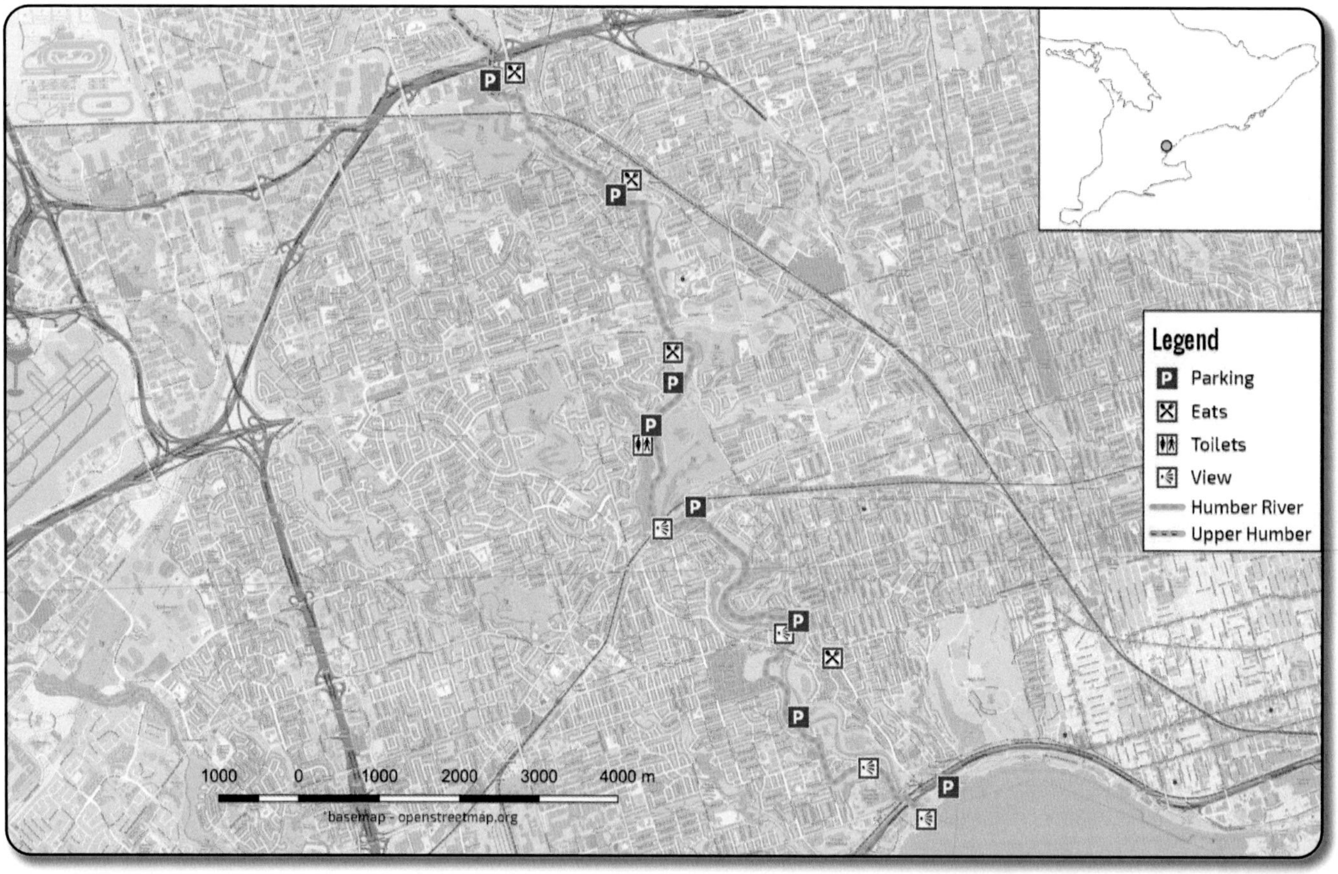

Legend
Parking
Eats
Toilets
View
Humber River
Upper Humber

1000 0 1000 2000 3000 4000 m
basemap - openstreetmap.org

Review:

The **Humber River** bike path is a favourite for locals on the west side of **Toronto** for good reasons.

This **13 km** trail offers an **easy, yet long ride** along the river, with an **ever-changing scenic landscape** on a **well-maintained paved route** with few hills. Plenty of **park benches, small waterfalls, fountains** to stop at along the way.

This path connects well with the **Lake Ontario Waterfront** bike trail network and ends on the north end briefly at the **Weston Road** and **St. Phillips Rd** detour.

At the top end, you can continue after climbing stairs, then riding **300 metres** on the street to go even farther north for **20 km more** of park trail cycling. Read my Upper Humber R. Review.

The lower section of the trail is more popular, yet I think the upper end is as enjoyable.

So **starting at the lake,** it winds up along the west side through a small park to a side street. Note the **Oculus Pavilion,** a bizarre, circular "spaceship" rain shelter.

Unfortunately, now there will be a **700 m detour** road ride along side streets – take **Stephen Dr.,** left on **Riverwood Pkwy.** Entrance on the right takes you through parkland and puts you back down into the river valley.

Passing under the **Old Mill Subway station**, you will cross over the **old stone bridge** to get to the other side of the river. Look to see if any fishermen may be out for the salmon run.

Notice that you can ride the **Home Smith Park Rd.** on the west bank on your return. This was a one-way road heading south that once had fine homes, until flood waters from a hurricane changed that.

Onward, you might find a few short, dirt side trails in **Lambton Woods**. Then, travel to **James Gardens** – as the flower gardens are worth looking at. It is also busy for wedding photos, hence the scarce parking on weekends.

You'll pass two golf courses before needing to cross the street at the lights at **Eglinton Ave. W.** Beyond this point, you will not see much of the river for a few minutes until the road descends to the valley parkland once more.

Finally, you end up at the stairs and the street detour. You can continue the second half of the **longest river trail in Toronto,** or you can just head back.

Taking the subway to the **Old Mill Station** is an excellent way to get to this ride from other areas of town, without having to worry about parking.

The paths are busy with bikes and walkers on any sunny weekend, so keep your speed and sanity. This route has many **opportunities to stop**, rest on the lawn, a bench or river rock, and watch the clouds drift by ... ahhh!

Long Sault – Park/MTB Trail

9293 Woodley Rd., North of Bowmanville

Length – 18 km

100% double-track park trail path

Elevation – Flat in sections with some ravines and gradual incline northward; also a few large hills.

Terrain – A wide trail of smooth dirt mixed with grass, leaves, roots, and some very sandy spots.

Skill – Easy for MTB; Advanced for two Park trails.

Traffic – Watch for hikers, dogs, and cross-country skiers in winter.

Maps – Found at parking lot, as well as plenty of signposts along the route.

Facilities – Lots of parking, outhouses, and picnic tables.

Highlights – A few lookouts and farms; fall colours and wildlife.

Trail Fee – $3.00/hr, $6.00 per day.

Phone – 905 579 0411

Website – Central Lake Ontario Conservation

Similar Trails – Heber Downs , Northumberland, Ganaraska

Local Clubs – Cobourg Cycling Club, Peterborough Cycling Club

Access – From **Bowmanville**, go north on **Hwy 57 to Waverly Rd.** for about 12 km, then turn east on **Hwy 20** for ten minutes to the end of **Woodley Rd., #9293.**

Aside from the park entrance, there are two small parking lots on the north side.

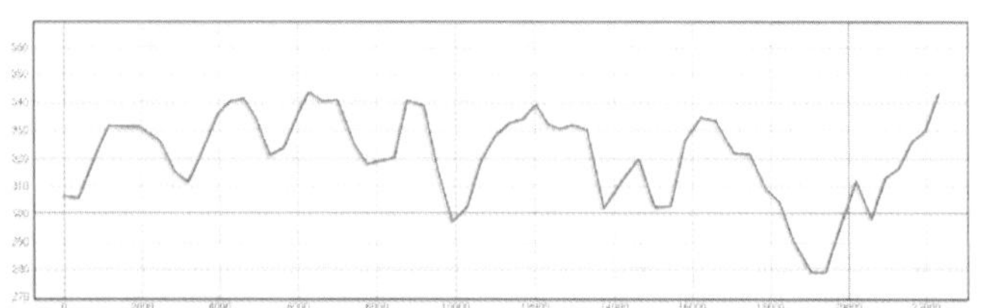

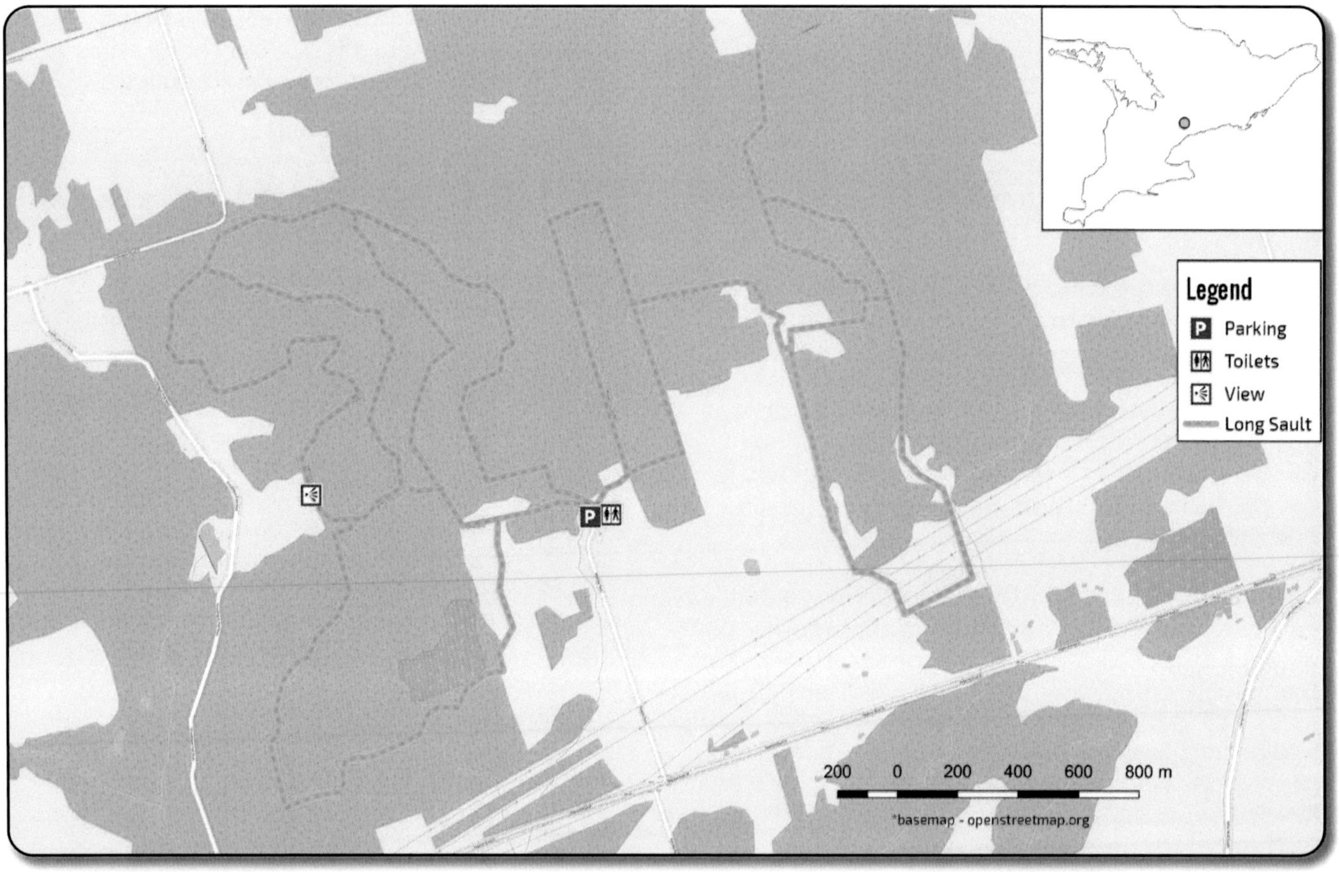

Review:

Long Sault Conservation Area is north to **Bowmanville**, on the side of a north-sloping hill.

Riders will find **five loops,** rated from **Beginner** to **Advanced** for a **Park trail** rider.

The **18 km** of paths are well-signed, wide, and have smooth soil with a leafy base and the odd root to keep you attentive. Any **fit cyclist** can easily do this as a day outing with friends or family.

The signs cleverly tell you to ride in the **opposite direction** of the hikers so they can see you.

Granted, there are a **few long hills** you may have to walk, but most riders with a decent bike and strong legs can manage.

The routes are shady, with the odd bench at which to sit and take in the occasional view. It is indeed a pretty place to visit in the **fall,** if you get there at the right time!

I suggest riding the west side first, completing the **Bluebird** and **Wild Turkey** loops. The east side is an open field with straighter paths.

Due to the larger hills and the occasional spot of loose sand, I recommend this trail for the **Advanced Park** rider.

The official site rates this as a **MTB trail,** but it is a bit **too easy** as the double-track path is straight. But as a beginner mountain biker, it's great.

The seasoned MTB crowd can still get a good workout with a fast, cross-country type run, but expect no twisty or narrow trails.

Also a great spot for **Fatbikes** any time of the year, so watch out for Nordic skiers and snow-shoers in the winter.

Plenty of path to ride here, and being close to **Oshawa** it is an excellent transitional step for harder MTB tracks elsewhere.

Lower Don – Park Trail

Lakeshore to Taylor Creek, Toronto

Length – 8 km (one way)

95% park trail path
5% roads, crossing, detours

Elevation – Flat as it follows the river with a few short inclines, one significant hill, and some bridges and tunnels.

Terrain – All paved asphalt, with some sand due to flooding.

Skill – Easy

Traffic – Bikes, hikers, rollerbladers, dogs. During summer weekends and commuter hours, it can be bustling with riders.

Maps – There is new signage, complete with maps and milestone markers.

Facilities – Be aware there are no close washrooms or amenities until you get out of the valley and into city streets.

Highlights – Large bridges, a sculpture garden, rapids, and lovely colours in the fall.

Trail Fee – Free

Phone – Toronto 311

Website – Don River Valley Park

Similar Trails – Humber River, Taylor Creek, Thames Valley

Local Clubs – Toronto Bicycle Network, Toronto Bicycle Club

Access – There are limited entryways and exits: at **Lakeshore Rd., Queen St., Riverdale Park** bridges, **Pottery Rd.**, and **Don Mills Rd.** It's best to use your bike to get there, as there is limited parking; only some at **Pottery Rd.** and **Taylor Creek.**

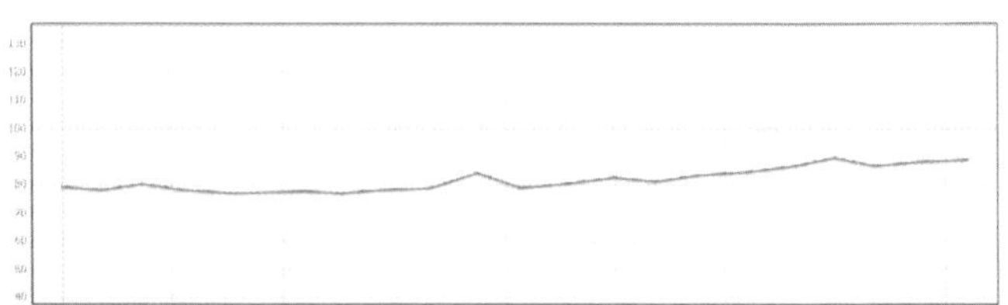

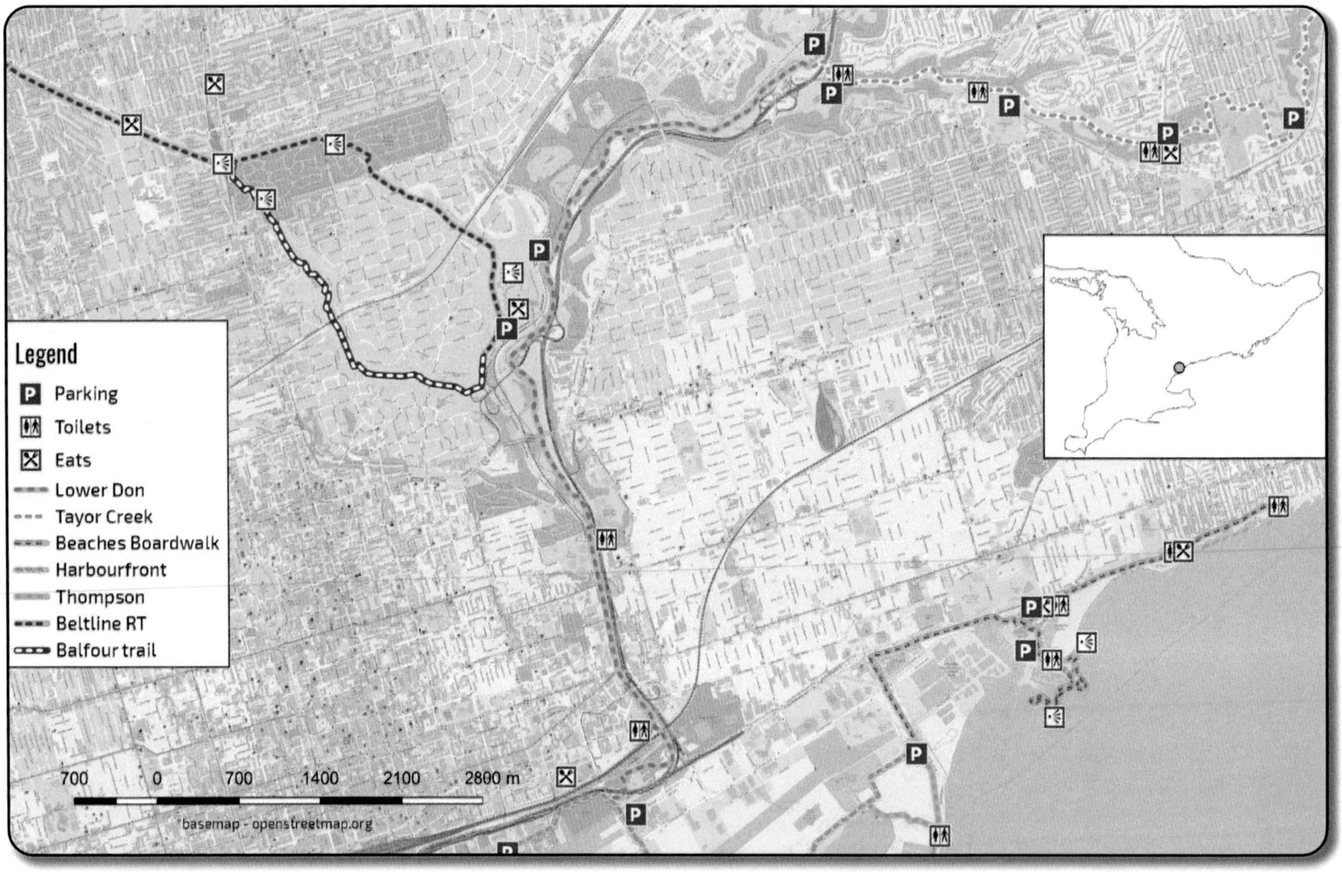

Legend
Parking
Toilets
Eats
Lower Don
Tayor Creek
Beaches Boardwalk
Harbourfront
Thompson
Beltline RT
Balfour trail

700 0 700 1400 2100 2800 m
basemap - openstreetmap.org

Review:

The **Lower Don River** path is one of the **main arteries** of Toronto's bicycle trail network.

It spans from the mouth of the **Don River** and north for **8 km**, connecting to many other routes at both ends. Other exits help riders get around and explore **the city.**

I am pleased to state **construction upgrades** are finally done this has made this path a safer and more pleasant ride. **New signage,** complete with maps, enhance the ride and help tourists find other routes and amenities.

Running up this large valley, the path is a very **popular bike thoroughfare**. Expect lots of bicycles, joggers and walkers with dogs on weekends, as well as work commuters during the week.

This **well-maintained path** has grown in nicely, it has a bit of a wild, natural feel to it, and in the fall the **colours are spectacular.**

If it were not for the drone of the **expressway traffic** beside you, it almost seems as though you are in the country; but then you spot another high rise building and think, maybe not.

As you cycle this path keep in mind **exit points are limited**, with the river on one side, fenced **train tracks** on the other, and the busy **Don Valley Parkway (DVP)** blocking the way.

Riding north from **Lake Ontario**, this ride is **all asphalt** and hugs the **Don River** on the west side. As the riverbanks were straightened and tamed many years ago, this starts as a flat, straight route.

This does little to stop spring **flooding,** so take note of closures and any loose sand washed up on the path.

Thankfully, this route has a few **bridges** and **tunnels** to take you elsewhere. The first along the route heading north is **Corktown Commons**, and there is a new park to explore if you go west through the tunnel.

There are bike-friendly stairs at the **Queen St.** and the **Riverdale Park** bridges to get you up and out. Not until **Pottery Road, 2.5 km** further up the route, will you find any exits that lead up the steep climbs out of the valley.

Past the **river rapids** (another good spot to rest), a crossroads further up goes west over parklands to MTB trails, or up **Beechwood Dr**. (a quiet, steep road) to **O'Connor Drive.**

I noted a new **sculpture garden** along the way; a strange curiosity that gets everyone to pause and perhaps rest, take a photo, and look back at the giant black bridge, the **Bloor St. Viaduct**. A nice addition by the city!

For about another **2 km**, the path meanders up the valley and under **another large bridge (Millwood Rd.)**, ending as you go under the **DVP** to a junction by what locals call the **Giant Molars.**

Here, riders can continue along the Taylor Creek path east, or head even farther north along the Don River to **Sunnybrook Park** or **Edwards Gardens**, all excellent rides.

Morrison Valley – Park Trail

Trafalgar Rd. & 8th Line, Oakville

Length – 4 km (one way)

95% park path trail
5% roads,crossings, detours

Elevation – Most of the route follows the creek valley, with a few steep hills (best to walk) that lead in and out of the valley.

Terrain – Made of an asphalt base, with some sections of crushed stone and gravel.

Skill – Easy

Maps – There is a map at the trailhead, with a few signs on the trail.

Facilities – Parking can be found on the street, with amenities close by.

Highlights – A quiet trail with bridges, forests, creeks, and lovely fall colours.

Trail Fee – Free

Phone – None

Website – City of Oakville

Similar Trails – Dundas Valley, Oshawa Creek, Taylor Creek

Local Clubs – Oakville Cycling Club

Access – In Oakville the path runs parallel between **Trafalgar Rd. & 8th Line.** There is lots of access from side streets, so refer to a map as well.

Oakville Municipal Building on **White Oaks & Trafalgar**.

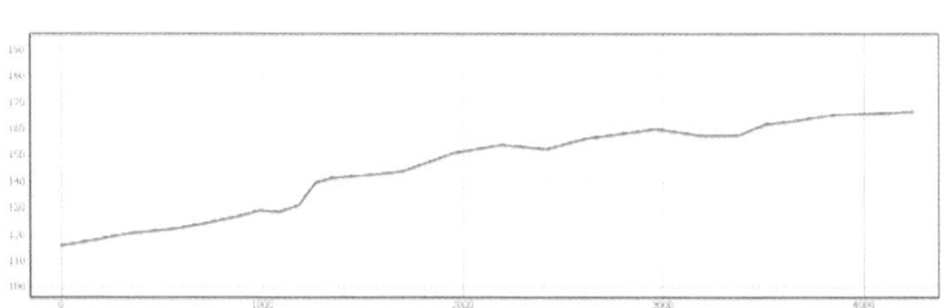

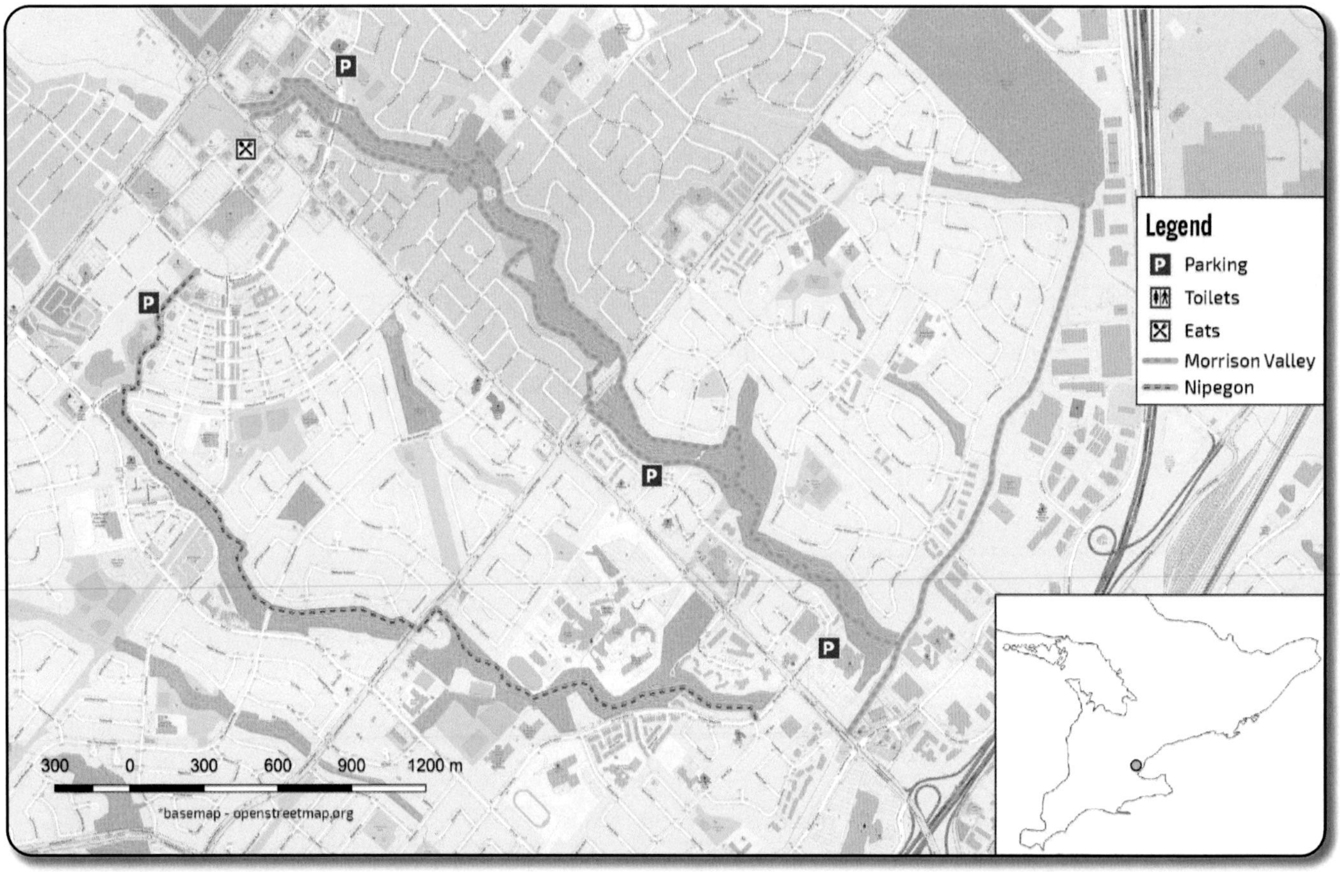

Legend
P Parking
Toilets
Eats
Morrison Valley
Nipegon

300 0 300 600 900 1200 m
*basemap - openstreetmap.org

Review:

The **Morrison Valley Park Trail** is a short yet pleasant **8 km bike ride** through the middle of **Oakville**. Most **paths run parallel to the water on each side**.

This makes for a fun, quick loop up one side and almost to **Dundas St. E.** and **Trafalgar Rd.,** then back down the other.

Although short, the route is not boring with ever-changing **sections of pavement and crushed stone**.

As some of the path is at **creek level,** a few bridge crossings will take you up and **along the valley ridge**.

As the path winds through a **narrow, treed ravine** that follows the creek, you will briefly experience a feeling of being **in the country.**

The total length is **family friendly**, at **8 km return-trip**. There are a **few steep hills** to contend with, so you may have to walk your bike at times.

Unfortunately, there are three **busy roads to cross** along the way so be cautious in your attempts.

If not a local, a suitable place to park is in the lot at the trail's south end at the **Oakville Municipal Building** on **White Oaks & Trafalgar**. Find the trail leading right in on the east side.

At the bottom of the **Morrison Trail** is a water-diversion channel; yes, it's ugly, but you can ride the bank east for a few more kilometres. It looks like it may have been a rail bed years ago, although I am not sure.

Oakville has many bike paths, although most are short and not connected.

Morrison Valley is one of the longer stretches you can ride without having to contend with much street traffic.

An **optional return route** is to head west at the top end and through the "large mall zone" to reach **Oak Park.**

Then, loop back down the **Nipigon Trail**. This will take you right back to **Oakville City Hall,** adding about **2 km** more to the **4 km** you had for the return trip.

Niagara River – Park Trail

Niagara on the Lake to Fort Erie

Length – 53 km (one way)

90% park path
10% roads, crossings, detours

Elevation – Follows a gradual slope up from Lake Ontario with a large switchback at **Queenston**, then level to **Lake Erie.**

Terrain – A wide path of paved asphalt, with some crushed stone and gravel; road-riding is available in **Niagara Falls.**

Skill – Easy

Traffic – Well-used by cyclists, with some walkers and tourists to watch for.

Maps – Plenty of signs and maps on the trail.

Facilities – Street parking and washrooms, with access to food, water, lodging, and bike rentals.

Highlights – A very scenic ride! Take in **Niagara Falls**, the large river and its many lookouts, as well as garden parks, sprawling estates, military forts, and historic towns.

Trail Fee – Free

Phone – 1 800 563 2557

Website – Niagara Cycling Tourism, Niagara Falls Tourism, Niagara Parks

Similar Trails – Hamilton Beach, Ajax Waterfront, Welland Canal

Local Clubs – St. Catharines Cycling Club, Niagara Freewheelers

Access – There are many parking lots, and a good spot to start from is along the **Niagara Parkway.**

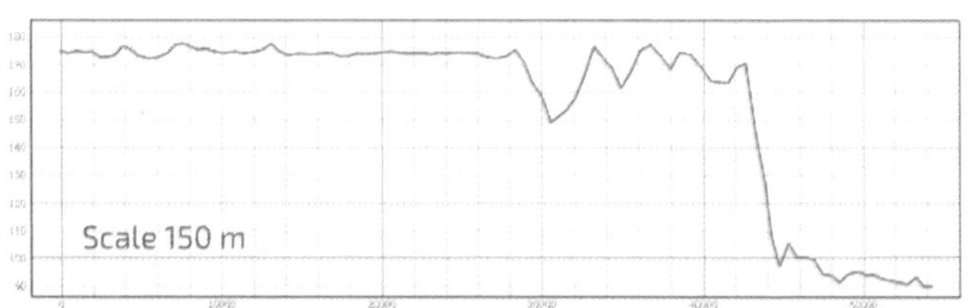

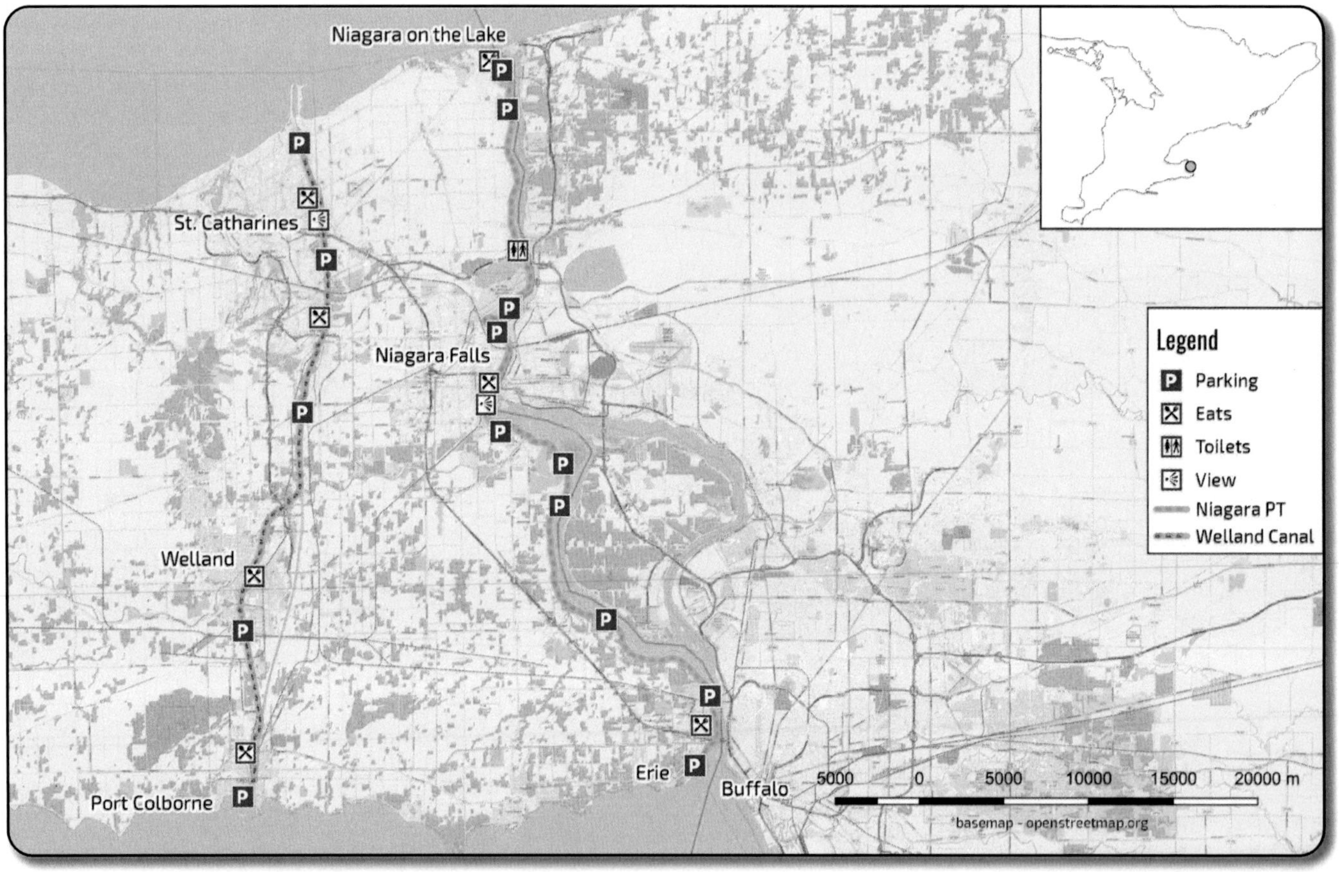

Niagara on the Lake
St. Catharines
Niagara Falls
Welland
Port Colborne
Erie
Buffalo
5000 0 5000 10000 15000 20000 m
basemap - openstreetmap.org

Legend
- Parking
- Eats
- Toilets
- View
- Niagara PT
- Welland Canal

Review:

The **Niagara River Recreation Trail** is one of the **best Park trails in Ontario**. As this **53 km** trail is paved, it is a well-used path that winds along the **Niagara River.** You'll never get bored of the **sights** and **attractions**.

The mighty **Niagara Falls** is undoubtedly the big draw and is located in the middle of this route.

Other highlights are **lookouts over the river gorge** and the **fast-flowing water,** as well as **stately homes, flower gardens, quaint eateries, historical statues** and **forts.**

Since it is **100 km return-trip**, I typically ride only from one end or the other—to the Falls and back.

There is one main difference between each section. Above **Niagara Falls**, riding in north from **Fort Erie**, the river flows just a few metres below the riverbank trail.

However, if you ride south from **Niagara-on-the-Lake** to the Falls, the trail starts close to the river and contains **an approximately 100 m switchback** at **Queenston**. From there to the Falls the now-turbulent river is way below in the gorge.

Take a moment to visit the **quaint** and **historic** parts of **Niagara-on-the-Lake** and **Queenston.** Or, you may like the buzz of tourists and bright lights of **Niagara Falls.**

Fort Erie is more of a working border town, with a Rail trail that carries on along **Lake Erie**.

This **well-maintained** paved path is free of cars and runs parallel to the road through picturesque parkland.

Watch for the many crossovers at side roads and driveways. Unfortunately, cycling through the town of **Niagara Falls** requires some road-riding to connect back to the natural trail.

There are plenty of places to eat or stay overnight along the way. I found a campground right on the path, and also saw numerous beautiful Bed & Breakfasts.

Make it a weekend with a circular route back along the Welland Canal. On weekends you can also take your bike on the **GO Train** (always check first).

If this is sounding like the ideal **Toronto getaway,** it is! Whether for a day trip or longer stay, this is a great place to play tourist or the romantic.

Nokiidaa – Park Trail

Aurora to Newmarket

Length – 18 km (one way)

90% park path
10% roads, crossings, detours

Elevation – Mostly follows the river in a gradual slope, with one hill—yes, only one medium sized climb.

Terrain – Smooth asphalt for the majority of the middle section, with some crushed stone and gravel at each end of the path; also some boardwalks and bridges.

Skill – Easy

Traffic – Nice weekends are busy, with the typical users of Park trails.

Maps – A map is found at the trailhead and there are signs on the trail; there are no signs where the trail splits.

Facilities – Washrooms are located in **Newmarket Park** and at two **Aurora Park** centres; places to eat can be found in **Newmarket.**

Highlights – Old **Newmarket**, bridges, locks, and wetlands; enjoy carved wooden statues and wildlife.

Trail Fee – Free

Phone – None

Website – City of Aurora, City of Newmarket

Similar Trails – Highland Creek, Greenway, Humber River

Local Clubs – Uxbridge Cycling Club, Newmarket Eagles Cycling Club

Access – There are numerous entry points; refer to map for parking locations.

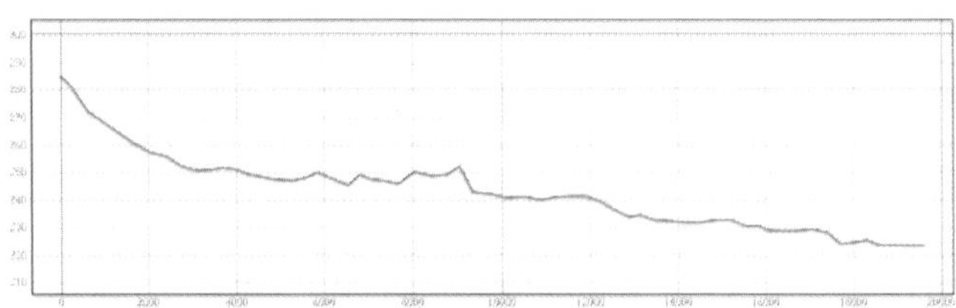

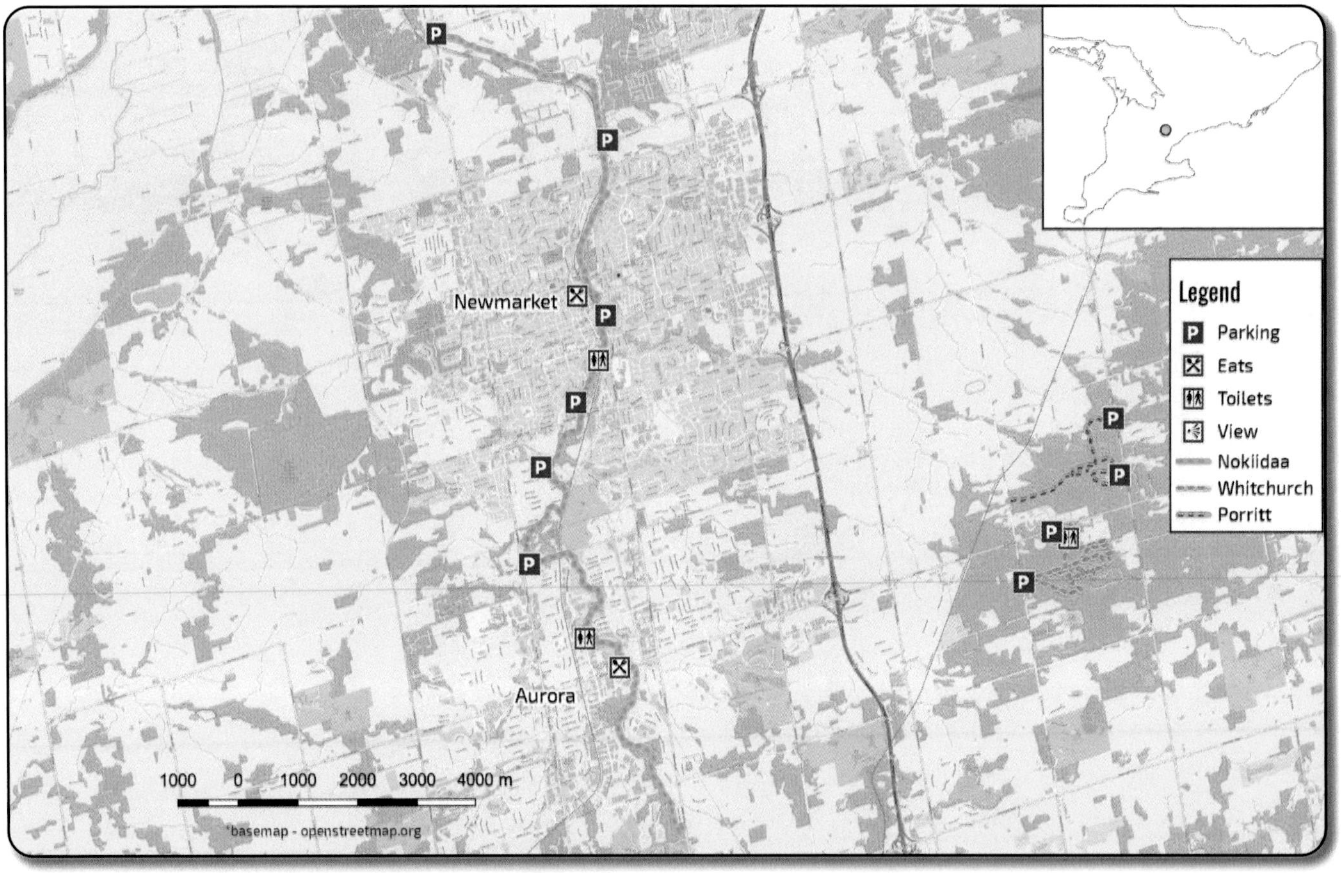

Newmarket
Aurora
Legend
Parking
Eats
Toilets
View
Nokiidaa
Whitchurch
Porritt
1000 0 1000 2000 3000 4000 m
*basemap - openstreetmap.org

Review:

The **Nokiidaa (Tom Taylor)** bike trail is a popular Park trail from **Aurora** to **Newmarket**. On any given weekend, locals cruise this path that runs along the creek and turns into the **Holland River**. **Nokiidaa** is an Ojibwa word that translates to "walking together".

Enjoy a **very scenic path** that changes landscape as it winds through the valley, among the subdivisions, and into pockets of wooded trees and fields.

This park path is very **well-maintained** consisting of smooth asphalt. You will find crushed gravel above **Green Lane** as well as in the south a few kilometres from the end of the trail's end in **Aurora**.

There is **only one moderate hill** to get around the golf course (near the middle); otherwise your cruise is free and easy as it meanders along the creek.

Starting in the south end, this Park trail has ample signage and connects well to other paths, going through many underpasses to avoid car traffic. There are a few crossings over roads that require you to jog over to reconnect.

About half of the pathway is **shaded,** with the rest open parkland. At some points the **path splits** and runs on either side of the creek. They are equally worth doing, and both are optional on the return.

I personally found the **west side** more to my liking. Here, the **trail splits** off several times and leads into friendly neighbourhoods. A lack of signs can have you question which way to go; if you have no map stick with the level path, closer to the water.

Historic downtown Newmarket has lots of charm, and I recommended this stop. It's convenient; just a block west of the path, after the pond.

At one point the creek was dammed, and the remainders of a **lock and swing bridge** harken back to a time when barges moved goods north to **Lake Simcoe**.

Distance markers at every kilometre are artful **wood sculptures**, which is a nice touch. Plenty of **park benches** dot the path for a rest, if you need one. This is undoubtedly an even more **beautiful ride in the fall.**

Due north and central to **Toronto**, this trail provides a great reason to get out of town and go for an outing with your favourite friend on your trusty bicycle.

North Simcoe + Tiny – Rail Trails

Penetanguishene to West of Barrie

Length – 32 + 30 = 52 km

90% rail trail path
10% roads, crossings, detours

Elevation – A flat grade with two gradual northward climbs, then descents into **Georgian Bay.**

Terrain – A wide path of crushed stone and gravel, with one detour along some side roads.

Skill – Easy

Traffic – Quite few users, with bicyclists, hikers, and horseback riders; snowmobiles in winter.

Maps – Signs are located at crossroads, and maps boards at parking locations.

Facilities – Street parking, as well as services in **Elmvale, Wyevale, Anten Mills**, and **Penetanguishene.**

Highlights – **Fort Willow, Mayer's Marsh, Minesing Station**, wetlands, **Penetang.**

Phone – None

Website – Simcoe Country

Similar Tails – Oro – Medonte, Victoria South

Local Clubs – Barrie Cycling Club

Access – Enter at any crossroad as there are a few parking lots to choose from: **Hwy 26** and **Flos Rd. 4** West, **Hwy 92** and the halfway point of **Elmvale** and **Heritage Park, Concession Rd. 3 East** and **Concession Rd. 5 East, Wyevale** and **Hwy 25** in **Perkinsfield**, and **Main St.** and **Beck Blvd.** in **Penetanguishene.**

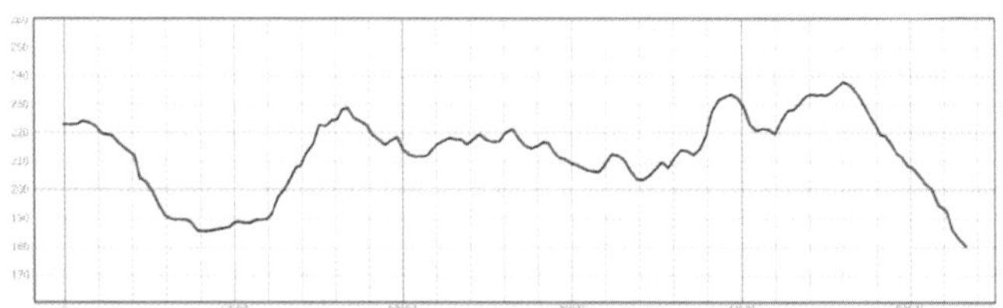

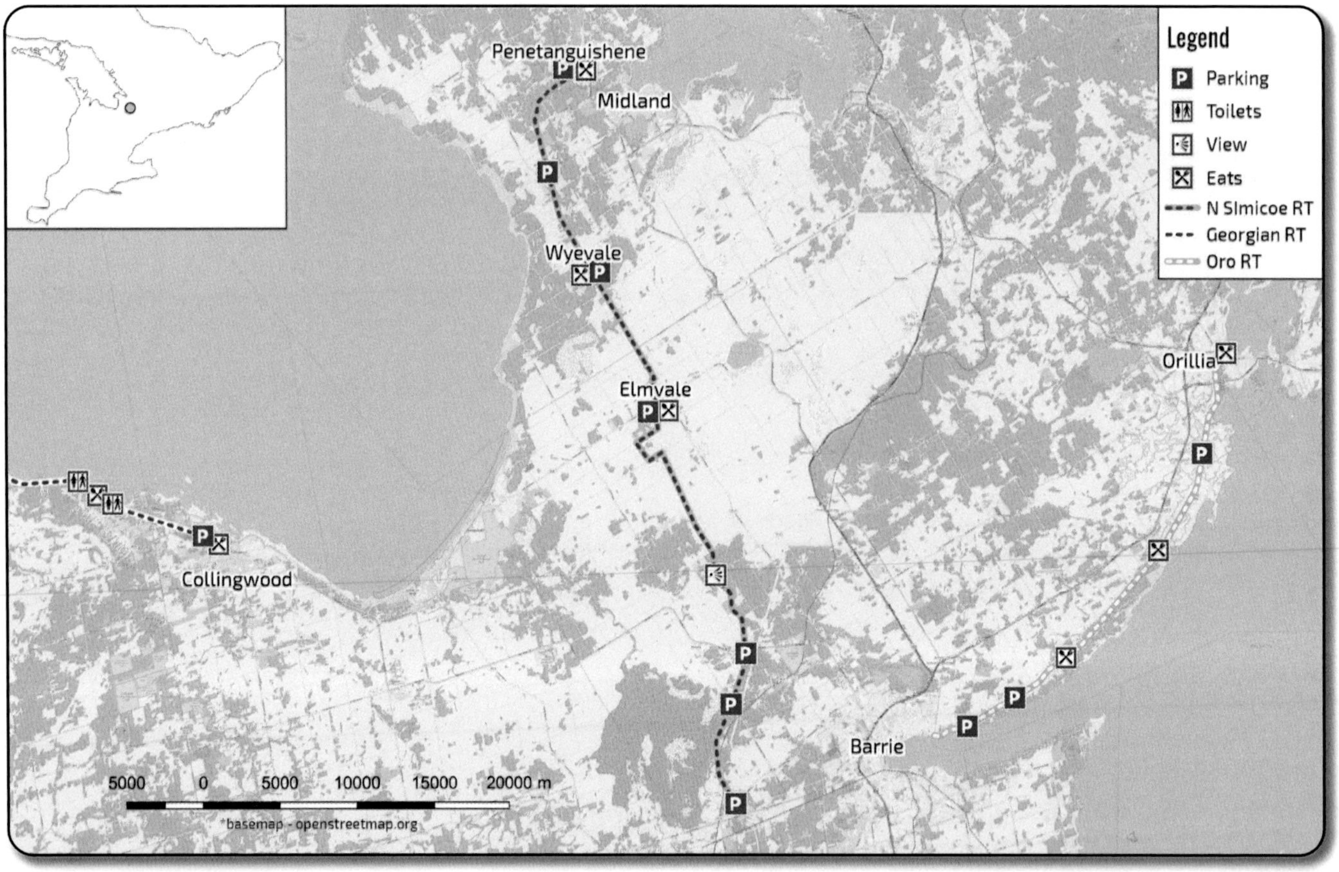

Penetanguishene
Midland
Wyevale
Elmvale
Orillia
Collingwood
Barrie
Legend
Parking
Toilets
View
Eats
N Simcoe RT
Georgian RT
Oro RT
5000 0 5000 10000 15000 20000 m
basemap - openstreetmap.org

Review:

The **32-km North Simcoe Rail Trail** also includes the **20-km Tiny Rail Trail** that heads north to **Penetanguishene** and was initially the route of the **North Simcoe Railway**.

This Rail Trail travels through **forests, large wetlands, scenic farmland, and small towns,** as well as by a **few historic points.** A tree-lined and shady route most of the way, the middle section north of **Hwy 26** and on to **Wyevale** has more to see, being more open to the sun's rays.

Part of the **Trans Canada Trail** you will see the occasional rider or hiker. The trails are mostly straight stretches, as this was the cheapest way to lay long tracks. The base is well-maintained and made of crushed stone dust, with some grasses coming through on the less accessible parts.

Along the route, there are **eleven interpretive signs of historical interest** to enlighten travellers.

The **south end** of the trail, just west of **Barrie,** does not have a definitive starting point or a parking lot (although it should). You can, however, find a right spot on the roadside.

South beyond **Sunnidale Rd.** things gets rough and the trail peters out. I find it better to catch the Rail trail here, or further up on **Pinegrove Rd.**

This route will lead you north to **Fort Willow, a small historical site** that once stored military supplies during the **War of 1812.** On the west side of the trail is the sizeable **Minesing Swamp**—which could mean bugs.

Further along, at **Hwy 26,** is a good starting point as it has a parking lot. Here, the trail continues and crosses through fields, as well as a golf course. It then climbs to an impressive view of the valley when you reach **Horsevalley Rd. West.**

A **detour** comes **4 km** north after the village of **Phelpston**. Unfortunately, someone sold the right of way and trail users now need to go around on this stretch of country roads. So, head west to **Ushers Rd.** and then back east on **Flos Rd. 8 W.** to pick up the line again.

If you've followed the path in this direction you'll now be at **Elmvale**, so check out the old homes from the time trains ran past, and find places to eat if you need them.

Beyond this, the path runs straight along **Hwy 6** for **12 km** past **Wyevale** and to the highest point of the trail, near **Perkinsfield.** The path then gradually curves and descends sixty metres to **Penetanguishene** through a quiet forest valley. Eventually, riders will emerge and come into a neighbourhood.

The trail ends at the bay, on the paved waterfront Park path. This provides a fine opportunity to have lunch and then head back, or make this, the largest town along the ride your starting point.

For a leisurely, mellow cruise, you'll enjoy biking this strip of history.

History – In the pioneer days, stage coaches ran a similar route north, adding a tavern every two kilometres or so for passengers to eat and rest. When the **North Simcoe Railway** was built in **1878,** this put the thirty-seven taverns along the route in jeopardy of losing most of their clientele.

Trains on this line primarily served the lumber businesses on **Georgian Bay**. In **1991** the track was abandoned by **CN Rail** to become a multi-use recreational trail.

Omemee – Rail Trail

Lindsay to Peterborough

Length – 35 km (one way)

95% rail trail
5% roads, crossing, detours

Elevation – Mostly flat, with a gradual slope.

Terrain – A wide path of crushed stone, gravel, and some sand; a large bridge is also on the route.

Skill – Easy

Traffic – A quiet ride, with some bicyclists, hikers, and horseback riders; cross-country skiers and snowmobiles in winter.

Maps – There are maps at a few trailheads, and proper signage on the trail.

Facilities – Street parking, with services in Omemee.

Highlights – A massive trestle bridge, the Lindsay locks and downtown, as well as the sights in Peterborough and Omemee.

Trail Fee – Free

Phone – None

Website – Trans Canada Trail

Similar Trails – Uxbridge, Victoria South, Kissing Bridge

Local Clubs – Peterborough Cycling Club, Kawartha Cycling Club

Access – There are many crossroads where you could find parking.

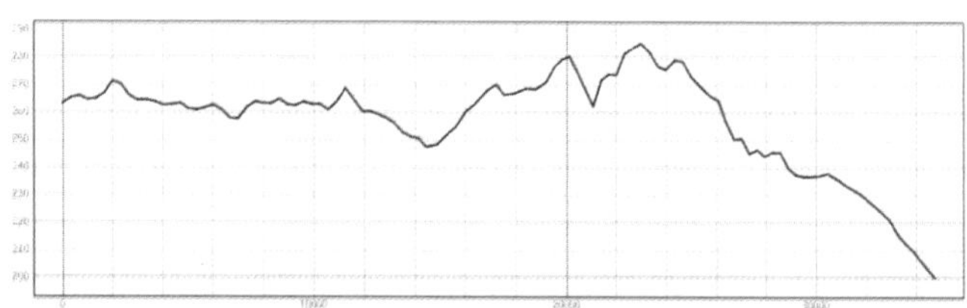

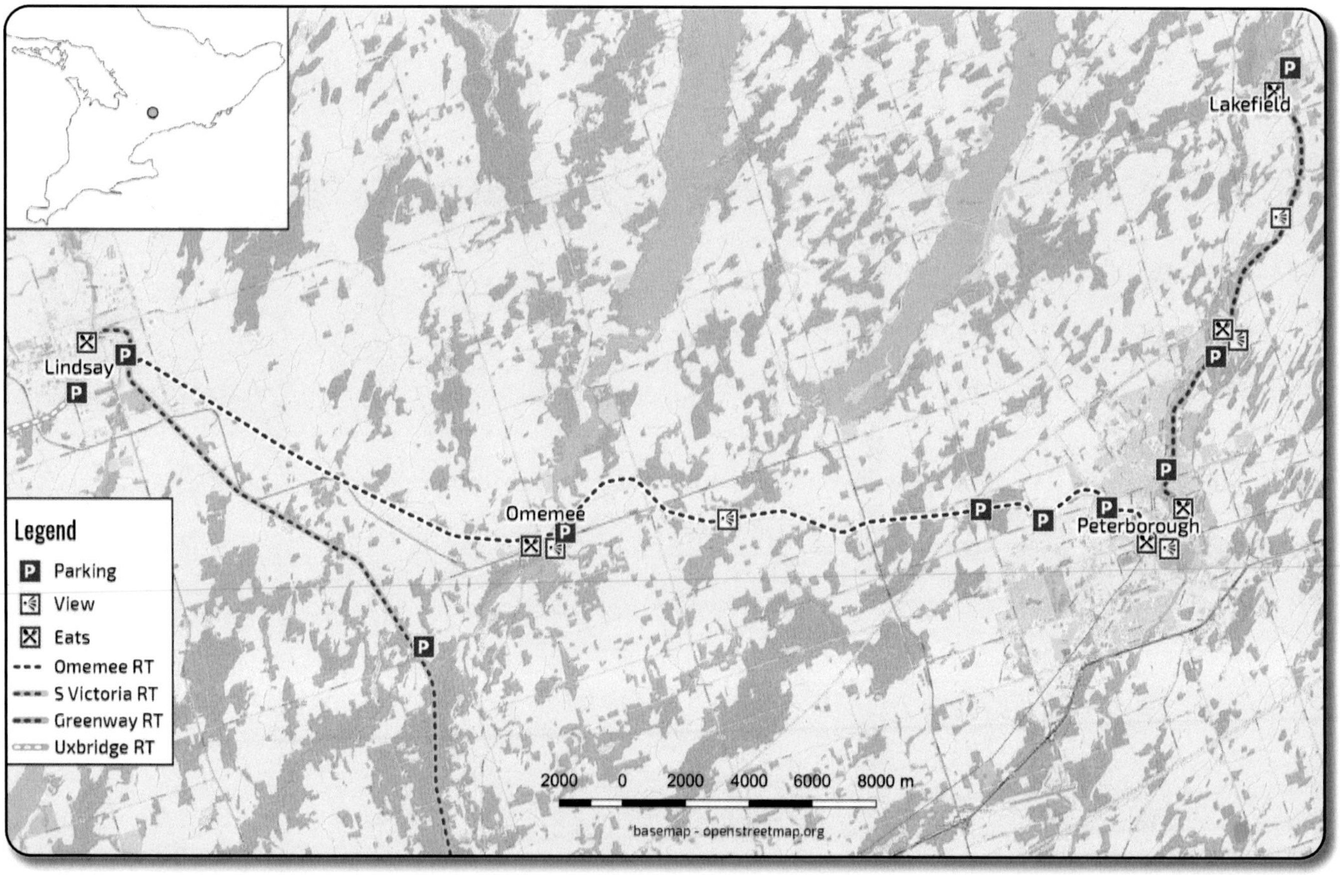

Lakefield
Lindsay
Omemee
Peterborough

Legend
Parking
View
Eats
Omemee RT
S Victoria RT
Greenway RT
Uxbridge RT

2000 0 2000 4000 6000 8000 m
*basemap - openstreetmap.org

Review:

The **Omemee Rail Trail** is a popular **35-km** ride running from **Lindsay** to **Peterborough.** It is an easy ride on crushed gravel and makes for a good outing with family or friends.

Being part of the **Trans Canada Trail**, the path is well-maintained and free of anything motorized during the summer.

This is **Southern Ontario farm country** so you will see plenty of **farms, fields,** and the **occasional woodlot** as this rail bed meanders along. Expect numerous road crossings on country roads; the busier crossings still have the **original bridges** and underpasses.

About midpoint along the trail, services can be found in **Omemee.** There is little else to be found in between, so pack water and snacks for the ride.

If biking just half the trail, I recommend the **Omemee** to **Peterborough** portion as I find this end more scenic than the **Lindsay** side. At **40 km return-trip**, that is plenty of trail for most!

Starting in **Omemee,** go to the north end of **Emily St. N.** to access the Rail Trail. Before heading off, take a quick peek just west to see the **Pigeon River** and the **iron bridge**.

Now, heading east into **Peterborough,** the highlight here is the **200 m** long **Doube's Trestle bridge** (at about the **6.5 km** mark). And what a view! At **29 m** above the **Buttermilk Valley,** I am thankful there are now guardrails!

As you get closer to **Peterborough** the path passes through some **wetlands**, gradually descending **80 m** into a ravine. Here is a lovely stretch of **shady riding** that takes you into an older neighbourhood.

Skip along the four short city sections of parkland before the rail bed ends at **Aylmer St. E**. You will find many places to eat just beyond in the downtown area.

If heading to **Lindsay**, the trail ends at a suburb but does join up to another Rail Trail (the Victoria South branch) and takes you into town via a short road detour. It ends at the **locks**, and once you cross the river there are places to eat downtown.

If you wish to camp at the halfway point, try **Emily Provincial Park** just north of Omemee.

History – The **Port Hope, Lindsay, and Beaverton Railway** opened this line in 1857 running first from **Lindsay** to **Omemee** and then south to **Port Hope.** (Some of the track bed now forms **Ski Hill Rd.** at **Hwy 38.**)

A direct link to **Peterborough** was still needed, and in 1883 the **Midland Railway** completed a route from **Omemee**. Originally, the trestle bridges along the trail were made of wood; later, portions were replaced with iron.

The last passenger train passed through **Omemee** in 1962, and the **Lindsay-Peterborough** line closed in **1988**. The trail was abandoned until **2010**, when the **Kawartha Trans Canada Trail** opened the path as a recreational Rail Trail.

2019 Reaboro - Beaver lodge - Trestle Bridge

2018 Lindsay - Pickard Access

Oro – Medonte – Rail Trail

Barrie to Orillia

Length – 28 km (one way)

90% rail trail
10% roads crossings

Elevation – Mostly flat, and follows the Lake Simcoe shoreline.

Terrain – A wide path of crushed stone with some loose gravel; bridges along the route.

Skill – Easy

Traffic – Not typically busy, but used by bicyclists, hikers, and horseback riders; may see snowmobiles and Nordic skiers in the winter.

Maps – There are signs at most crossroads.

Facilities – Street parking and lots of amenities marked on the map at the trailhead.

Highlights – Historical signage on the path, and picturesque marshland and farms.

Phone – None

Website – Lake Country Oro

Similar Trails – Victoria South, Millennium, Kissing Bridge

Local Clubs – Barrie Cycling Club

Access – There are two parking lots, one at each end of the trail; you can also park at most crossroads along the path. Find some at **Line 15 S., Line 2 S. (aka Shanty Bay Rd.), and 15th Line.**

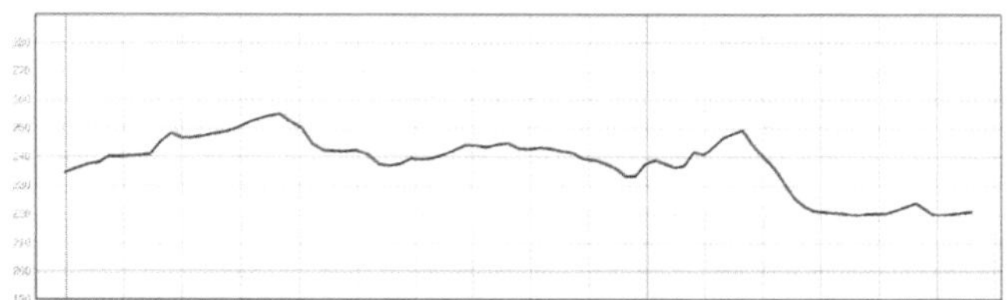

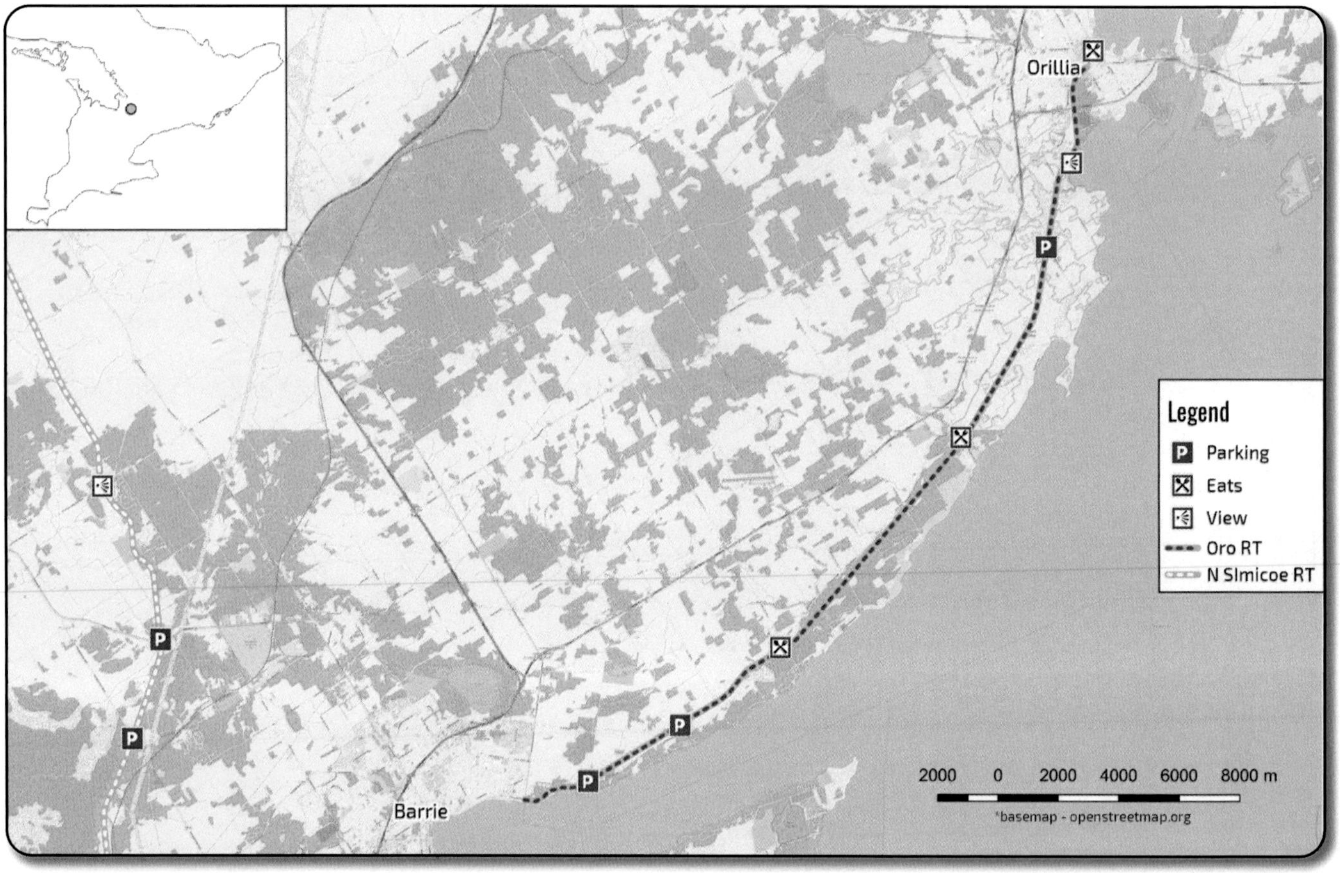

Review:

The **28 km Oro - Medonte** Rail Trail connects **Barrie** to **Orillia** through quiet forests and wetlands. A **very straight** path, it is easy enough for anyone to do on a hybrid bike.

This old rail bed has crushed-stone dust laid down as a level base, and there are no climbs to be concerned about.

There is plenty of **shady forest** on this route, with a few **bridges** spanning creeks. Past **Shanty Bay** you will see a few homes, and closer to **Orillia** is a **long stretch of wetlands**. You may see herons and possibly beavers!

Although this rail bed runs parallel to **Lake Simcoe**, riders will not see any water until they get close to **Orillia**. There, the path skirts by the lake as it turns into town. (See if you can spot Osprey nests on top of hydro poles.)

If you want a peek of the shore, take any side road you pass for ten minutes south; they all lead to the waterfront.

This is not my favourite Rail Trail, but is surely one of the better **maintained** and long enough to get some easy exercise. It is **suitable for a family outing**, and I saw couples towing little ones in trailers. Any road traffic at the many crossings is light, but do take care.

To add some interest, the county has added **historical placards** along the path; it's a nice touch if you're into local history.

There are few spots to refresh, buy food, or find shelter as you pass the communities of **Shanty Bay, Oro Station,** and **Hawkestone**, so be self-reliant and pack wisely.

I do recommend a great loop on **Ridge Rd. E. - Hwy 20.** Just when you think you are about halfway through your ride, take the next crossroads to connect. The loop provides a **more open, picturesque** return that has little car traffic.

Need some more trail to ride? The path along the **Barrie waterfront** is delightful or, on the other end down **Line 14 South**, head to **Carthew Bay** and loop around **Eight Mile Point** (not 8 miles long?) to see the lake—and get some ice cream!

Heading into **Orillia** there is another Rail Trail north of town. This is the **Uhthoff Rail Trail**, which goes **50 km** into **Midland.**

Enough choice for you? Which route will you take first?

History - A major community at the time, this section of the rail line through **Hawkstone** was completed in **1871** and helped shift commerce from lake steamer to rail.

Due to this, the town started to move inland toward the tracks. As a vital rail centre, there were plenty of stockyards, a freight shed, and a water tower, although there is little visible now at the site.

Eventually, as with most rail traffic in **Ontario,** lack of use and high maintenance costs forced **CN Rail** to close the line by **1996**. The local county took ownership and converted the route to a recreational trail in **2001.**

Oshawa Creek – Park Trail

Oshawa

Length – 7 km (one way)

90% park path
10% roads, crossings, detours

Elevation – Enjoy a gentle incline along the Oshawa Creek to Lake Ontario.

Terrain – A wide path marked with a centre with line, it is mainly asphalt with a few wooden bridges.

Skill – Easy

Traffic – Busier on weekends in the summer, expect bicyclists, walkers with dogs, and joggers.

Maps – There is a map at the trailhead, as well as signs along the trail.

Highlights – Botanical Gardens, the Lake Ontario shoreline, and many bridges and underpasses.

Trail Fee – Free

Facilities – Parking and washrooms are at either end of the route, as well as local services and places to eat.

Phone – 905 436 3311

Website – City of Oshawa;

Similar Trails – Highland Creek, Humber River, Upper Etobicoke

Local Clubs – Oshawa Cycling Club

Access – Park at the north end at the **Botanical Gardens**, or in the south end at **Lakeview Park.**

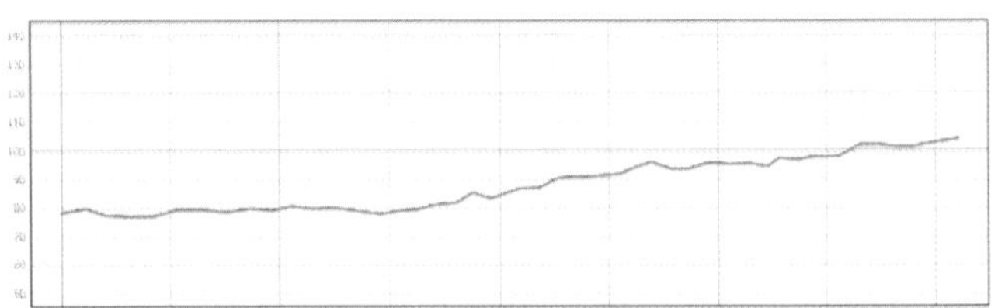

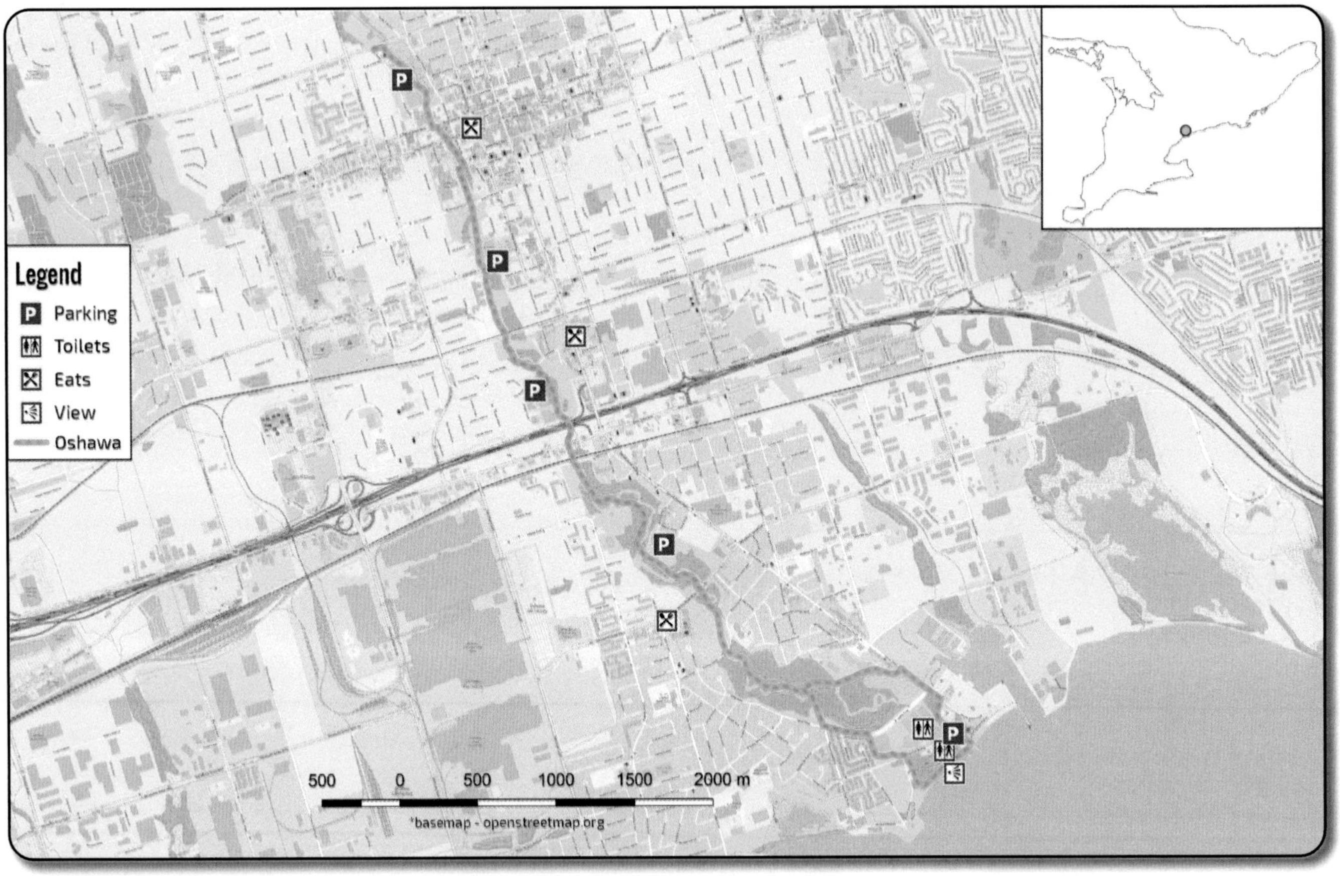

Review:

I was happy to discover this short but excellent Park trail in the centre of **Oshawa**. Although not too long at **7 km** (one way), the **Oshawa Creek (Joseph Kolodzie) Bike Trail** has such **varied scenery** that it deserves mention.

What makes this trek so interesting are the endless **bridges** and **tunnels** as it works its way along the creek and down to **Lake Ontario**.

The bike path is well-treed and shady; you could forget at times you're still riding through the city.

Having ridden many Park trails, this one is definitely **not boring.** It flows well and **weaves under roads** and **through tunnels** and over **bridges**, from one side of the creek to the other.

An **easy, paved trail,** it is well-marked; simply follow the **yellow centre line.** There are some **narrow stretches** and **tight corners**, so gauge each for yourself.

From the top, this path starts at the lovely **Oshawa Valley Botanical Gardens** and crosses a few roads, including **Bond St.** and **King St.** It then travels behind an ugly mall, where another bridge brings you back to nature.

Once you cross, not only does the scenery improve, but the trail avoids roads until it ends at a large park on the lakefront.

After a quick crossing over **Valley Drive,** it then splits two ways at **Lakeview Park Ave.**

I recommend heading down to the water, where you are greeted with a grand view of **Lake Ontario.**

Rest awhile at the many benches, take a walk on the beach, or check out the small group of **historic homes** at the **Oshawa Museum.**

There is also a play area for the kids if they are restless, as well as a lookout point and a chance to go for a swim.

Upon return, riders can opt to catch the trail off **Simcoe St. S.,** located 600 m north.

Connecting east or west along the shoreline is the **Waterfront Trail**, with so much more riding to be had if you have more in you! (I recommend going west.)

This was a pleasant find while out scouting, and I am pleased to know there is good trail riding in Oshawa. It would be especially lovely in the fall.

Palgrave – MTB/Park Trail

17580 Duffy's Lane, Palgrave

Length – 22 km

70% single-track MTB trail
20% hiking trail
10% double-track access roads

Elevation – Rather hilly on the single-track MTB trail but it flows well; not as much climbing for wider forest paths—riding counter-clockwise is easier.

Terrain – Smooth soil with some sandy spots and gravel, although it can be muddy; watch for a few roots and rock piles; log hops, structures, and berms installed.

Skill – Intermediate

Traffic – Quiet during the week and light on weekends; typically bicyclists and hikers.

Maps – Found at trailhead; signposts along the route, but I felt they were too varied.

Facilities – There are three parking lots, but I recommend the Duffy Lane entrance.

Highlights – Picturesque ponds, with the longest, continuous single-track loop in the area.

Trail Fee – Free

Phone – 416 661 6600

Website – Toronto & Region Conservation Authority

Similar Trails – Albion Hills, Glen Major, Dufferin Forest

Local Clubs – Caledon Cycle Club

Access – Drive north **11 km** past **Bolton** on **Highway 50,** just beyond Albion Hills. Turn west on **Patterson Side Rd.**, and then north up to **17580 Duffy's Lane** for **2 km**. Look for the parking lot down the road, on the right and just past the curve.

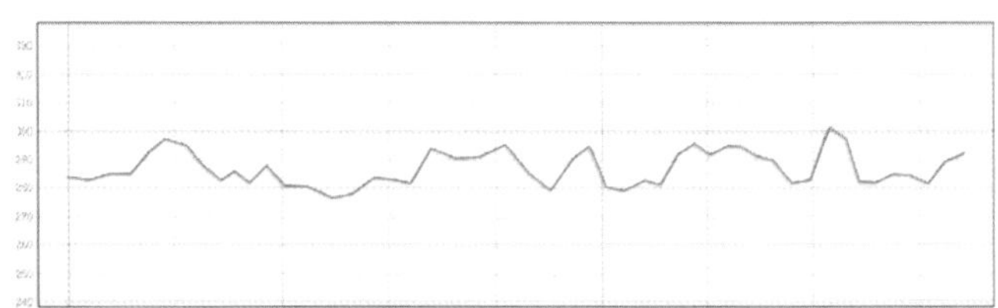

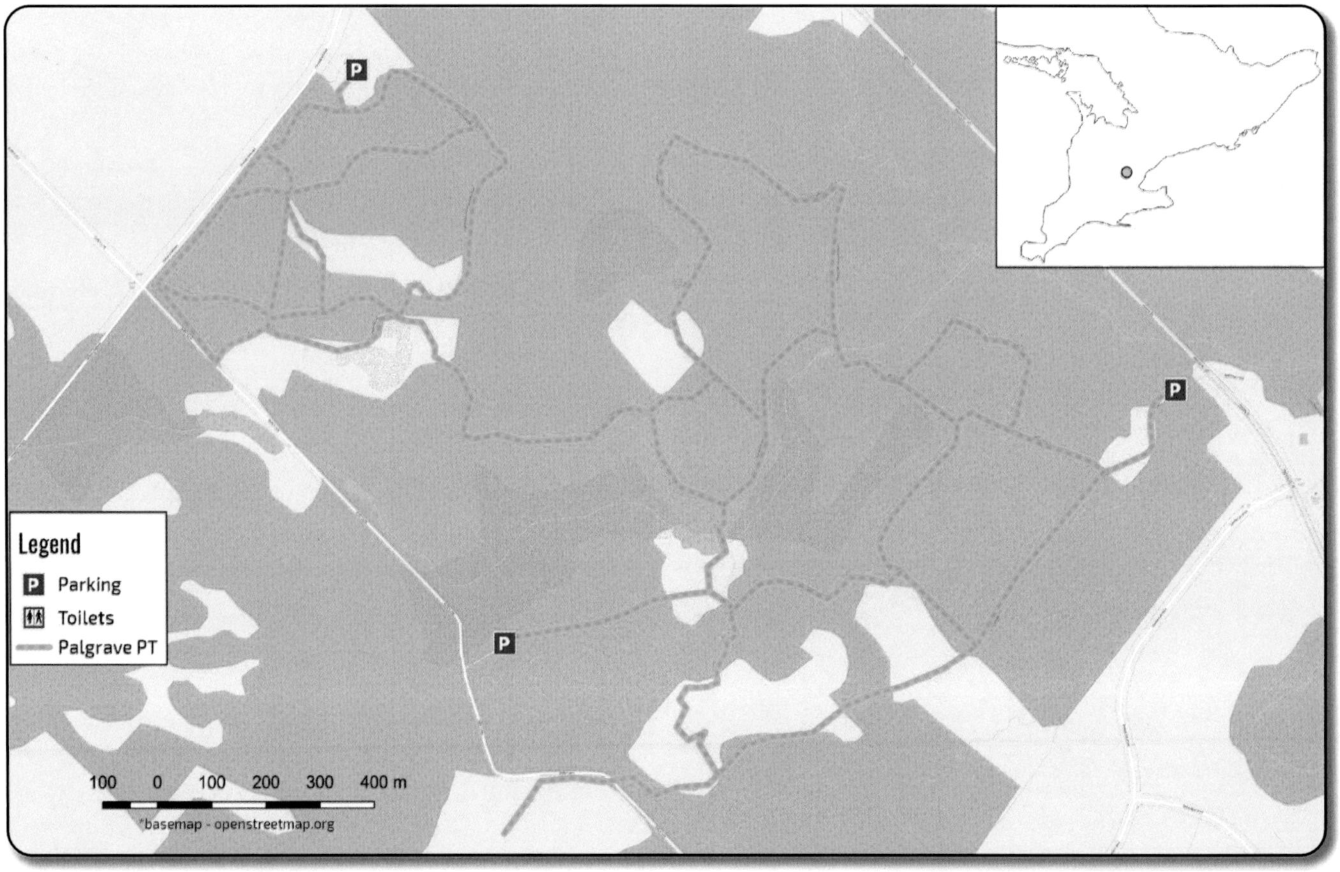

Legend
P Parking
Toilets
Palgrave PT

100 0 100 200 300 400 m

*basemap - openstreetmap.org

Review:

Palgrave Forest offers MTB riders near **Toronto's west side** some extra trail in which to let loose. This somewhat secret spot has plenty of **long and hilly cross-country** type tracks to really get your legs burning.

This intense, fast **cardio ride** consists mainly of one continuous loop. I find it keeps getting better over the years, as racers cut better trails and signs are now popping up to clarify what was once a somewhat confusing forest trail. (Although at times it still is.)

The terrain consists mainly of black loam soil that does get a little muddy after a rain. There are also a few **sandy patches.**

Due to tree farming, much of the forest is straight **rows of pine** mixed with native trees. As a result, there are some open areas, as well as a pond.

Expect plenty of **winding climbs**, but riders are rewarded with quick bombers down. (Making this place a favourite!) Most **ride counterclockwise**, as it's easier and flows better.

This continuous, uninterrupted trail is unusual, as most **MTB areas** have trails which intersect too frequently. Here, once you get going, you rarely have to stop to sort out which way to turn.

With switchbacks and berms, most of this **mega loop** flows well. There are a few simple **structures, rock piles,** and **logs** to keep it interesting, although if you ride it often nothing here is going to wing you.

An **Intermediate Park ride** for hybrid bikes would be to stick to the wide and straight old hiking paths. The **Oak Ridge** and **Bruce** trails are about **9 km,** and not so demanding on the hills.

The scenery is pleasant, but nothing more than green forest. It is **a quiet, empty** place on weekdays.

Numbered posts have recently been added, and although you may get turned around you'll never get

lost.

In the northeast quadrant of **Palgrave** there are signs of **old cross-country ski paths** you could also explore. However, these routes are not on the map and are rather overgrown—but isn't that part of the fun?

Make your way here for some serious enjoyment and exercise soon!

The official start and end points of the trail are a bit odd. From the parking lot (#24 on the map board), you can ride straight to #26 along the route. ***A better starting point*** *is to ride down the road to #5, where you will find a* ***map board****. From there you can start a more logical loop.*

Rouge Waterfront – Park Trail

Port Union to Pickering, GTA

Length – 9 km (one way)

80% park path
20% roads, crossings, detours

Elevation – Flat along the water's edge with a few short hills over the bluffs.

Terrain – Mostly paved with some gravel and sand, as well as a few bridges.

Skill – Easy

Traffic – Well-used by bicyclists, joggers, and dog-walkers.

Maps – Plenty of map boards and trail markers.

Facilities – Find parking, toilets, and snack bar at Rouge River, as well as benches, picnic tables, and a rain shelter along the path.

Highlights – Views of Lake Ontario, bridges, river marshland, and trains.

Trail Fee – Free

Phone – None

Website – Great Lakes Waterfront Trail

Similar Trails – Ajax Waterfront, Hamilton Beach, Cornwall

Local Clubs – Toronto Bicycling Network, Toronto Bicycle Club

Access – There is plenty of parking at **East Point Park**, as well as at the end of **Beechgrove Dr.**, the mouth of **Rouge River**, and the **Petticoat Creek Conservation Area**; parking can also be found on side streets.

It is a very convenient place to get to from the **GO Train** station at **Rouge Hill.**

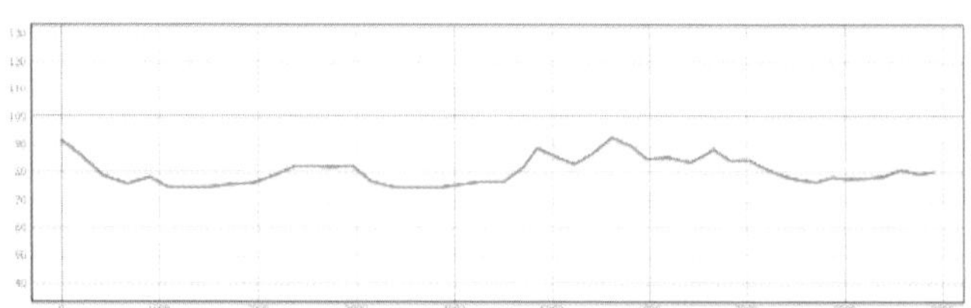

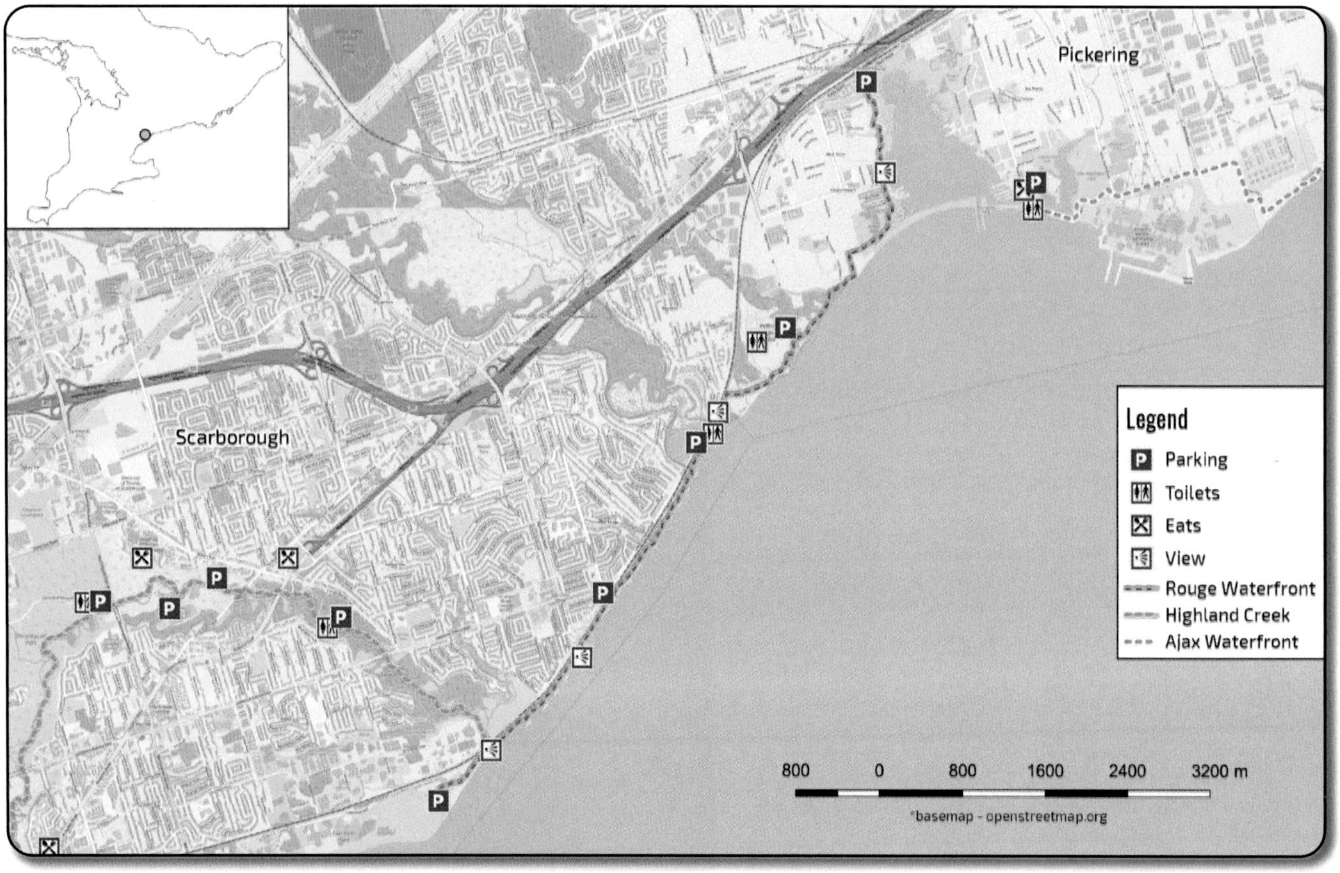

Pickering
Scarborough
Legend
Parking
Toilets
Eats
View
Rouge Waterfront
Highland Creek
Ajax Waterfront
800 0 800 1600 2400 3200 m
*basemap - openstreetmap.org

Review:

One of the best sections of the **Waterfront Trail**, this route traverses the east side of **Toronto**, from the far end of **Scarborough** and into **Pickering.**

This **9 km scenic, paved Park trail** has serene views of Lake Ontario and crosses over both **Highland Creek** and the **Rouge River.**

The **landscape is ever-changing**, and although the elevation is mainly flat at the lake, **it does rise** over the bluffs and while crossing bridges. Well-marked, it is for good reason a popular and busy route.

Starting from the **west end** at **East Point Park** the path descends a long, steep hill to meet up with three bridges at Highland Creek. (Also a great trail ride for another day.)

One bridge is for the train tracks that separate the trail from the neighbourhood exits at **Port Union** and the **Rouge Hill GO station**.

Note that there are signs asking riders to walk the bridges, which I found odd as they were as wide as the paths themselves.

Passing by many stone breakwaters and beach inlets, riders eventually come to the mouth of the **Rouge River**. There is a buzz of activity here on weekends, with kayakers, fishermen, and families out for a BBQ.

Take the white pedestrian bridge up and over the river, which leads to **Rodd Ave.** This is one of **a few short road detours** along the route.

After a quick run across the parkland in **Petticoat Creek Conservation Area,** you will again need to detour. Take **Marksbury Rd.** to **Surf Ave.,** around the block then on to **West Shore Blvd.**

The last detour is much more significant at **Frenchman's Bay.** Unfortunately, there is no bridge at the channel, so riders will need to go up and around.

In this review, I included the section which leads to the top, as it then continues as a pleasant trek through parkland with two connecting (and quiet) street detours.

When you get to the top at **Bayly St.,** and can hear the **Hwy 401**, it is now all road riding to the **Pickering marina.** If you do choose to continue on, there are many more similar paths to **Ajax, Oshawa,** and beyond.

As it is always cooler by the lake, be sure to pack a windbreaker. As you can see from the photos, on a beautiful day this route is **a joy to cruise.**

Taylor Creek + Warden – Park Trail

Don Valley to Warden Ave., Toronto

Length – 6 km (one way)

80% park path
10% gravel path
10% roads, crossings, detours

Elevation – Flat, with a few dips at the water and a gradual incline up from the creek.

Terrain – Mostly asphalt and smooth soil, with some gravel and sandy patches; alternate water crossing.

Skill – Easy to Intermediate

Traffic – Well-used by bicyclists, hikers, and dog-walkers.

Maps – A map is found at the trailhead, as well as signs along the trail.

Facilities – Four parking lots, as well as washrooms and benches along the trail.

Highlights – Bridges, ponds, and lovely colours in the fall.

Trail Fee – Free

Phone – Toronto 311

Website – City of Toronto

Similar Trails – Highland Creek, Humber Valley, Morrison Valley

Local Clubs – Toronto Bicycling Network (TBN)

Access – Find parking lots at: **Pharmacy Rd.**, **Dawes Rd.**, the bottom of **Haldon Ave.**, and by the DVP when entering from **Don Mills Rd.** (but check a map, as the entrance has no sign!).

From the other end, the subway stops at **Warden Woods** if you wish to use the TTC.

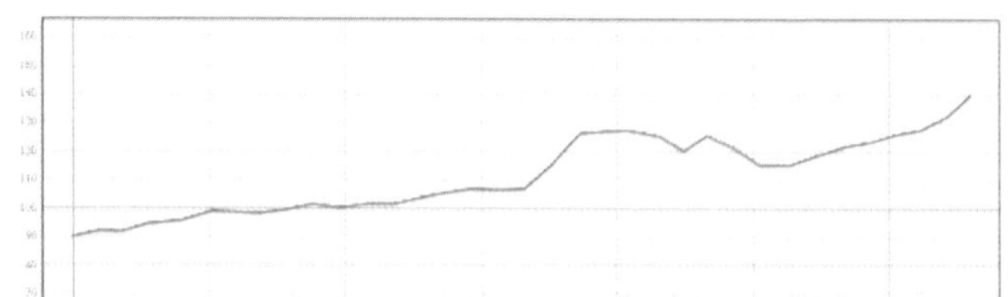

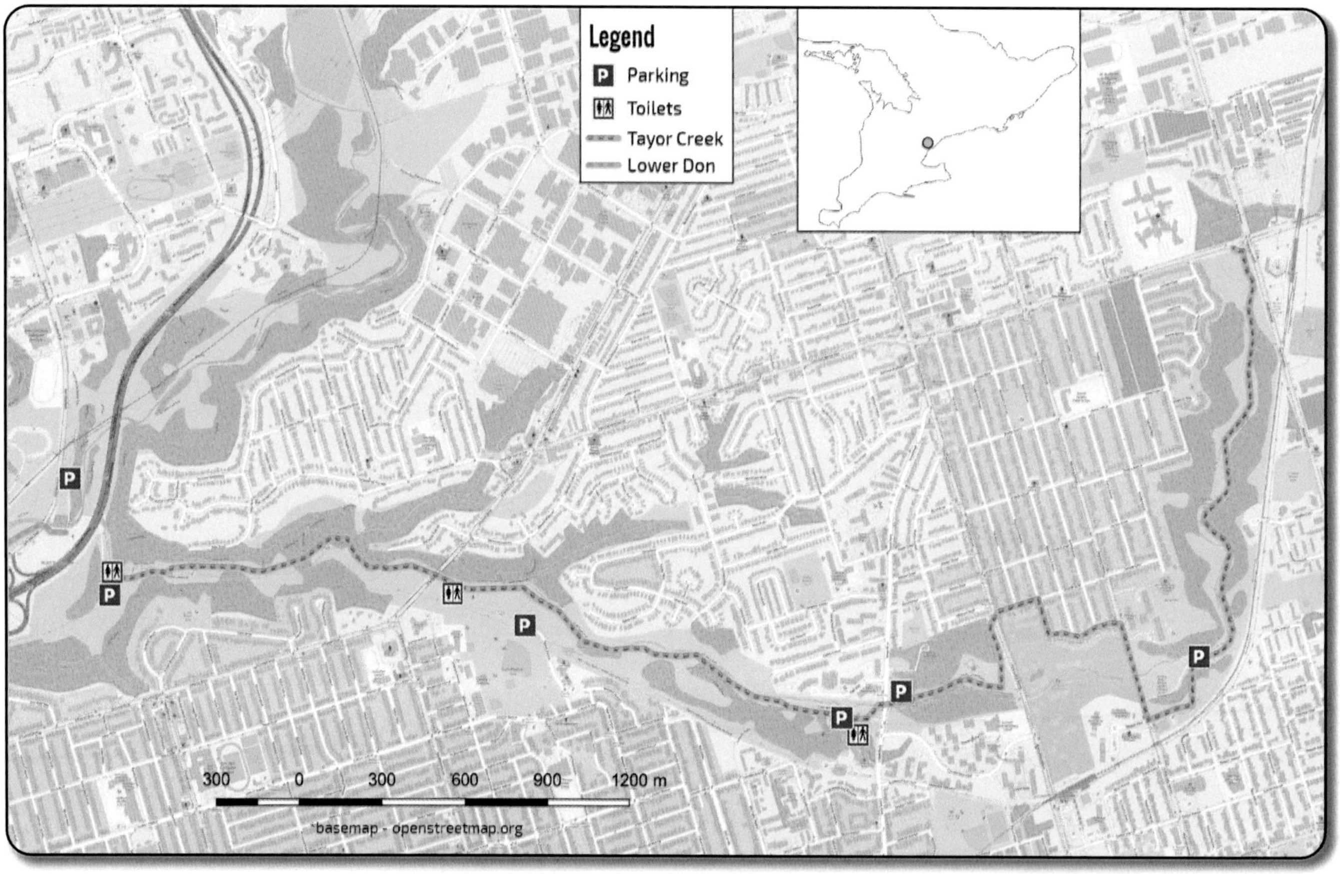

Legend
P Parking
Toilets
Tayor Creek
Lower Don

300 0 300 600 900 1200 m

basemap - openstreetmap.org

Review:

Taylor Creek and **Warden Woods** are beautiful stretches of parkland trail that continue from the **Don Valley** trail system. Although short, it has interesting bridges, alternate paths through the ravine, and gorgeous colours in the fall.

The trail is mostly **paved** and **well-used,** but there are some spots that are sandy or have water runoff. Set in a small valley, enjoy an ever-changing landscape as you follow the water.

Starting from the **west end,** where the trail meets the **Don Valley**, riders leave the drone of the highway as they ride along the winding creek.

The path also contains some **wooden bridges**, and a few new metal ones that should last longer (in the past, flash floods have taken out a few).

You may see signs of this flooding if you come across sand on the path. Annually water tends to spill over the banks in spring and can fill the valley on occasion.

An unusual part of this ride are the **alternate paths** through the **creek**. Rather than take a bridge, riders can take a route across the water along the **concrete waterways** built for park maintenance vehicles. One is covered by only a trickle of water, but the other two cross the main creek and are typically ankle-deep. If the water is low they are easy enough to traverse; cross in a **straight line,** at **moderate speed** and in a **low gear**. Otherwise, if you go too fast or too slow, you will get wet or fall. It's your call and fun too!

Halfway along the trail, on the north bank of the creek, is a wide **dirt path** that provides a good loop back for **hybrid bikes**.

Beyond **Dawes Rd.**, young kids will likely want to stop at the **duck pond** to find frogs and turtles (and see ducks!).

Unfortunately, once you reach **Victoria Park Ave.** there is a **long, steep hill** up to street level, which then takes you to **Warden Woods.** It's a tough climb, but well worth it.

Take this **short detour** to get around the golf course: **Donside Dr.** to **Maybourne Ave.,** then along **Dolphin Dr.** and south on **Pharmacy Ave.;** the park trail again starts on the east side of the road, after the bridge.

Warden Woods has less parkland and more of a beautiful, natural ravine setting. The path curves up for a few kilometres to end at **St. Clair Ave.**, near the **Warden Subway Station**. The last half of this section is all gravel.

Park benches, BBQ pits, fountains, and **two washrooms** along the route add to the comfort of this ride.

This is a very **popular, enjoyable** route that connects to the Don trails for those who desire more riding. (Located just north of where I live, it gets plenty of use!)

Tommy Thompson – Park Trail

1 Leslie St. & Unwin Ave., Toronto

Length – 12 km, or 5 km to point (one way)

70% road (closed to vehicles)
30% park path
10% hiking trail

Elevation – The road is pancake-flat, but dips to cross a bridge; climbs required to get to the light beacon.

Terrain – A wide asphalt main road, with gravelled side roads; watch out for construction waste.

Skill – Easy

Traffic – Quiet on weekdays, but on summer weekends a busy place with bicyclists, people roller blading and skateboarding, as well as hikers.

Maps – Map at gate, as well as road signage.

Facilities – Street or lot parking, outhouses, and a welcome centre (under long-term construction).

Highlights – The Toronto skyline, with lots of opportunities for nature photography, bird watching, hiking, or swimming.

Hours – Weekdays: 4 p.m. – 9 p.m.; Weekends & Holidays: 5:30 a.m. – 9 p.m.

Tommy Thompson Park is open all holidays except Christmas Day, Boxing Day, and New Year's Day.

Trail Fee – Free

Phone – 416 661 6600

Website – TRCA, Tommy Thompson Park

Similar Trails – Beaches Boardwalk, Hamilton Beach, Ajax Waterfront

Local Clubs – Toronto Bicycle Network, Toronto Bike Club

Access – The gate is located at the foot of **1 Leslie St. and Unwin Ave.**, south of **Lakeshore Blvd E**. Parking can be found on the street or at the lot inside, on the west side.

A new Bike trail entrance is also at **Unwin Ave.**, where you may park by the bridge.

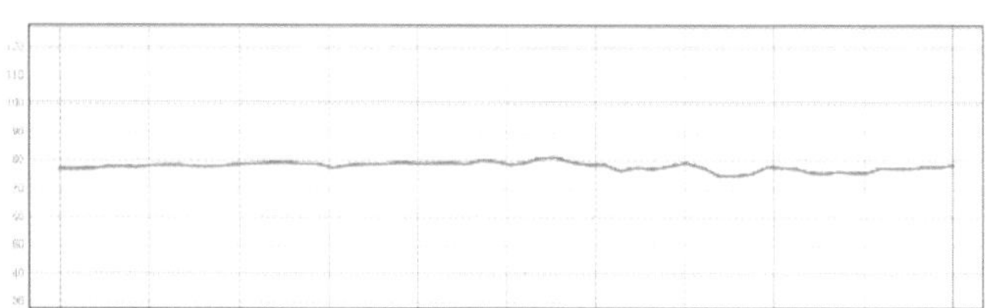

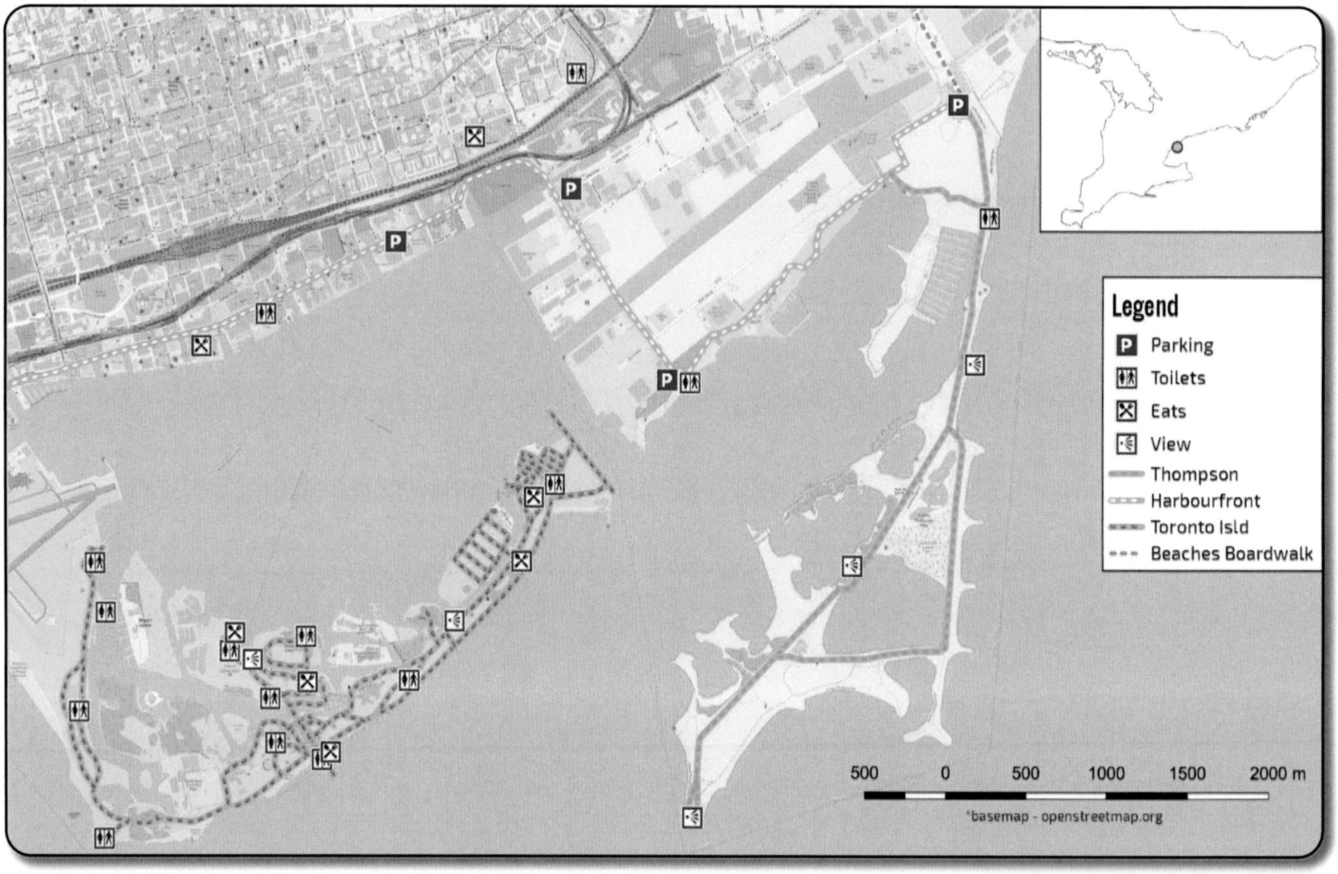

Legend
Parking
Toilets
Eats
View
Thompson
Harbourfront
Toronto Isld
Beaches Boardwalk

500 0 500 1000 1500 2000 m

°basemap - openstreetmap.org

Review:

Tommy Thompson Park (Leslie Street Spit) is a **long, flat bicycle cruise** out to **Lake Ontario.** It's an oasis in the middle of a busy city to which cyclists can retreat.

The path is mainly a **straight asphalt road**. Thankfully, there are no longer any dump trucks running along it to make this man-made **peninsula**.

It is flat—with a few speed bumps, what? Take a short, **5 km** to the point with the **lighthouse** on the hill. Sadly, it is not an historic lighthouse, just a simple light beacon, yet the view is worth the climb. Once you reach the floating bridge, you are two-thirds there.

Being a paved road, some find this route a bit dull. Yet it does offer an **escape** from hectic city life and vistas.

The air is fresh and the surrounding **land serene.** The scenery provides numerous **views of the Toronto skyline,** as well as the **Beaches** shoreline.

Built over the last **60 years**, this peninsula is made of **landfill** from construction sites. Hence, it is slowly transforming itself from a waste zone to a **wildlife and recreational area.** Birding, hiking, and photography opportunities abound.

However, care must be taken as the ground has numerous waste material hazards which may puncture your tire if you wander off the paved Park trail.

There is an **alternate, triangular route** you may use to return. Exploring this gravel road will take you around the wetlands and to the inner harbour currently being built.

Although you may see other narrow gravel paths, **none** are for cyclists! City park planners have designated these more scenic, meandering routes to walkers only, so they stay out of the way of bicyclists. (They definitely got the better deal.)

Tommy Thompson Park is open every day, but only in the evenings on weekdays. This is better than it has been for years when it was open only on weekends.

More riding can be found west towards the Harbourfront, or east along the Beaches Boardwalk.

An excellent family outing, be sure to pack a snack, some water, and a windbreaker, as there is nothing to buy on this trek.

Remember, it will be **cooler** and **windier** than inland, which is a wonderful advantage on a hot summer day. (But it can be really strong if you pick the wrong day!)

Give yourself a break and cruise the "Spit" to **free your mind** and get some light **exercise** in. Granted with no hills, it's not that much.

Toronto Islands – Park Trail

Toronto Islands, Toronto

Length – 15 km (5.5 km from end to end)

30% park path
70% road

Elevation – Flat, like the prairies.

Terrain – Wide asphalt roads with a few local service vehicles, as well as patches of gravel and sand.

Skill – Easy

Traffic – Busy in the peak season; watch for park vehicles and wandering tourists.

Maps – A few signposts and maps along the trail.

Facilities – Public washrooms, restaurants, patios, as well as a bike rental, picnic areas, and opportunities for swimming.

Highlights – Take in the city skyline, a small amusement park, the lighthouse, old cottages, yacht clubs, and four beaches, including Hanlan's Beach (an optional nude beach).

Trail Fee – Free; $4.00+ for the ferry, depending on ticket type.

Phones – Toronto 311

Website – City of Toronto

Similar Trails – Harbourfront, Ajax, Hamilton Beach

Local Clubs – Toronto Bicycle Network (TBN)

Access – Ride in from any of the three island ferry docks.

Bringing a bike on the ferry is allowed, but on **busy and long weekends** it will be tricky with the crowds to get it there. If you can, it is better to go on a weekday in the summer.

Some years, the lake level is too high during the spring. This may cause flooding on parts of the island and delay the opening.

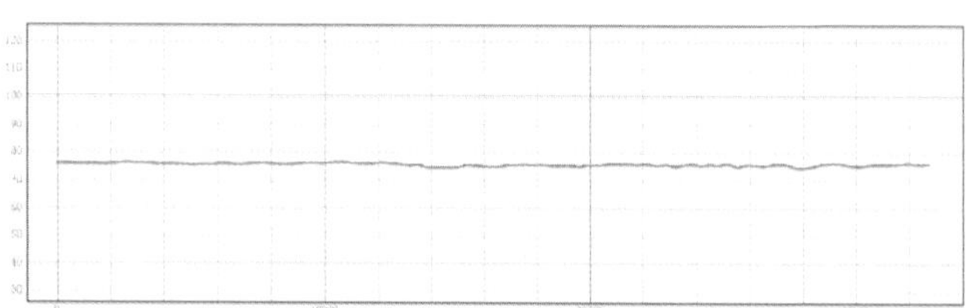

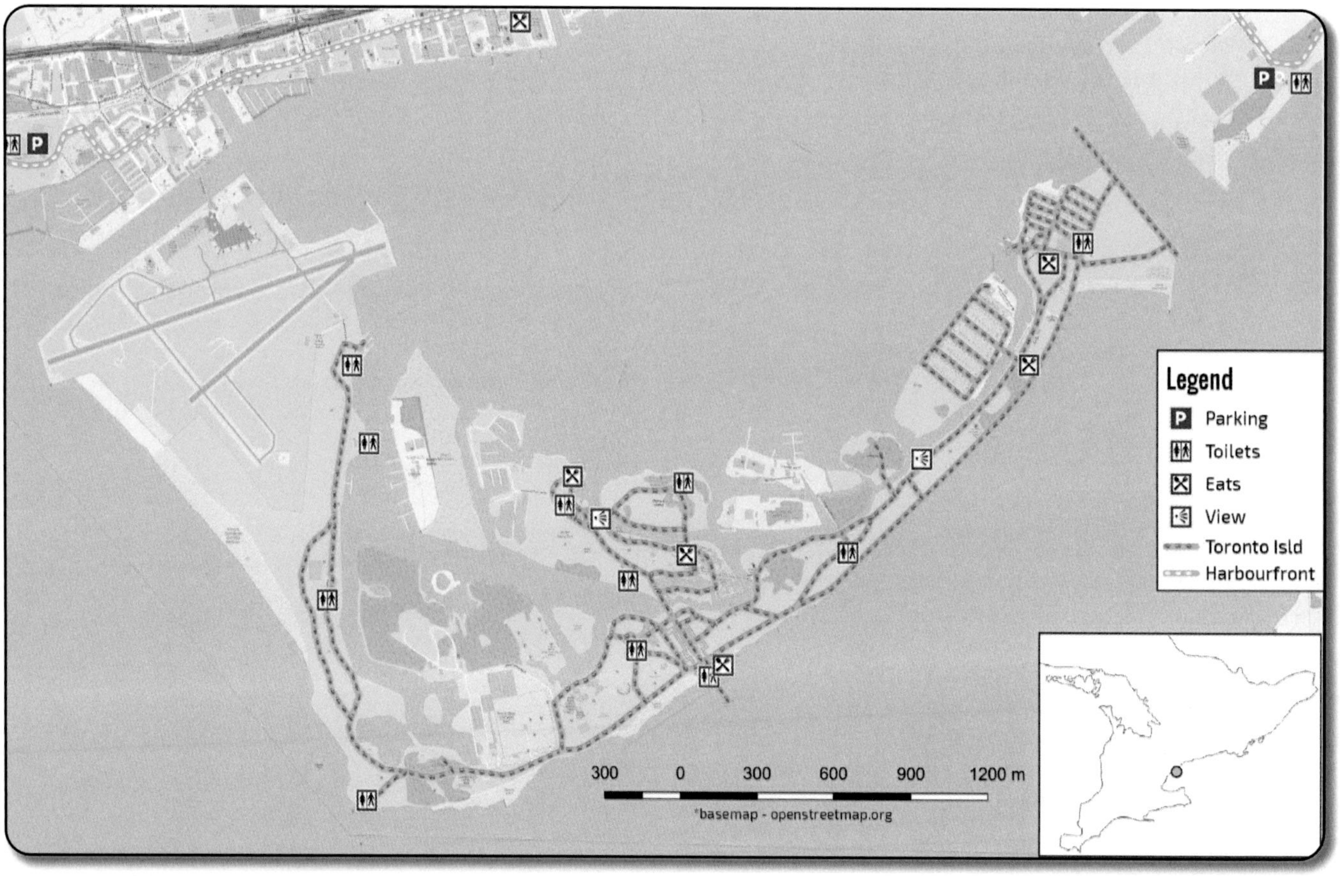

Legend
Parking
Toilets
Eats
View
Toronto Isld
Harbourfront

300 0 300 600 900 1200 m
*basemap - openstreetmap.org

Review:

With an **enjoyable ferry ride** to the **Toronto Islands**, there is **15 km** of trail to discover, with plenty of **fresh air** and **open spaces.** It's a bit of the **country in the city,** spanning a flat trail network.

This **popular cycling destination** is a joy to ride and a great day trip. **Traffic is light**, with only a few service vehicles and us cyclists, walkers, and seagulls.

Most of the Park trail is **paved asphalt**, but there are many side trails that take you onto crushed-stone paths and wooden boardwalks. A **direct line** from one end of the island to the other is about **5.5 km**; triple that distance by wandering down the different paths.

The Toronto Islands consist of (I counted) fifteen small islands, some of which are private sail clubs or animal sanctuaries.

There are **three ferry routes** to the island, and taking any one of them will be a great start to your island adventure. But note they are different.

If wanting to only cycle half the islands, I recommend the ferry to **Ward Island** on the eastern half to see the **quaint, old cottage homes.** (Sadly, there was once three times as many.)

The west side of the islands has a few **marinas, some parkland,** and the **airport**. It is perhaps a bit less appealing, but **more tranquil** for a picnic lunch. On this end, you will find the longest beach in the area, **Hanlan's Point.**

In the **central area** are the **public gardens, more parkland,** a small kids' amusement park, and the pier jutting out from the beach. **Gibraltar Point Lighthouse**, circa **1808**, is the oldest lighthouse on the Great Lakes (and they say haunted!).

The Toronto Islands have a long history, and were formed from the sands from the **Scarborough Bluffs.** (First by a shifting sandbar and then, after many storms, the islands were formed.)

Bikes may be rented on the **far south side** of the island by the pier (yet not by the island docks, which is odd). Therefore, you will need to walk first or rent a bike by the ferry docks on the mainland.

Pick a fair-weather day to go, as the **temperatures are always cooler** than in the city and it can be windy on the islands.

The crossing on the ferries is a treat. These **restored century old ships** bring you back in time when the city folks flocked to the island to watch **baseball games** and **rowing regattas.** That was their entertainment before TV.

A wonderful outing for tourists and locals to quickly get away from the city. It is a relaxing bicycle cruise that will reveal numerous picturesque locations to stop for a photo of the harbour and **Toronto skyline.**

Upper Etobicoke – Park Trail

Brampton

Length – 20+ km (one way)

90% park path
10% roads, crossings, detours

Elevation – Follows the Upper Etobicoke Creek and is rather level, with a gradual incline going north; a few dips under bridges.

Terrain – All asphalt with some gravel patches and a dirt path at the south end.

Skill – Easy

Traffic – Average volume; cyclists; walkers, with dogs, with strollers.

Maps – Found at some intersections, as well as signs along the trail.

Highlights – Parkland, bridges, picturesque homes, and exercise stations.

Trail Fee – Free

Facilities – Parking, benches along the trail, and local services.

Phone – 905 874 3601

Website – City of Brampton (map page), Walk and Roll

Similar Trails – Upper Humber, Nokiidaa

Local Clubs – Caledon Cycling Club, Brampton Cycling Club

Access – A large parking lot can be found at **58 Church St. E.** and **Ken Williams Dr.**

There are also many other starting points with parking available.

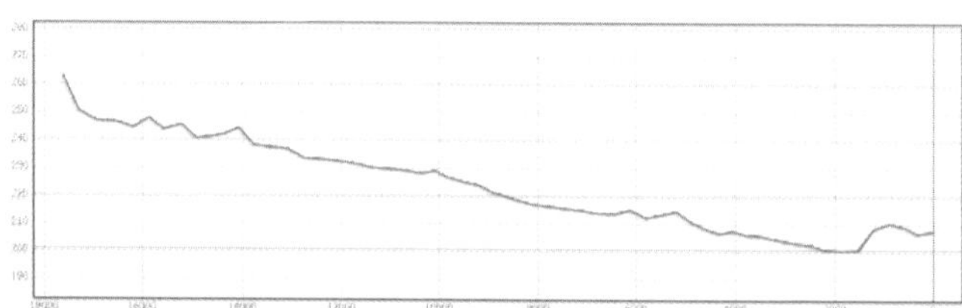

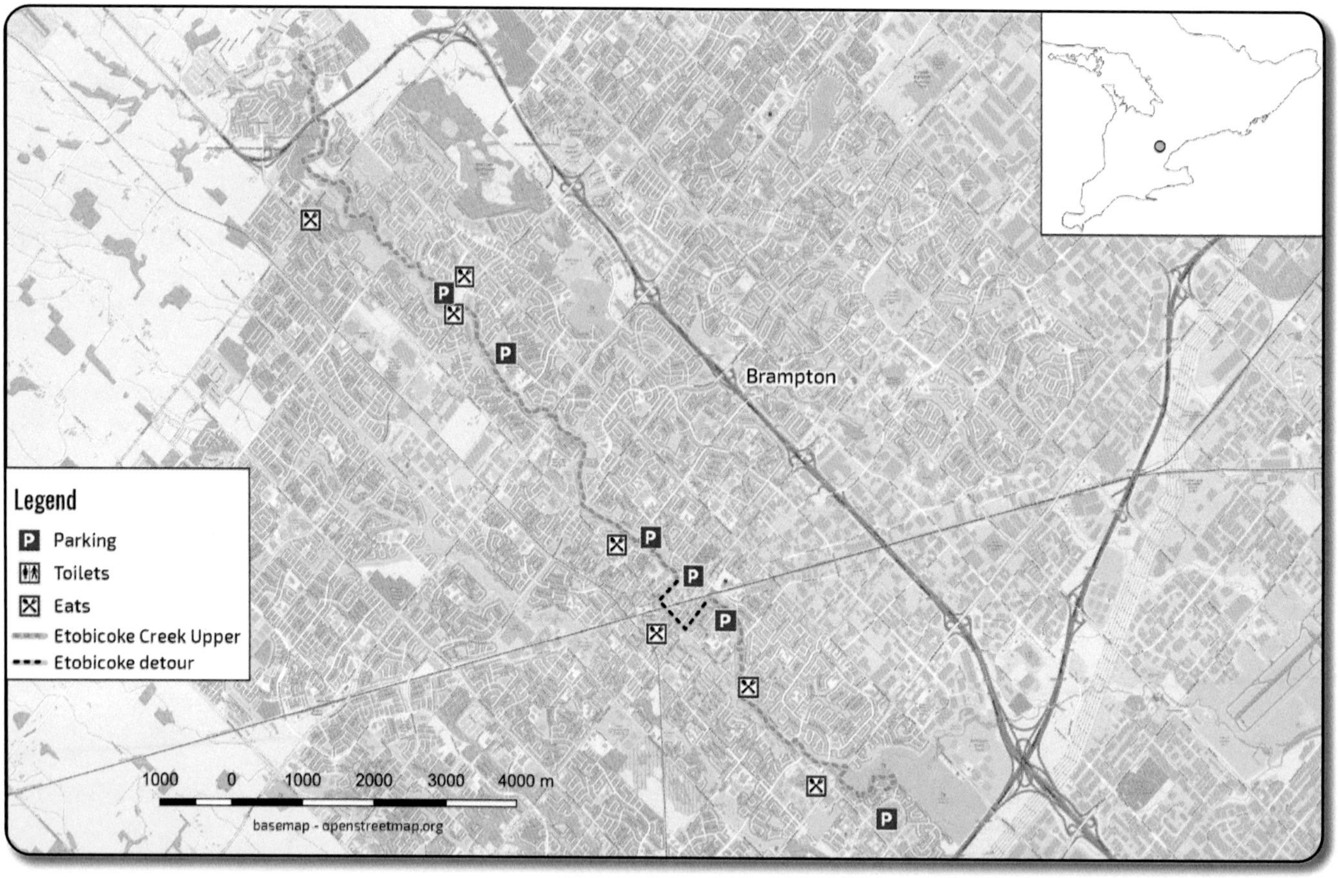

Review:

This is the longest Park trail in **Brampton** and runs **20+ km** along the **upper Etobicoke Creek**. This meandering route is perfect for riders looking for a **cruise** on a weekend afternoon.

The path is all paved and **easy to pedal,** as there are only a **few small hills**.

Most of the ride is **manicured parkland,** with small wooded areas giving the occasional shade. One passes through many neighbourhoods, providing views of **homes, playgrounds,** and **sports fields**.

One section is unusual; it has **exercise stations** with fancy metal workout equipment you may use. Add a few bench presses to your outing, or just relax on the many **park benches**.

There are plenty of malls nearby to get lunch or take a washroom break; good to note as I did not see any "relief" on the trail.

Although **well-marked with signage** most trail **arrows are very small** (too small), so pay attention to the many paths branching off that simply lead to the top of the valley and then end.

This Park trail is **split into two sections,** of about equal length due to a rather abrupt **1.4-km detour** through the centre of town. This was done to get around some water culverts the city put in. Perhaps, one day I hope, this concrete disaster will be naturalized, and the trail will carry through, as it should.

I suggest first doing north **10 km**. This route connects well with the bridge underpasses and has few road crossings. To add more distance to your ride, head **south** beyond the detour and bike the **8 km** of similar Park paths as well.

To do the **official detour,** one has to leave the path and ride the road down and around the busy downtown core for a few blocks. This connects to some stairs leading down to the southern section. To get there, go west on **Church St.**, south on **Main St.**, and then take a left at **Wellington St. E.**; the stairs are at the end of this street.

This path, and the creek, eventually takes cyclists under the **Hwy 410 – Hwy 407** interchange, which is a bit noisy. For an even longer, **mega pedal,** you can ride most of the **Etobicoke Creek** down past the airport and right to the lakefront.

Perfect for a Sunday cruise, put this on the top of your list to ride with friends or for a chance to visit Brampton.

Upper Humber – Park Trail

Humber River, Toronto

Length – 20 km (one way)

90% park path
10% roads, crossings, detours

Elevation – Level as it follows the river, with a gradual slope in the valley.

Terrain – A wide path of paved asphalt, with a dirt path at the end.

Skill – Easy

Traffic – Popular with local walkers and joggers.

Maps – Good signage with a few maps along the trail.

Facilities – Parking can be found at many parks along the trail, as well as benches and play sets. There are only three restrooms at Rowntree Mills Park, Ester Lorrie Park, and the arboretum.

Highlights – Bridges, a natural park setting, an arboretum, and a dam.

Trail Fee – Free

Phone – Toronto 311

Website – City of Toronto

Similar Trails – Humber River (south section), lower Don Valley, Highland Creek

Local Clubs – Toronto Bicycle Network, Toronto Bicycle Club

Access – The best place to start is at the south end, from the parking lot at the end of **Dee Ave.**

There are also other lots at local parks: **Pine Point, West Humber Parkland, Esther Lorrie Park, Humber College, Blue Haven Park,** or **Rowntree Mills Park.**

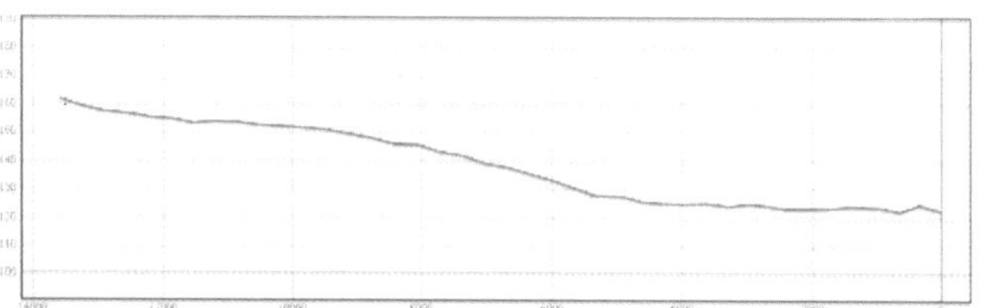

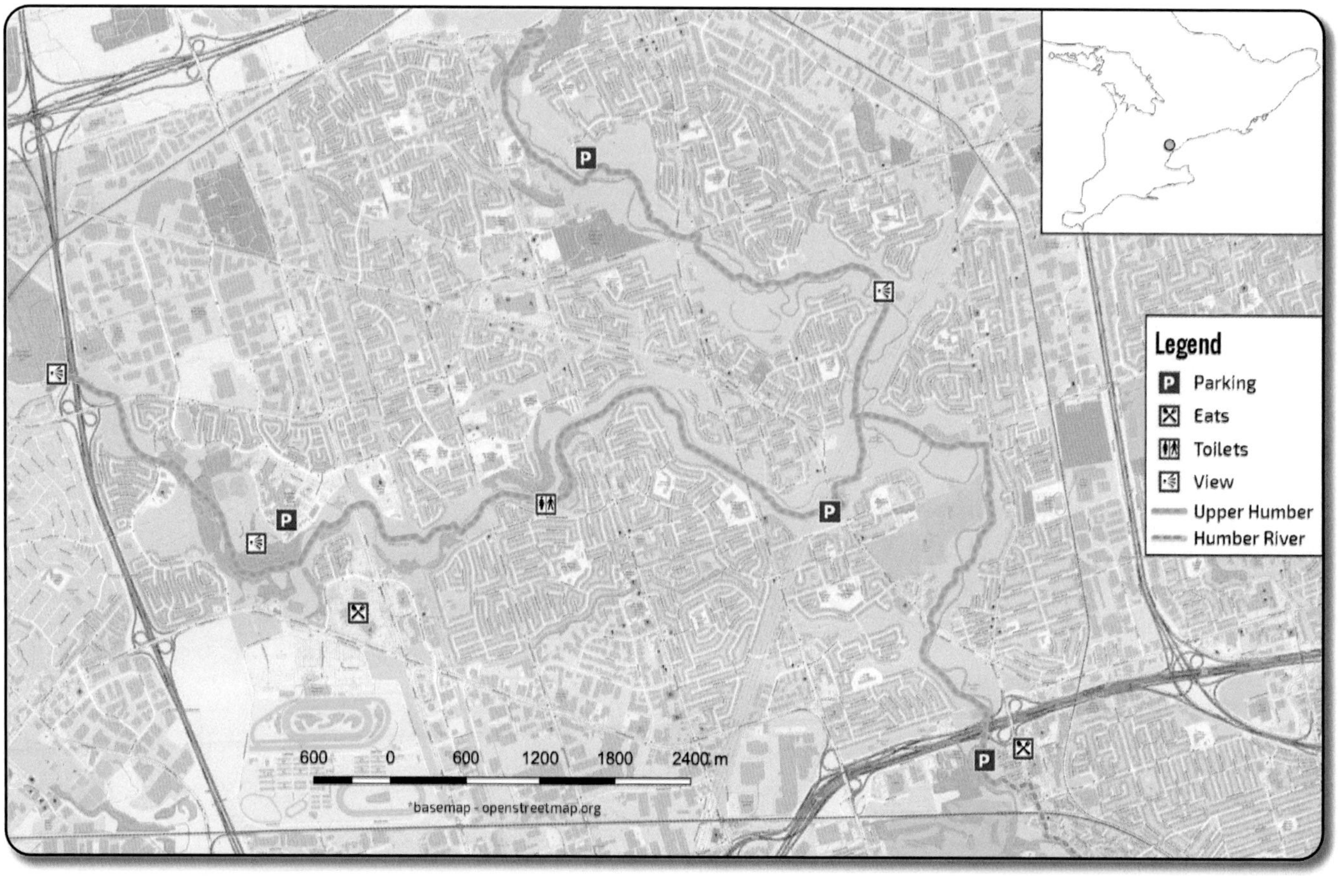

Legend
Parking
Eats
Toilets
View
Upper Humber
Humber River

600 0 600 1200 1800 2400 m
°basemap - openstreetmap.org

Review:

The upper forks of the **Humber River** offer **20 km** of some of the **best Park trails** to ride in the city. Here, in the **northwest corner of Toronto,** runs an **easy, long, and enjoyable** bicycle route that branches off in **two directions**.

Starting just below **Hwy 401** the path winds north for **4 km,** where it forks west for another **10 km;** or, take the right way north for **6 km** more.

The ride is enjoyable and varied with no outstanding features, just your typical open, and somewhat **natural parkland setting**, complete with mowed greens and park benches.

Bridges take you across the river a few times, and numerous **spur trails** lead into local neighbourhoods. I doubt riders will get lost if they follow the river and avoid any side paths. Thankfully, the signage seemed adequate.

The trail goes under most road crossings, with only **Albion Rd.** requiring you to cycle up to the roadway and cross at the lights.

Taking the west branch of the **Humber River Trail** will lead you to the dam at the **Claireville Reservoir**. On the way, there is the **Humber College** Arboretum, which may be of interest to some. (I found it a nice break to walk about the gardens.)

The **other north branch** meanders in a similar way, through the valley and ending as a dirt path at **Steeles Ave. W.**

Aside from the view of a few towering apartments, this is an **idyllic ride** with little to remind riders they are still in the city. (Which is often the goal!)

Although the sides of the river's valleys are well-treed, the path itself has **little shade**. Also, I only remember seeing one restroom spot on each route.

The best part is the fact this **trail continues south** to the lake for another **13 km;** take a short road detour along **Weston Rd.** for about **300 m**. Adding this part to your route makes for **one long day-trip,** but that may be what some of you seek.

Highly recommended as a great bicycle ride for a weekend cruise with the whole family, or for a solo distance ride.

Uxbridge Lindsay – Rail Trail

Uxbridge to Lindsay, or Woodville

Length – 64 km

90% rail trail
10% roads

Elevation – Quite a flat route.

Terrain – A wide path with crushed stone, gravel, and asphalt, as well as wood bridges and open wetlands.

Skill – Easy

Traffic – Bicyclists and hikers, as well as snowmobiles in the winter.

Maps – Maps and signage can be found at key points.

Facilities – No services close to the route except at Uxbridge, Lindsay, Sunderland, Cannington, and Woodville.

Highlights – Various marsh wildlife, old bridges, quiet stretches.

Trail Fee – Free

Phone – None

Website – Toronto to Algonquin Greenway, Trans Canada Trail

Similar Trails – Oro – Medonte, Caledon, Elora Cataract

Local Clubs – Uxbridge Cycling Club

Access – There are many entry points; in **Uxbridge** start at the park, on a side street by **2nd Ave.** and **Rosena Lane.**

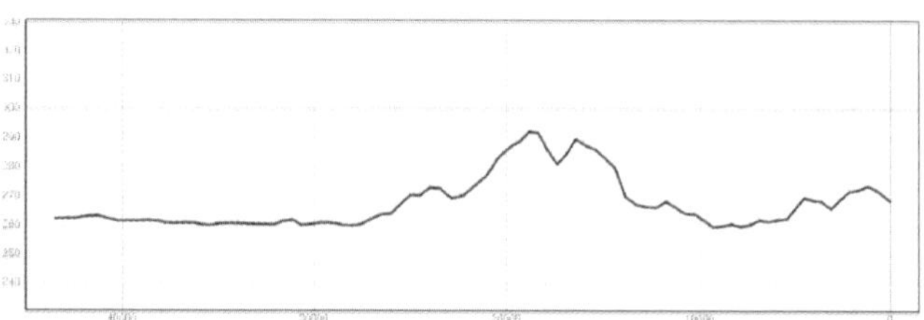

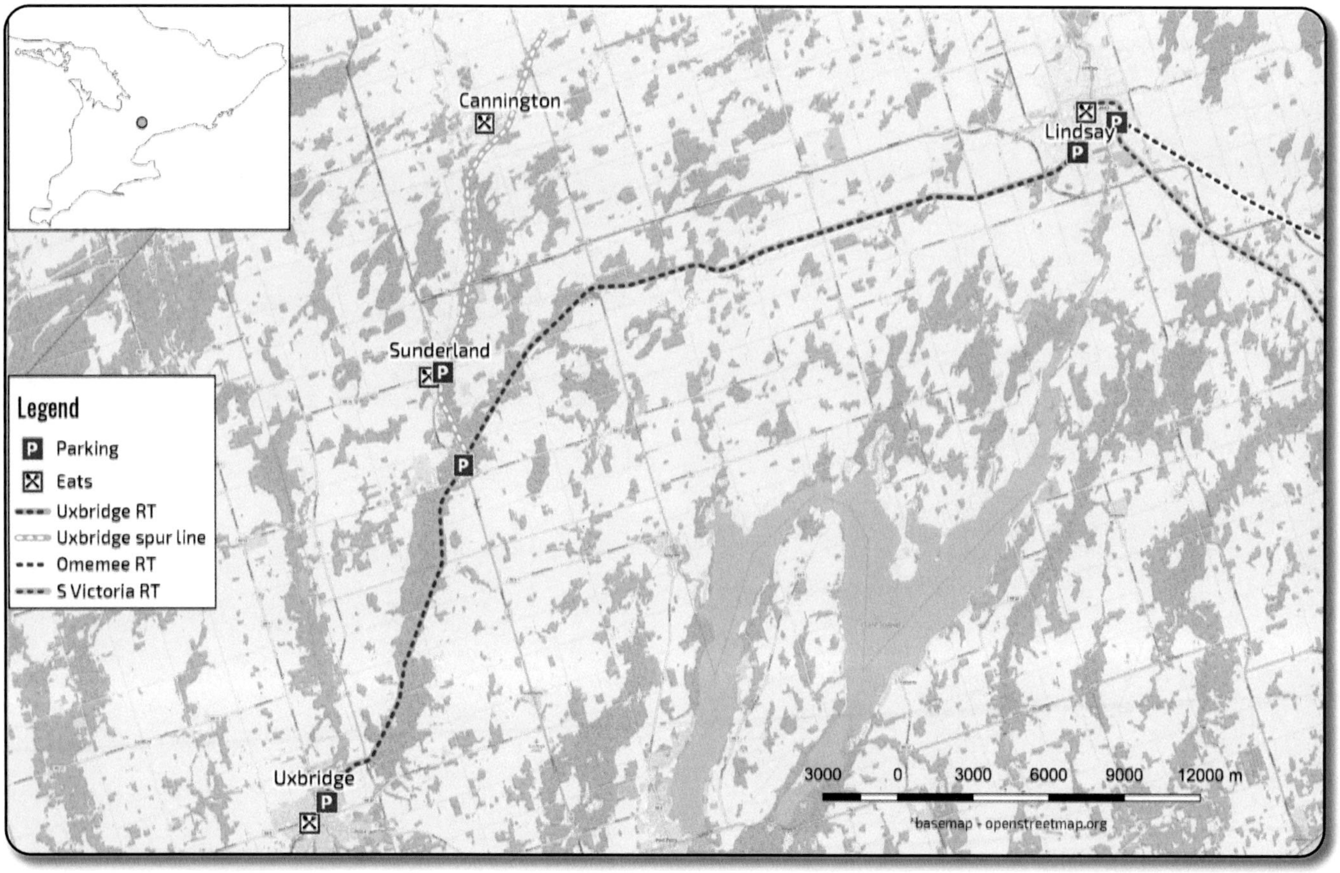

Cannington
Lindsay
Sunderland
Uxbridge

Legend
Parking
Eats
Uxbridge RT
Uxbridge spur line
Omemee RT
S Victoria RT

3000 0 3000 6000 9000 12000 m
basemap - openstreetmap.org

Review:

The **44 km Uxbridge to Lindsay** Rail trail is the closest for bike riders to try on the **east side of Toronto**.

Most is **well-maintained,** as it is part of the **Trans Canada Trail**.

A good and fast ride, this route stays away from traffic. It is also **not muddy** at all, considering much of it passes through **wetlands.** However, high water levels may flood the path in the spring.

Currently, the starting point in the town of **Uxbridge** is by the **historic trestle bridge** that was just rebuilt. From there, the path goes a few kilometres northeast along a shady, crushed-gravel route.

The trail then opens up to an extensive, **long wetland,** with the path going alongside and across for **12 km.** There is **plenty of solitude**, with endless marsh grasses and wide-open vistas.

Make the occasional stop at small ponds or bridges to look for wildlife. This will help break up a pretty straight and otherwise uneventful stretch.

I suspect the railroad once followed this route because the land could not be farmed, was unclaimed, and cheap to own. Yet, to lay a rail bed down for heavy train traffic must have cost plenty on the soft, marshy base.

The **railway splits** as it passes over **Hwy 12** and **7** at **Blackwater Junction,** which is about **15 km from Uxbridge**. The right arm goes another **29 km to Lindsay**, where the scenery changes to woodlots and farm fields on a very linear route.

The other direction curves **north** on the left branch and was recently graded. This route has more marsh scenery (if you wish for that), as it goes along the **Beaver River Wetlands Conservation Area**.

The path also does pass close to **Sunderland** and **Cannington,** ending at **Woodville 20 km** away. On this route, you are likely to find a few amenities in these small towns.

The main route, however, has **no communities** along the way. Bring what you need, as **Lindsay** is a long way from the starting point.

Although there were no **biting bugs** on our fall ride, I am sure they are out in the spring—especially in the marshland.

If you want a more extended adventure, stay overnight in **Lindsay** as there are **three other Rail trails** that go beyond to Omemee, Victoria South, and **Victoria North**. I met some Europeans **Bikepacking** this route, heading for **Ottawa** and most of it on done on old Rail Trails.

Looking for some real train action? From south of Uxbridge to Stouffville, a vintage train pulls tourists along this rail line.

History – Uxbridge was once the headquarters of the **Toronto and Nipissing Railway (T & NR)**. In **1871** trains ran from **Scarborough** to **Uxbridge,** and eventually to **Coboconk,** to pull lumber from the **Gull River.** It never made it, as planned, to far away **Lake Nipissing.**

This route carried mainly passengers, grain, and firewood for the owners to their **Gooderham and Worts Distillery** in **Toronto.**

By **1882** it was sold to the **Midland Railway** and years later, as the route was not needed, only the track in the south was kept and was divided for train travel between **VIA, GO Transit**, and the **Durham Heritage Railway**.

In **1874** the **Port Whitby & Port Perry Railway** built a connecting line to **Lindsay** at **Blackwater Junction,** but the **Grand Trunk Railway** soon took ownership. Trains ran on this section until its closure in **1991**.

Victoria South – Rail Trail

Lindsay to Bethany

Length – 29 km (one way)

80% rail trail
10% park trail
10% roads, detours

Elevation – Very flat, as most rail lines are.

Terrain – A mix of crushed stone, loose gravel, and sand, with some asphalt paths close to town.

Skill – Easy to Intermediate.

Traffic – Not busy, with the occasional bicycles, hikers, and horseback riders, you may see the occasional ATV or snowmobiles users.

Maps – There is a map board at the trailhead in Lindsay, with signposts on the trail.

Facilities – Food and washrooms in Lindsay and Bethany.

Highlights – Scugog and Pigeon Rivers, old bridges, downtown Lindsay, and marshes.

Phone – None

Website – Kawartha Lakes

Similar Trails – Oro – Medonte, North Simcoe

Local Clubs – Uxbridge Cycling Club

Access – Start your ride at:

- **30 King St.** in **Lindsay**
- **Mount Horeb Rd.** and **Pigeon River** (the halfway point)
- **Ski Hill Rd.** and **Jackson St.** in **Bethany**

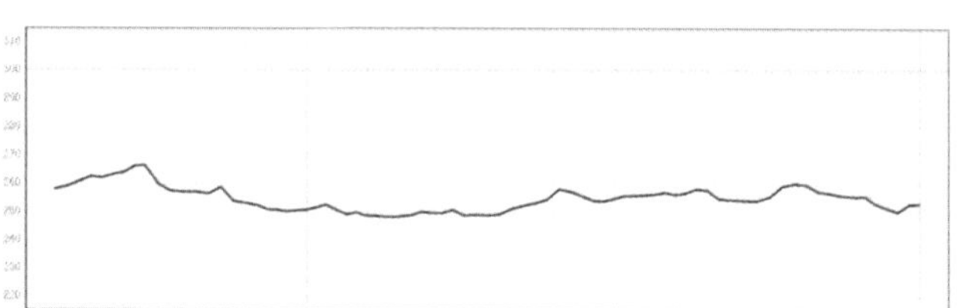

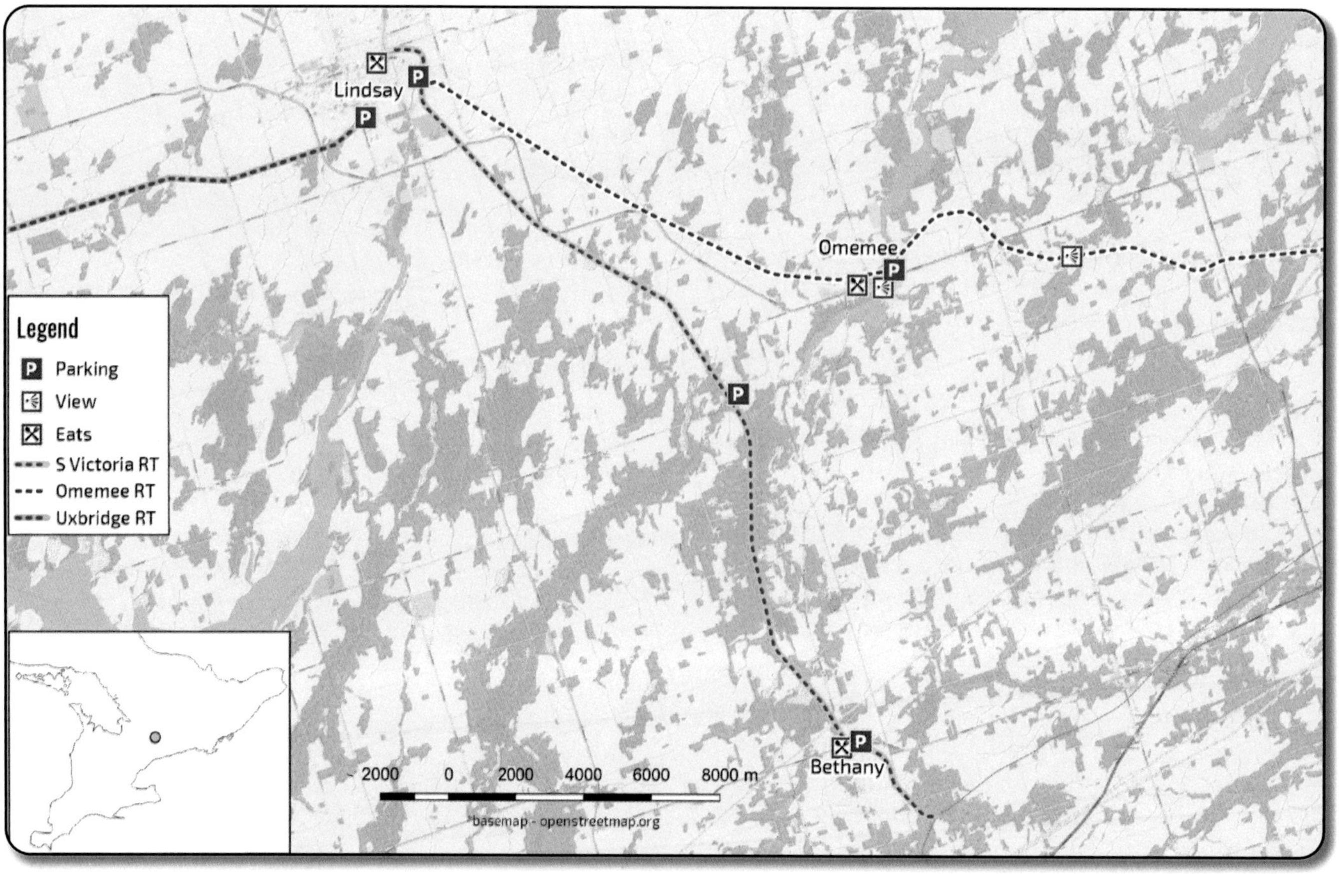

Review:

The **29-km Victoria South Rail Trail** runs southeast from **Lindsay** through farm country and on to a maintained flat stretch of rail bed, then down to the village of **Bethany.**

A quiet cycle through Ontario farm country and wetlands, this route offers views of fields, farms, and country homes.

The surface of this trail is a little rougher and looser than other Rail Trails. A by-product of this is that ATVs can use this route, although I did not see any.

As a more open, lesser-treed path the Rail Trail gives you much to look at, although perhaps **too much sun.**

The best part of this bicycle trail starts in **Lindsay,** by the **locks** and the **old mill.** The route follows the **Scugog River** on a paved, treed Park trail for **1.5 km**.

Riders will pass a few **old bridges** and soon veer off toward the river's edge where they'll meet the road at **Dobson St**. At the end of this street is the start of the **Omemee Rail Trail**.

Cross the road and follow the **Victoria South trail** into an open, straight section passing a **golf course** and **farm fields.** It then continues through a **few woodlots,**

and bridges cross two branches of the **Pigeon River.**

The other appealing part of this ride is the **12 km** of wilderness through the **Fleetwood Creek Valley** wetlands. Well, enjoyable as long as the bugs are not biting.

Once out of the marsh you arrive at a **Ski Hill Road** (Hwy 38) in the village of **Bethany.** Years ago, this road was another rail line coming down from **Omemee.**

There is a small gap in the trail in **Bethany**, but it does continue south of **Hwy 7A.** From here is an optional **3 km** of seldom-used pathway that meets up with another working rail line.

In **Bethany**, riders can find a general store and a few places to eat before heading back; or make this town your starting point and have lunch in **Lindsay.**

As an alternate return route, take part of the gravelled **Old Mill Road** or cut over to the **Omemee Rail Trail**.

History – In 1857 the **Port Hope Lindsay and Beaverton Railway** started running trains from **Port Hope** through **Millbrook** and on to **Lindsay**. In **1869** the new owners, **Midland Railways,** extended the line to **Beaverton** on **Lake Simcoe**, and eventually as far as **Midland** by **1878**.

Ownership changed again, moving to the **Grand Trunk Railway,** but the line still never made much money. The last passenger train ran in **1951**, with freight trains occasionally using the track until the **Canadian Pacific Railways** decommissioned the route in the mid-**1970s**.

Regrettably, much of the southern half of this trail was sold off, and other sections serve as part of the **Ganaraska** hiking trail.

Welland Canal – Park Trail

St. Catharines to Port Colborne

Length – 42 km (one way)

95% park trail
5% roads, crossings, detours

Elevation – Hilly at each lock in the north end, but flattens out beyond Thorold.

Terrain – A wide, paved path with a bridge and a few short road detours.

Skill – Easy, rated Intermediate level to do the hill by the locks.

Traffic – Not crowded, with mainly bicyclists, and a few people walking or roller blading.

Maps – Good signage throughout.

Facilities – Food and lodging is available along the way, as well as restrooms and bike-repair stations.

Highlights – Freighters, locks, and bridges.

Trail Fee – Free

Phone – None

Website – Niagara Cycling Tourism

Similar Trails – Niagara River, Hamilton Beach, Rideau Canal

Local Clubs – Short Hills Club, Bikefit Sunflowers

Access – Parking at the north end starts at **Charles Ansell Park**; in the south end it starts at **HH Knoll Lakeview Park**, the **Welland Canal Centre** and Museum, or the **Allanburg** bridge.

There are also many parking spots along the route.

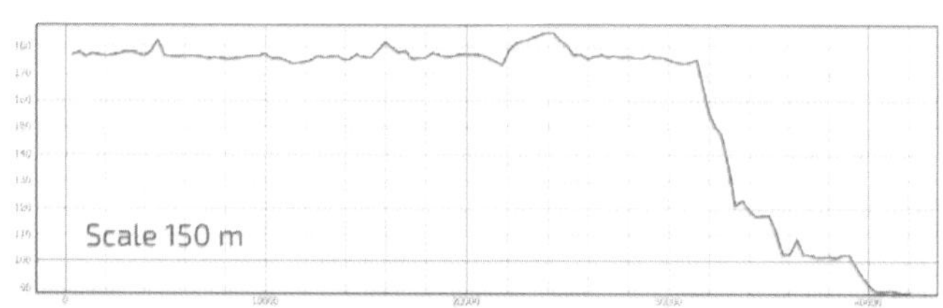

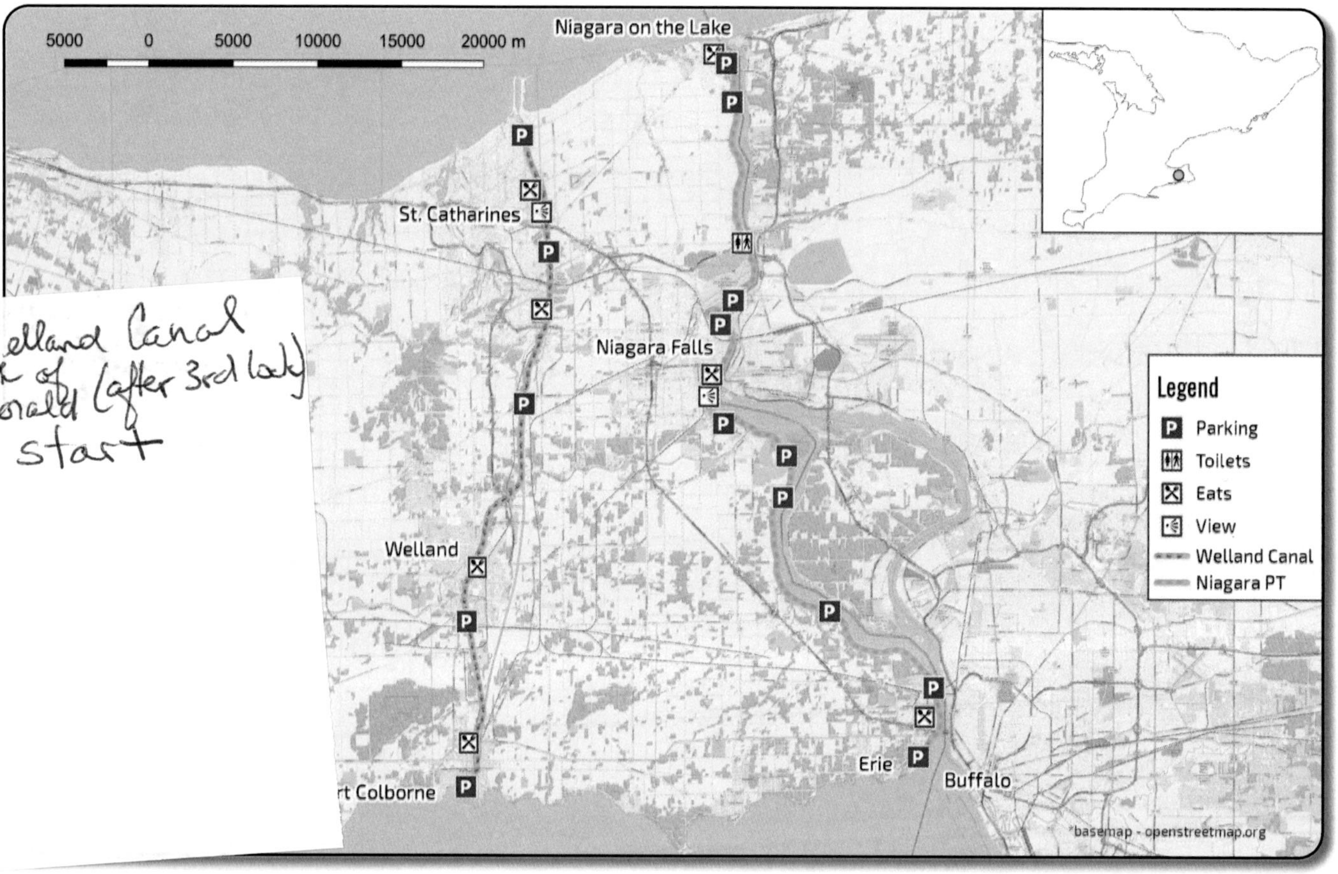

5000 0 5000 10000 15000 20000 m

Niagara on the Lake

St. Catharines

Niagara Falls

Welland

rt Colborne

Erie

Buffalo

Legend
Parking
Toilets
Eats
View
Welland Canal
Niagara PT

basemap - openstreetmap.org

Welland Canal
South of Thorold (after 3rd lock) to start

Review:

The **42 km Welland Canal** bike path makes for a **great weekend outing**—or two! This **historic canal** from **Lake Ontario** to **Lake Erie** is a beautiful, scenic, and established route along the water's edge.

The sights vary along the way, but the **large freighters** drifting down the canal and the **giant locks** are definitely sights to see. There are stretches of homes, industries, and open parklands, as well as the occasional bridge to cross.

On the **west side**, the route follows the canal for most of the way. It is spacious paved path that is well-marked with a few detours.

From the **north end**, you can start at **Lake Ontario** by including the **George Nicholson Trail** for another **3 km;** officially, it begins at the first bridge/lock on **Lakeshore Rd.**

As you cycle along the edge of **St. Catharines** and the canal, you will **pass two locks** and start to climb. By the town of **Thorold** and the third lock, you will have to climb the **Niagara Escarpment** which is a **good-sized hill.** Continuing south, the rest of the ride south is a flat and leisurely cruise.

Further on, riders will cross a few bridges and end up at an island with natural parkland and wooded areas.

The path diverts away, through the city of **Welland,** to run along the older, closed **canal for 14 km** before rejoining up to the main one. On the return, there is an option of riding a path along the **opposite side**. **Downtown Welland** is a perfect stop to take a few pictures and find something to eat.

Along this old section are signs of industry, with rusty bridges no longer in need. At one point the canal has been filled in to create a still surface for the boat races at the **Flatwater Centre;** you can see people training with kayaks and canoes.

As you ride south to **Port Colborne**, the path jogs for a bit onto an **island**, then across and back to the west side to end at the edge of **Lake Erie,** at a marina and park. (Hungry, need ice cream? They got it!)

There are numerous small towns with amenities along the way to plan a lunch or to stay over. I also saw a few **free bike-repair stations,** if needed.

Doing the entire length and back clocks in at **84 km.** Many of you will opt to ride one end or the other; I suggest the middle section.

This trail can also be made into a much more substantial **140-km loop** to meet up with the **Niagara Parkway**; this makes for a great weekend! With some road riding along **Lake Ontario** and using the **Friendship Rail Trail** along **Lake Erie**, you have a complete circuit.

With so many choices and so little time, pick a trail and get moving.

Whitchurch + Porritt – Park/MTB Trail

3749 Aurora Rd. and Warden Ave., GTA

Length – 4+5 km (both areas)

60% double-track access roads
30% hiking trail
10% single-track MTB trail

Elevation – Rather flat, with small rolling hills at the back end.

Terrain – Smooth soil, with some gravel and sandy areas.

Skill – Easy for MTB; Intermediate for Park cyclists.

Traffic – A quiet place, with the occasional bicyclists, hikers, and dog walkers.

Maps – None at the trailhead, although a few signposts along the way.

Facilities – A rather small parking lot, with outhouses and a shelter.

Highlights – A pond, as well as big estates beside a horse ranch.

Trail Pass – Free

Phone – 905 895 1281

Website – Lake Simcoe CA

Similar Trails – Eldred King, Bendor, Midhurst

Local Clubs – Durham Mountain Biking Association

Access – There is a parking lot on the south side at **3749 Aurora Rd.** near **Warden Ave.** There is also access south on **Warden Ave.**, around the corner; the lot is smaller but you can also ride in.

Porritt has two parking lots north of **Aurora Rd.** on **Kennedy Rd.**

You could easily ride from one woodlot to the other on this ride, and I recommend you do!

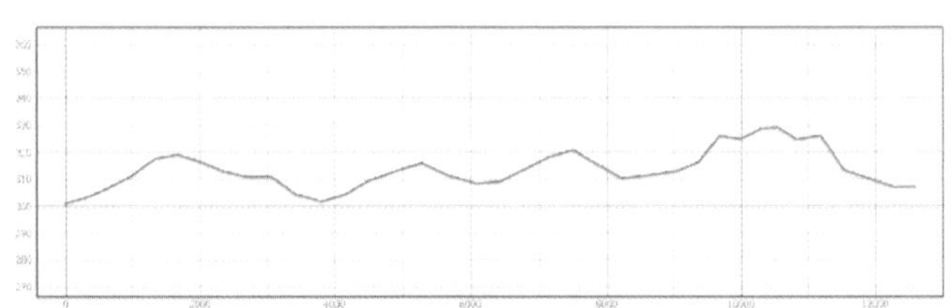

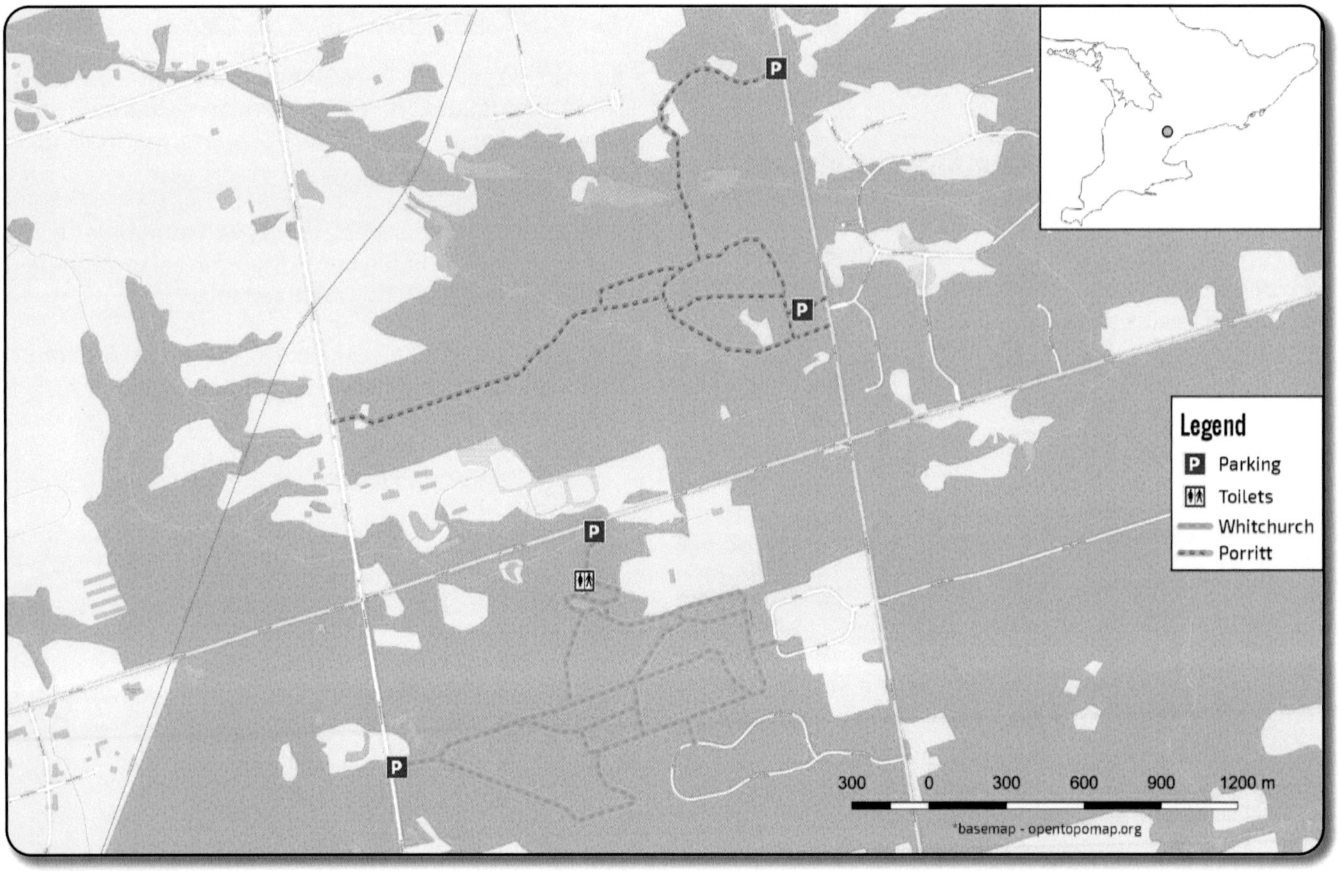

Legend
P Parking
Toilets
Whitchurch
Porritt

300 0 300 600 900 1200 m

*basemap - opentopomap.org

Review:

Whitchurch & Porritt Conservation Areas make up a short, **8 km** circuit of off-road riding east of **Aurora.** Running through a wooded area, this route has a relatively flat terrain made of wide access roads.

This is a decent spot for a little bit of light family adventure trekking through the woods. And so close to Toronto, I just have to mention it.

It is rather rustic, as none of the trails are paved; therefore it is rated as **Intermediate Park** forest, and may not even be that hard. It is all shaded, with no open spots except at the small pond.

This area is larger than the small conservation area you might see on a map. The trails extend beyond to the **south** and **west**, into what is called the **Robinson Tract.**

From the **Aurora Road** car lot, the path goes to the pond and a rain shelter. Enjoy this picturesque spot, then go south by the water as it turns into a thin hiking trail.

Once into the back end, paths are again wider. If coming in from **Warden Ave.,** around the corner, this will give you a smother gravel base to start the ride.

There are not many directional signs, and as paths are old and connect at odd intersections, there is not much logic to the layout.

If you arrive at the back fence and the large homes, turn back and try another way. (It may be tricky, but you cannot get too lost in here.)

This is a favourable spot for **newbie mountain bikers** to learn to handle unpaved terrain, with a few short hills at the back; veteran MTB riders will find no challenges here as I only saw **one narrow, single-track trail.**

Watch for the odd hiker, dogs, and mud when it's a wet season. However, the bugs here are never a problem.

The **5 km** at **Porritt Tract** trails are included on the map north of here. I recall it being hillier, though just as short a ride. Doing both will make for a good outing.

This is one of my favourite hidden spots just out of town, where I go when I need to escape the big city for a quick spin on my steed.

Elora Cataract – Rail Trail

Elora to Cataract

Length – 47 km (one way)

95% rail trail path
5% roads crossings, detours

Elevation – As with most Rail Trails, there is a gradual slope.

Terrain – Consists of crushed stone, as well as some gravel and grass; detours to an asphalt road.

Skill – Easy

Traffic – Bicyclists, hikers, and horses, as well as cross-country skiers and snowmobiles (mostly mid-trail) in the winter.

Maps – There are signs at the gates, as well as milestone markers.

Facilities – Parking is on the street, with amenities and lodging in Elora, Fergus, Belwood, and Erin.

Highlights – There is a large dam at Belwood Lake, the historic towns of Elora and Fergus, the Elora Gorge, the Forks of the Credit River, and the Elora Quarry.

Trail Fee – Free

Phone – None

Website – Elora Cataract Trailway, Grand River C. A.

Similar Trails –Kissing Bridge, Caledon, Uxbridge

Local Clubs –Waterloo Cycling Club

Access – Most side roads have ample parking space; try: **Gerrie Rd.** and **Beatty Line** in Fergus, Gartshore St. in **Belwood**, and towns of **Orton** and **Erin.**

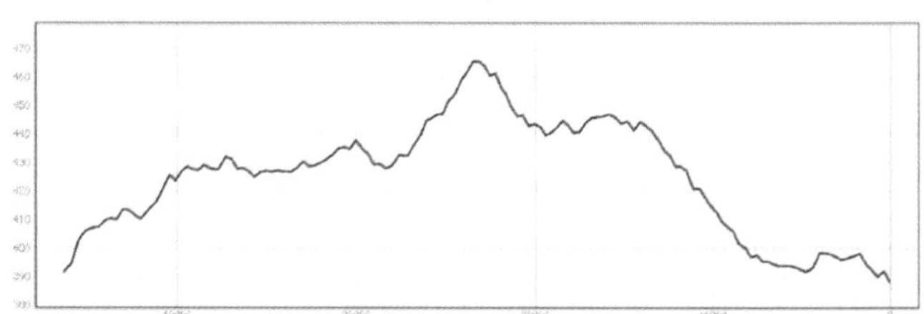

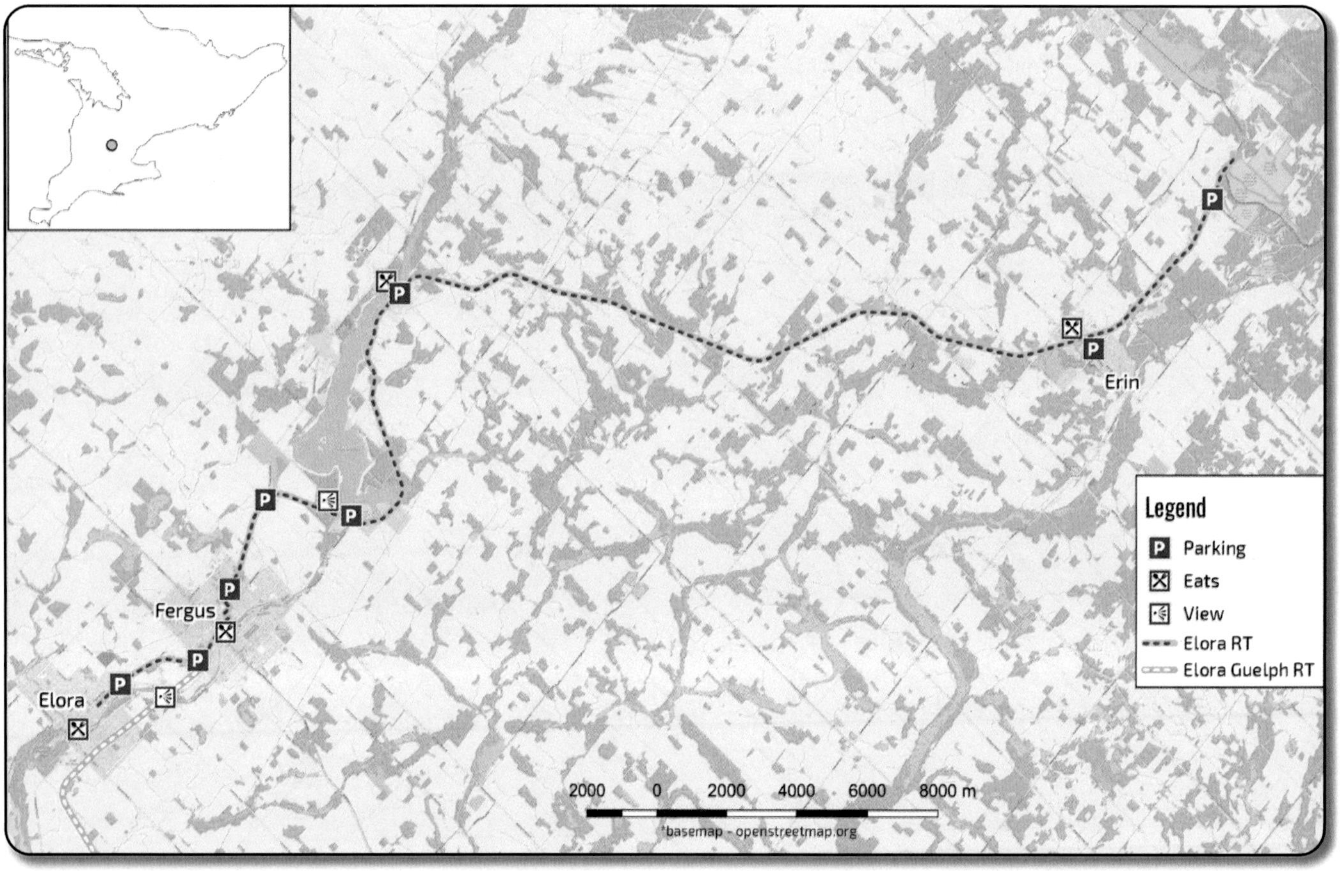

Erin
Fergus
Elora
Legend
Parking
Eats
View
Elora RT
Elora Guelph RT
2000 0 2000 4000 6000 8000 m
basemap - openstreetmap.org

Review:

The **Elora Cataract Rail Trail** is close to **Toronto** and offers a mellow bicycle ride on a **well-maintained** crushed-stone path. North of **Guelph,** it runs east from the historic town of **Elora** to the tiny village of **Cataract**.

At **47 km** in length, **my favourite section** is the **west end** of the route, which is more scenic and has more amenities.

From **Elora** the Rail Trail starts its way out of town but truly gets going at the parking lot, where it crosses **Gerrie St.** Both **Elora** and the next town, **Fergus,** have built streets over what was once the rail line, so the route is not consistent.

After a short, **3 km** ride you enter **Fergus**. Here, you need to take side streets for **2 km** through the town, then again meet up with the old rail line near **Gzowski St.** and **Forfar St. E.**

Onward, this stretch of trail curves around and crosses over the **Grand River** at the **Belwood Lake** dam.

The lake and river below is a majestic sight to see while **riding over this large dam,** where trains would have once crossed.

One can follow the path up the river and past cottages to eventually head inland through rural Ontario farmland and into the town of **Erin**.

Ride another **7 km,** and you reach the end at **Cataract,** finishing next to the Forks of the Credit River Provincial Park. This park makes for a **great fall hike.** It has some parking, but problematically, the village at the trailhead has none.

While out, make an effort to visit the **old historic centres** of **Elora and Fergus**.

You can also find **great hiking trails and camping sites** at the very popular (yet busy) Elora Gorge Conservation Area. Take a dip in the old quarry watering hole, especially after a hot day of riding. It's an unusual place, but worth a visit.

By the way, if in **Fergus** and you find yourself where the path ends coming into town at **Beatty Line,** you can opt to take another Rail trail to loop back to **Elora;** the **Elora Guelph Rail Trail** starts just 100 m south, crossing a large bridge spanning the **Grand River.**

There are plenty of great options to turn these towns, and trails, into a **good daytime outing** or **weekend stayover.** With plenty of **shops** and **patios** to check out, it's sure to be a good time while you're there.

History – Built in **1879** for the **Credit Valley Railway**, this branch line meets up with the main route running from **Toronto** to **Orangeville**. It served the local populous, farmers, and other industry for many years.

From **1884**, **Canadian Pacific Railways** leased the line and ran trains until **1988**. This abandoned rail corridor was developed into a recreational trail five years later.

Fanshawe – MTB/Park Trail

1424 Clarke Rd., London

Length – 22+ km

15% MTB single track
65% hiking trail
20% access roads

Elevation – Flat sections with gentle, flowing hills.

Terrain – The road is paved while trails are smooth soil, with a few rocks, roots and some gravel sections; watch for mud puddles after a rain.

Skill – Easy to Moderate

Traffic – Cyclists, hikers and dog walkers; not too busy.

Maps – Found at trailhead; follow blue hiker markers.

Facilities – Include parking lot, outhouse, camping, swimming, park store.

Highlights – Views of the small lake and farms.

Trail Fee – Pay at gate – $7 cyclists if you ride in, or $13 per car.

Phone – 1-866-668-2267

Website – Fanshawe Conservation

Similar Trails – Ganaraska, Minnesing, Wildwood

Local Clubs – London Cycling Club

Access – Entrance at **1424 Clarke Road, London, Ontario**. Go past the front gate, first parking lot by the dam, trailhead is nearby at the treeline.

If camping, the campgrounds have paths close by.

Parking also exists at Fisherman's Point on **Rebecca Road.**

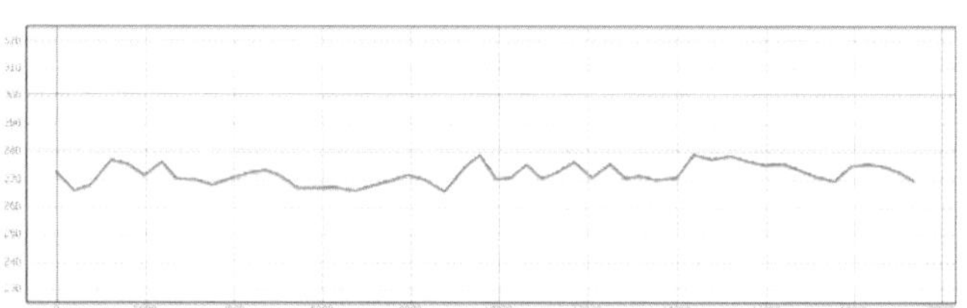

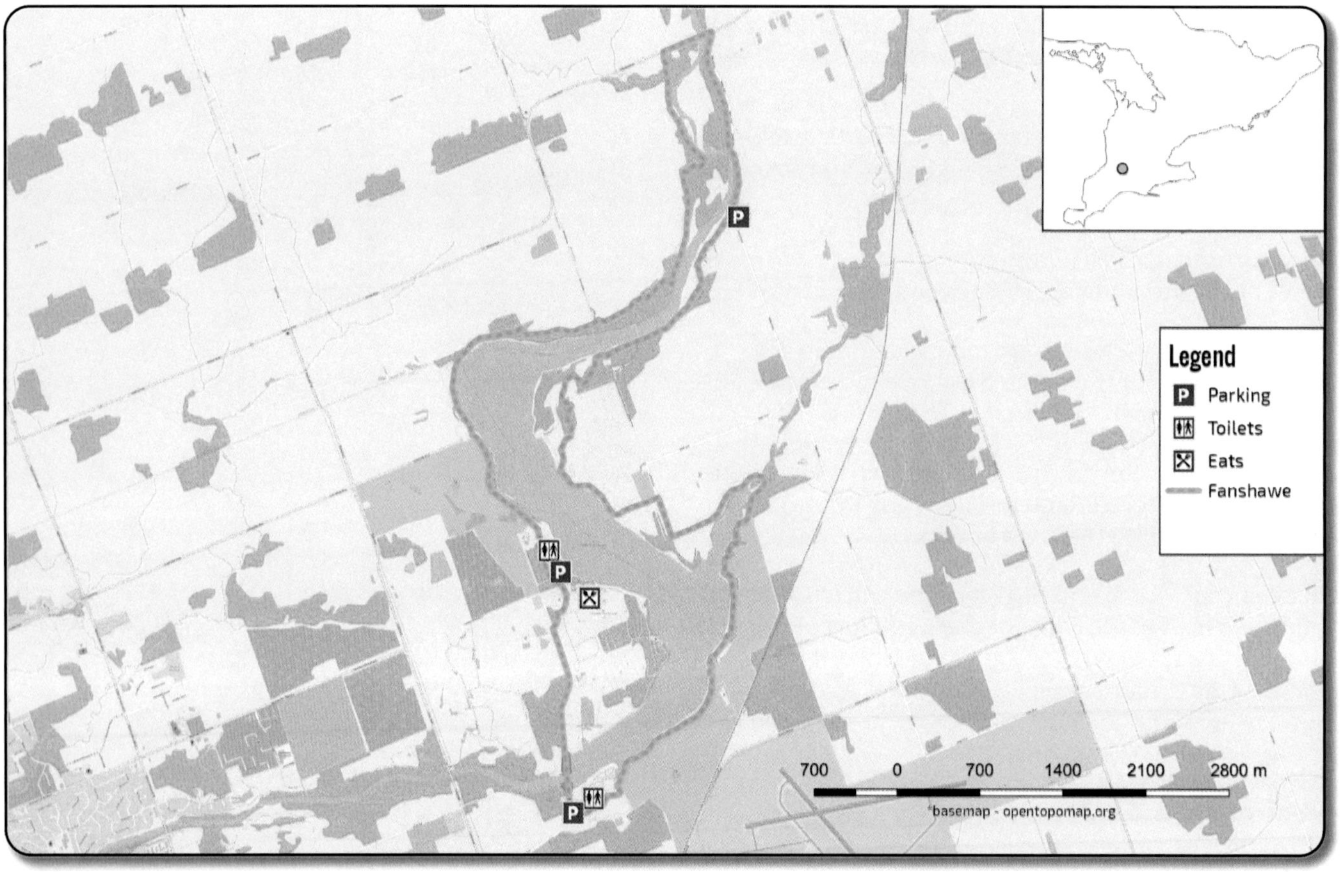

Legend
Parking
Toilets
Eats
Fanshawe

700 0 700 1400 2100 2800 m
basemap - opentopomap.org

Review:

Fanshawe Conservation Area has a **large bike trail loop** that circles the reservoir on its banks. This is an easy but long **cross-country style** ride at **22 km**.

As a **scenic ride,** it is ever changing as you work your way around the lake. This can be a **fast ride if you like it that way,** or a slower **family outing,** although **a bit long for kids.**

What this loop does not have, is a **shortcut**. So are you up for a 20+ km outing? If you have to bail and double back, please let riders pass.

Most of the single track is a **hiker's path** that is rather straight with **smooth soil** and the odd root or rock. Inclines are **short hills** and not too steep for any seasoned rider to manage.

By following the **blue diamond hiker symbols** as you go around, you can't get lost.

Cyclists are asked to **alternate directions depending on the day**. [Which is clockwise on even numbered days & counter-clockwise on odd days.]

Expect to ride a few sections on **paved side roads** - over the dam, past the camping area and behind two golf courses.

There were **4 Black Diamond side loops** (two are not seen on the park map) that are a little bit harder and are **cut the way MTB riders like,** with a few cool **structures** too... but really not that tough.

The **Dragon's Cur** trail was the best of them and **Monkey Wrench** is twisty fun.

Yet by Ontario MTB standards, they all felt like just a harder **Blue** trail. Hmmm sorry guys, Sudbury is more the **Black Diamond** country that can kill ya!

Expect to get mud on you and the bike, as there are many **small mucky puddles** that cannot all be avoided. This means you should **pass on a ride after it rains or in early spring**. I would prefer more maintenance to fill these holes and a few more boardwalks to cross... please.

There are two **small creek crossings** you ride through, (kind of fun) but not too fast or your shoes will get wet.

If you are out this way, there are not too many choices to ride trail. So this long loop is welcome, to give you a **few good hours** on your steed.

Georgian – Rail Trail

Collingwood to Meaford

Length – 32 km (one way)

90% rail trail path
10% roads crossings (some crossings are rather busy), detours

Elevation – Flat and straight, with some bridges, shaded woodlots, and farm fields along the way.

Terrain – A wide path of crushed stone, some gravel, as well as a little asphalt.

Skill – Easy

Traffic – Watch for bicyclist, hikers, and horses; cross-country skiers in the winter.

Maps – Plenty of signpost and milestone markers.

Facilities – Parking with outhouses, as well as local services in Collingwood, Thornbury, and Meaford.

Highlights – Georgian Bay, Thornbury Bridge, and Craigleith train station. Views of the Niagara Escarpment hill.

Trail Fee – Free

Phone – 1 888 227 8667

Website – Georgian Trail, Cycle Simcoe, Georgian Bay Tourism

Similar Trails – Caledon, Hamilton to Bradford, Millennium

Local Clubs – Collingwood Cycling Club

Access – Parking by trailheads at many locations where roads cross the trail.

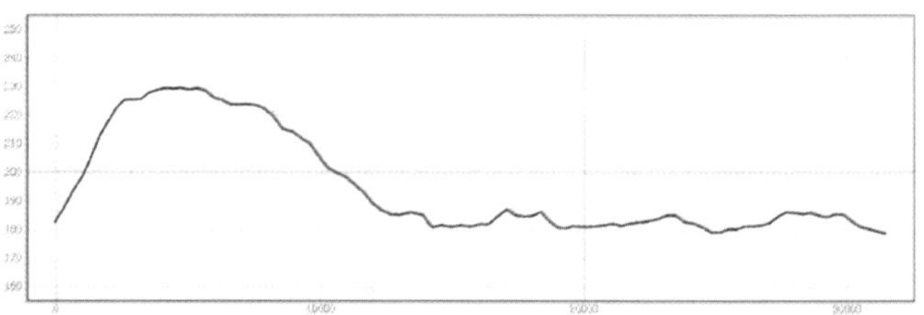

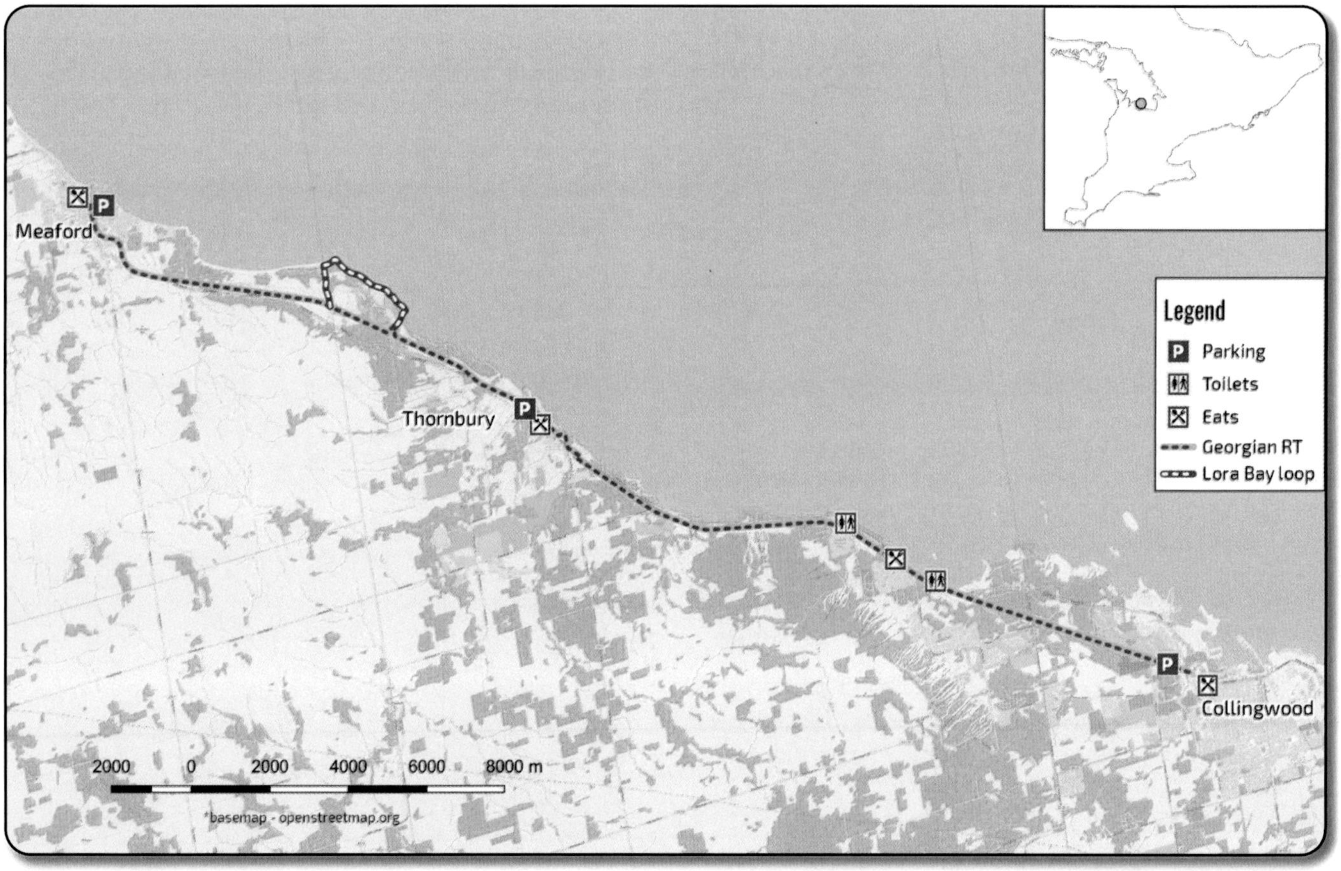

Meaford
Thornbury
Collingwood
Legend
Parking
Toilets
Eats
Georgian RT
Lora Bay loop
2000 0 2000 4000 6000 8000 m
*basemap - openstreetmap.org

Review:

The **Georgian Rail Trail** goes from **Collingwood** through to **Thornbury** and **Meaford** and is one of the more well-known bike rides for both locals and tourists. This pleasant **32 km** ride is an easy bike path that follows the coast of **Georgian Bay**.

It offers glimpses of the water, and travels through shaded woodlands, marshes, and farm fields, with the towering **Niagara Escarpment** as a backdrop.

This path has a **well-maintained** base of **crushed gravel**, with little overgrowth. There are plenty of signposts to keep riders informed as to how far they are from their destination.

Collingwood has many bike paths, and taking one along the water's edge will bring riders to the back of a mall on the west edge of town, where the Rail Trail starts.

Following this straight trail **6 km** through a forested area, passing a golf course, you then see the shores of the bay.

Near **Craigleith**, note the **old train station** that once brought vacationers in from the big city. This is also a good area to go for a dip in the bay during a hot summer ride.

We chose to ride what I believe is a shorter, more interesting section from **Thornbury** to **Meaford;** one way is a comfortable **13 km.**

Thornbury has a dam with an **old trestle bridge,** which we used as our starting point. As with most Rail Trails, the going was very straight until we descended into **Meaford** for lunch.

As you enter town, the Rail Trail goes into a wooded section that is rather enjoyable, ending at the harbour by the sailboats. The **old main street** is worth having a look around and is a nice spot to eat.

Alternatively, you could start your ride in **Meaford** and have lunch in **Thornbury** for some samples of cider at the **local distillery**. (Yum!) Or, go the full distance of **32 km** and find plenty of eateries in **Collingwood**.

Collingwood is the **largest town in the area,** which is doing well as a retirement community and recreation area. Nearby **Blue Mountain Village** has some serious **downhill MTB runs.** Visitors will also find the **downtown charming,** and full of life on the weekends.

Anyone looking for a **getaway** should consider trying this Rail Trail. It is about a two-hour drive from **Toronto,** and it is worth staying overnight to enjoy the many **festivals** and **events** in the area.

The **Lora Bay Loop** is an **alternate side route,** just to keep it interesting, north of **Thornbury.** I took this down to the water and found plenty of fancy cottages to gawk at, as well as a few parks with beaches where one can stop and go for a swim.

This **4 km** side route follows **Sunset Boulevard**. It's a small, enjoyable detour except for a **sizable hill** that one will have to face on the way back up the Rail Trail. (Of course, going down it is a blast!) On the **east** side, take **Lora Bay Dr.** down the hill. Or, on the **west** side of the Rail Trail, look for **Christie Beach Rd.**

History – This rail line was constructed in 1872 by the **North Grey Railway**, travelling between **Collingwood** and **Meaford.** Trains carried timber, quarried stone, and oil to markets in the south. (Yes, **Craigleith** had oil in its shale beds for a time.)

Passengers and tourists travelled north to **Craigleith** station, many for **ski holidays** at **Blue Mountain** until passenger service ended in 1963. **CN** eventually stopped running freight, and by 1985 the tracks were removed to become this recreational trail.

Grand River – Park Trail

Brantford

Length – 20 km loop

60% park path
30% double-track paths
10% roads, crossings, detours

Elevation – Flat along the dikes and floodplains, with a few short hills and bridges to cross.

Terrain – Paved, with some rough patches and gravel-based paths.

Skill – Easy

Maps – Plenty of map boards and trail markers.

Facilities – Parking lots and toilets, as well as benches, picnic tables, and rain shelter; restaurants and lodging are close by.

Highlights – The Grand River, dams, old rail bridges, and treed pathways.

Trail Fee – Free

Phone – 519 759 4150

Website – City of Brantford

Similar Trails – Thames Valley, Speed River, Greenway

Local Clubs – Brant Cycling Club

Access – Parking can be found at many lots on this loop. A suggested starting point is at **Mt. Pleasant St.** and **Gilkison St.** Also, try **D'Aubigny Park** at **Spalding Dr.**, and the beautiful **Glenhyrst Gardens**.

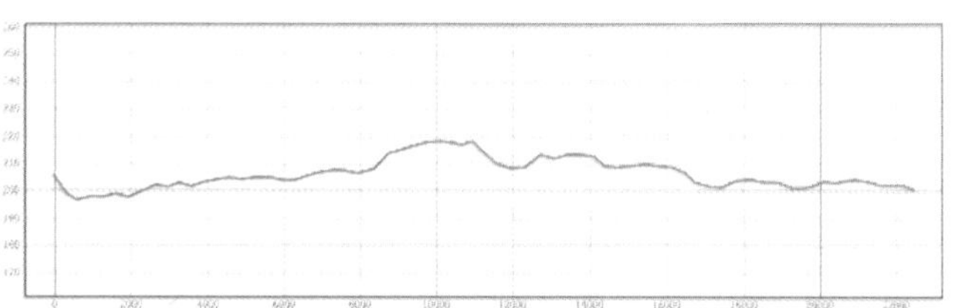

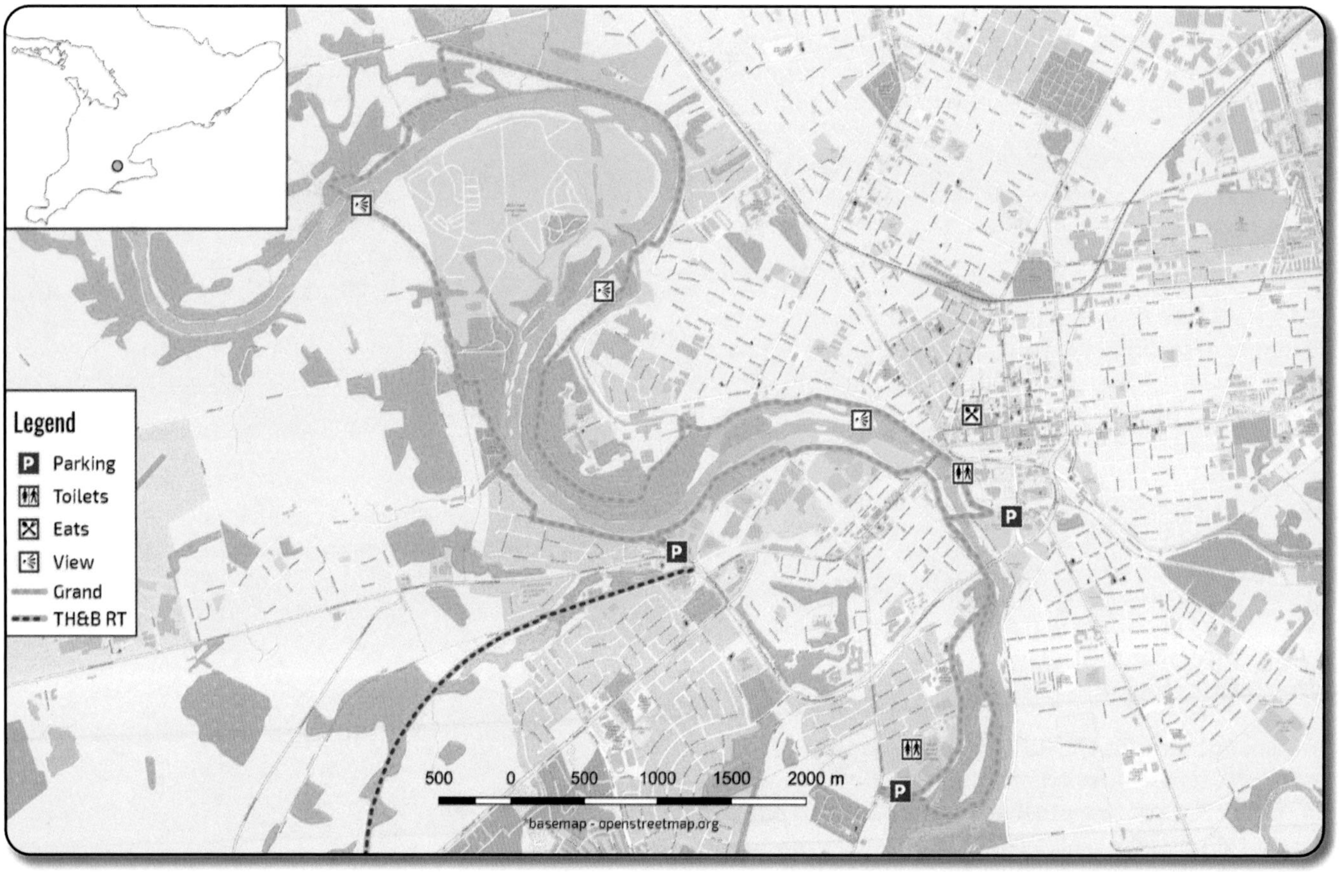

Legend
P Parking
Toilets
Eats
View
Grand
TH&B RT

500 0 500 1000 1500 2000 m

basemap - openstreetmap.org

Review:

Here is an enjoyable **20 km Park Trail loop in Brantford,** which follows the **Grand River** up one side and then back down on the other. Part city parkland, part repurposed **old rail lines**, this trail makes for a pleasant path to cycle.

With no single, long intercity park path in Brantford this provides a great **combined loop.** Although the path's name changes a few times, there are **plenty of maps** and **signposts** to guide you around and back again.

With only a few climbs, it is fairly flat riding that is easy to do. The scenery is a **mix of parks, woodlots, old rail beds,** and **floodplains,** with glimpses of the river when you look over your shoulder. You will be also riding on **top of dikes**, which keep the city dry during spring floods.

Part of this ride crosses over the **Grand River** via **two old bridges;** the north one is very long with great views—watch for canoes and fishing boats on the river.

I noted that some of the path's asphalt surface needed **repair**, and made for a rough ride. Although most of it is paved, there are sections with smooth dirt and crushed-gravel too. While riding the loop, I counted **three road detours** that were straightforward connections.

Looking on a map, you will see the starting points are numerous. I found the parking at **Mt. Pleasant St.** and **Gilkison St.,** by the baseball diamonds, a good choice. Starting from there, floods had closed **Gilkison's Flats** for repairs, so we took the upper park path along the sports fields instead.

As you follow the river it connects to the **Fordview Trail,** where you can cross at the **first old train bridge**. (The second bridge is closed.)

Continue up along the **east bank,** on what is now called the **SC Johnson Trail,** toward the town of **Paris,** located on top of the dike embankments. At first, I thought these mounds were old train routes, and some may have been, but other parts had turns too tight for any track to follow.

When you get to **Wilkes Dam,** a short detour takes you up to the route of an old rail bed. Just before **Hardy Rd.**, branch off left to get to a long bridge which takes you back to the other side of the **Grand River**. This part feels as though you are in the country for about fifteen minutes of cycling but then ends abruptly at a suburb (and back to reality).

Here you detour along the road for a few blocks to **Kerr Shaver Tr.** then **Oakhill Dr.**; this gets you back to **D'Aubigny Park** on a wooded path and then back out onto **Ballantyne Dr.**; this is a one-way street and your last detour, and also **has a bike lane.**

Pass an odd one-way intersection to connect back to **Lorne Park;** you will soon be back at the first bridge you crossed. The rest of the ride is a return to your car along the same path.

If you are into more riding out this way, the city maps promote other **Rail Trails** that lead out of town, such as the LE & B, the Hamilton to Brantford trail, and the Rail Trail to **Paris** and then **Cambridge.**

Guelph Lake – MTB/Park Trail

7673 Conservation Rd., Guelph

Length – 20 km

50% single-track MTB trail
50% hiking trail

Elevation – Consists of gentle hills, with a high point in the middle that slopes on the sides.

Terrain – Smooth soil, with a few rocks and rock gardens, as well as tree roots.

Skill – Intermediate MTB and Park trails.

Traffic – Bikes, hikers, dog walkers

Trail Maps – Found at the trailhead with a few signs on the trail, but they are not well laid out.

Facilities – A parking lot, with basic services in park's camping area.

Highlights – Enjoy a fast ride, a rock garden, and lakeside views, including a dam.

Trail Fee – Free

Phone – 519 824 5061

Website – Guelph Lake Conservation Area

Similar Trails – Palgrave, Fanshawe, Wildwood

Local Clubs – Guelph Off-Road Bicycling Association (GORBA)

Access – There are numerous entry points near the conservation area:

- across from the dam on **7673 Conservation Rd.**
- by the river on **797 Victoria Rd. N.**
- and at the end of **Kaine Hill Dr.**

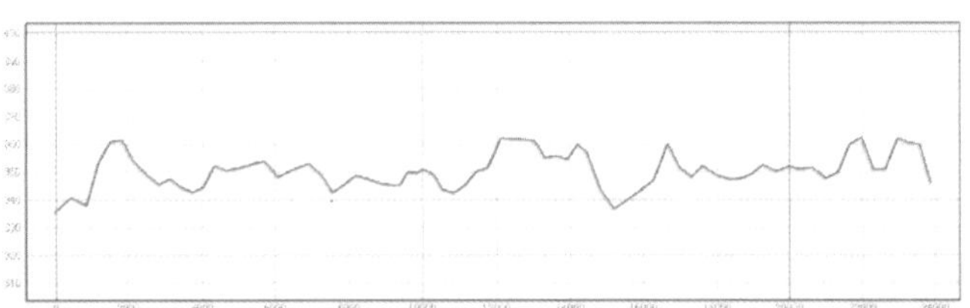

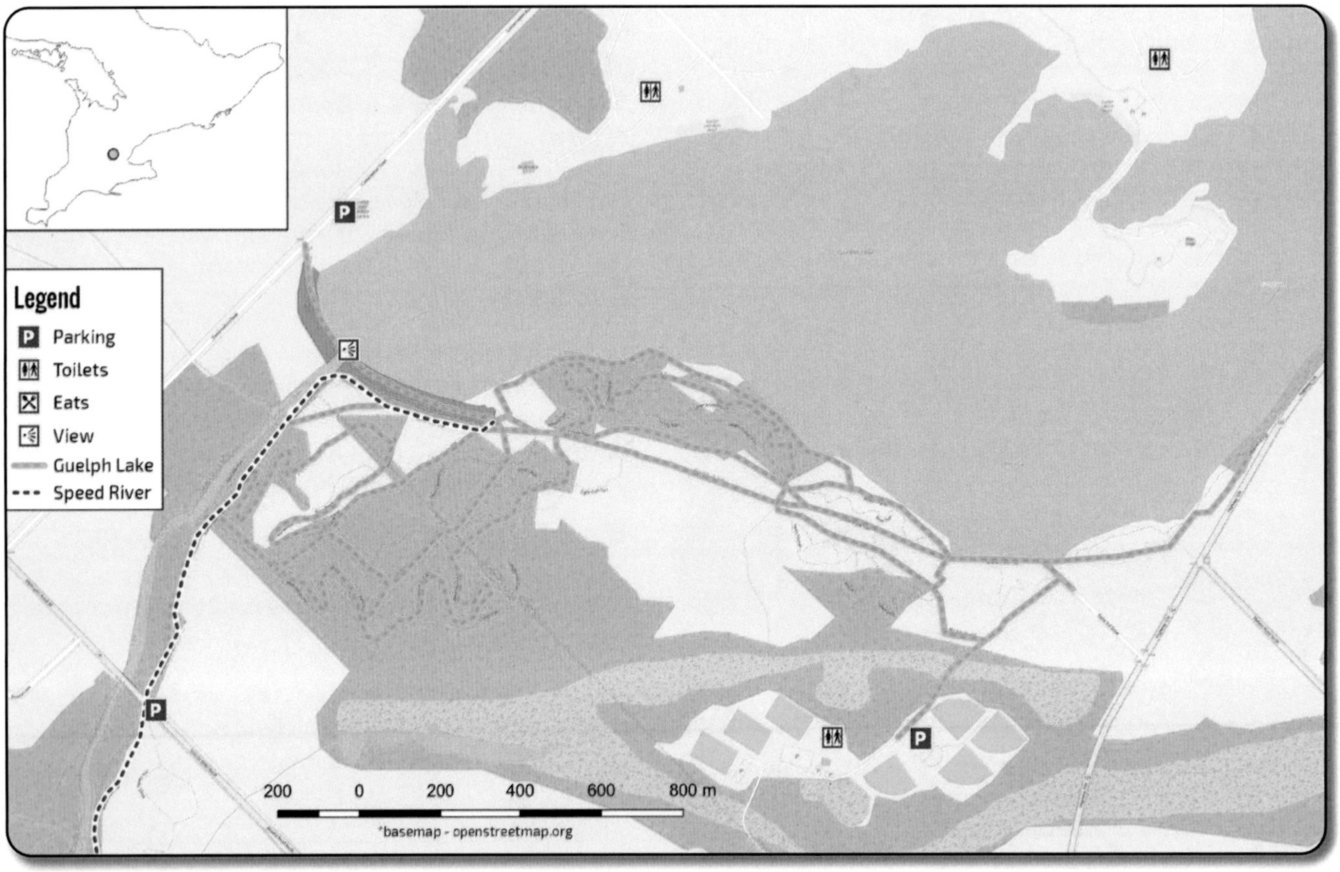

Legend
P Parking
Toilets
Eats
View
Guelph Lake
Speed River

200 0 200 400 600 800 m

*basemap - openstreetmap.org

Review:

The **GORBA** trails, near the **Guelph Lake Conservation Area,** has **20 km** of relatively **mellow** bike trails for beginners to **mountain bike**.

Anyone looking for **nothing too surprising** on their ride, and are more into quick lines through the woods will enjoy this route. You will also find plenty of loops along the way—over 30!

There is the **odd rock garden** and a few **tree roots** to manage, but most of the area consists of smooth, fast-winding trail through the pines; nor is it too hilly.

I found a few tricky side trails not listed on the map at the far end, but most of the **area is tame.**

Hence, **Intermediate Park** trail riders could also enjoy these loops too. (I recommend sticking to the broader main routes.)

Guelph Lake is a great spot to wander with your **Fatbike,** any time of year. The **2 km South Park** trail was a favourite for its sweet, long descent.

I really wanted to love this place based on what I had heard, but felt **two issues need work:**

Firstly, as I rode through this trail system with my son, I hoped for **more thrills**, but any man-made structures were few and old. I don't even recall any log jumps!

A refresh that includes some new features to enhance the MTB experience, such as boardwalks, bridges, rocks, logs, or berms, would be welcome additions.

Secondly, this trail system **lacks enough or proper signage** that logically guides riders through.

That said, you can't get too lost, but you may have to **stop at every junction** and determine which way is the best route. It becomes a bit of a guessing game, which is a tad frustrating as it interrupts your flow.

This area has enormous potential, and I hope they one day put some fun and challenges back in.

The local MTB club, **GORBA**, actively manages these trails, but they ask riders to stay off when conditions are muddy.

If you follow the **Speed River** down from the dam, the trail crosses **Victoria Rd.** There is more riding to be had beyond, although the trail now becomes a park path leading right into **Guelph;** mellow, but enjoyable.

This trail has no fee, as it is not located inside the conservation area, which is across the lake.

However, there is also **good camping** there if you wish to make a weekend of it. The sandy beach and warm water are perfect for an after-ride dip.

Island Lake – Park Trail

673067 Hurontario St. S., Orangeville

Length – 8 + 4 km

80% park path
20% single-track MTB trail

Elevation – A level path around the lake, with one long climb and a few quick inclines.

Terrain – A wide path with varying sections of crushed stone, gravel, and wooden boardwalks and bridges; there is also a single-track dirt trails with boulders.

Skill – Intermediate Park trail with extra Easy MTB trail.

Traffic – Cyclists, hikers, and kids; never too busy.

Maps – A map is found at the trailhead, and there are signs along the trail.

Facilities – Parking with washrooms and picnic tables, as well as swimming and boat rentals.

Highlights – Plenty of bridges and boardwalks, Island Lake, and downtown Orangeville.

Trail Fee – $5.00 (less for kids)

Hours – Open 8 am – 9 pm mid-summer.

Phone – 519 941 6329

Website – Island Lake Conservation Area

Similar Trails – Guelph Lake, Beaches Boardwalk, Hamilton Beach

Local Clubs – Caledon Cycling Club, Team Van GO

Access – From **Hwy 10** in **Orangeville**, head up **Buena Vista Dr.** to the end of **Hurontario St.**; marker **#673067** on the left.

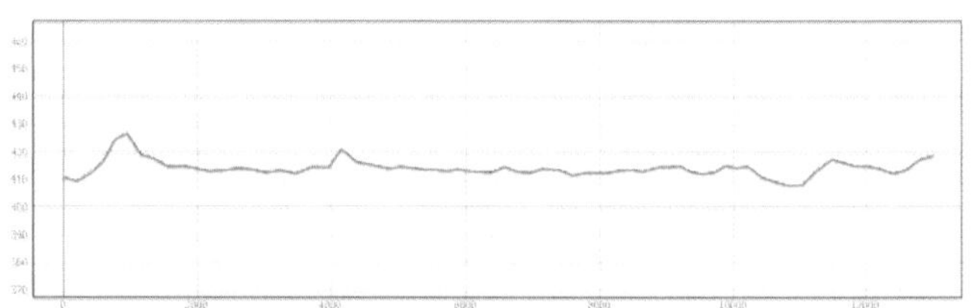

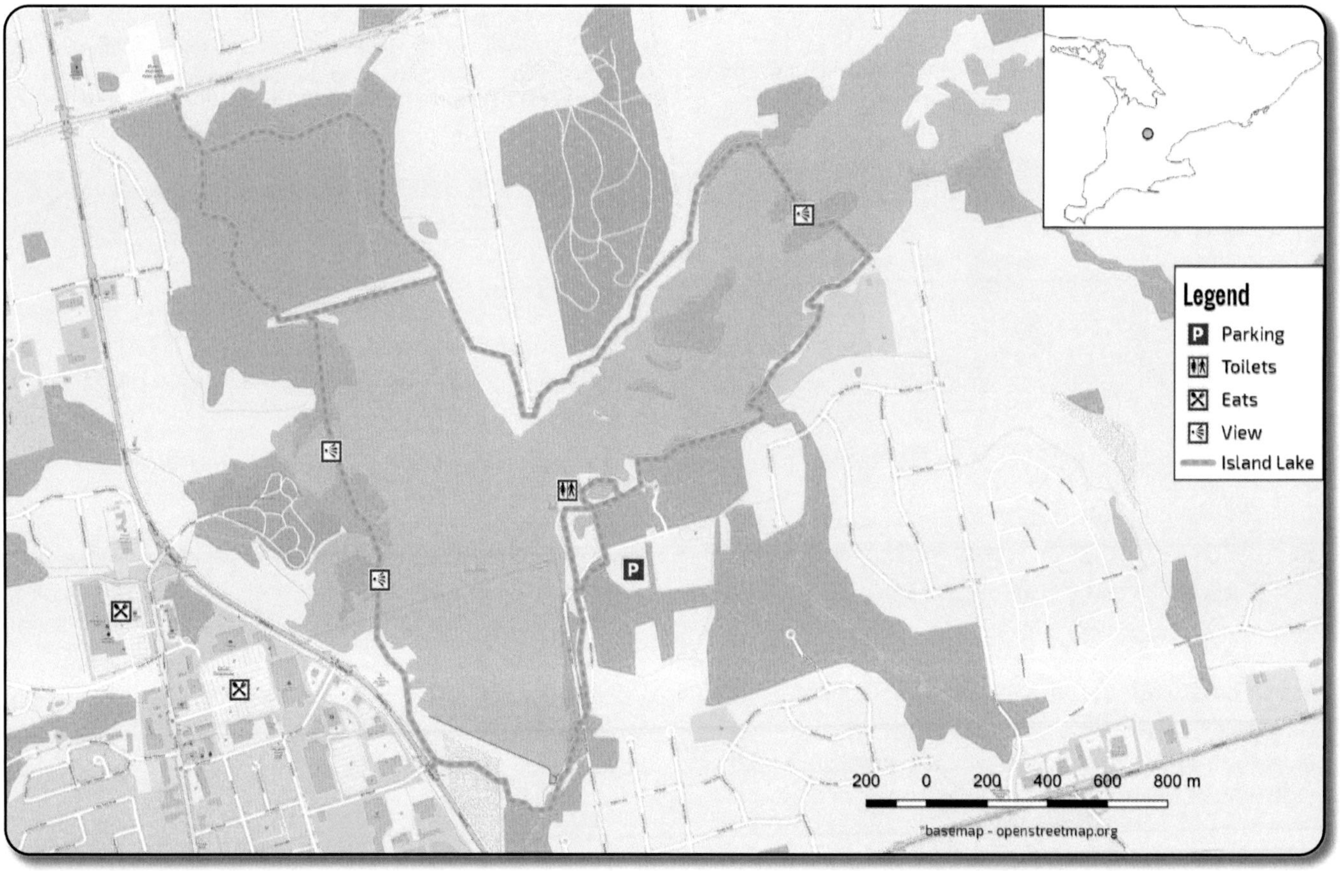

Legend
Parking
Toilets
Eats
View
Island Lake
200 0 200 400 600 800 m
basemap - openstreetmap.org

Review:

The **Island Lake Conservation Area** in **Orangeville** is an **8 km** Park trail that loops around the lake to make for a very pleasant day outing for any avid, Intermediate Park cyclist.

The lake is ringed by a **gravel path and wooden boardwalks,** with few hills.

There is the option of making the ride a little longer, by taking alternate loops instead of the straight trail across the dam at the north end.

In addition, next to this main lake (reservoir) circuit are a few short, **single-track MTB trails** through the woods at the south side. (Behind the parking lot.)

A bit harder to manage, these wind through the trees and contain random rocks to navigate around. It is, however, what I would **rate an Easy MTB** ride.

The most striking feature on this ride are the many **wooden boardwalks** and **bridges**. I counted upwards of six, crossing the water many times.

Some boardwalks even go through the forest. Frankly, this is the most bridges I have ever seen. I think they cut down a whole forest to build them, so enjoy!

Most of the ride is fairly level going, but there is **one long, gradual hill** and **one very steep section** as a detour to avoid any cars on the road (you may opt to walk it).

I rode the lake loop counter-clockwise, but think **clockwise might be easier** on the hills.

There are many opportunities to stop and take in the scenery. **Great places for viewing** are on the bridges, or while sitting down on a bench to gaze out at the water. Plenty of signs keep you on track.

After your outing, take a **swim**, have a **picnic,** or check out the **historic town** of **Orangeville**. It's a lovely walk down the main street, **Broadway**, just on the other side of **Hwy 11.**

On a summer day, this is a wonderful and easy ride for any fit rider, and there are few Park trails such as this one to be found in Ontario.

Rather unique in its trail design and construction, **highly recommended**, I'm sure you will love it.

Kissing Bridge – Rail Trail

Guelph to Millbank

Length – 45 km (one way)

95% rail trail path
5% roads, crossings, detours

Elevation – Mainly flat as rail lines go, with a gradual hill down to the covered bridge.

Terrain – Made of crushed stone and gravel, with rocks, grasses and tall weeds, and gopher holes!

Skill – Easy to Intermediate; west end gets wild and rough.

Traffic – Bicyclists and hikers; cross-country skiers and snowmobiles in certain sections in winter.

Maps – There are signposts on the trail and map boards at the gates, with milestone markers throughout the route.

Facilities – Parking lots, a few outhouses, and some food and lodging.

Highlights – See the **Montrose** (Kissing) covered bridge, large farms, and the Mennonite community of **Elmira** and **St. Jacobs.**

Trail Fee – Free

Phone – None

Website – Kissing Bridge Trailway, Goderich to Guelph Rail Trail

Similar Trails – Millennium, Omemee, LE & N

Local Clubs – Waterloo Cycling Club,

Access – Parking can be found in **Ariss, West Montrose, Elmira, Wallenstein, Linwood, Millbank** on side roads.

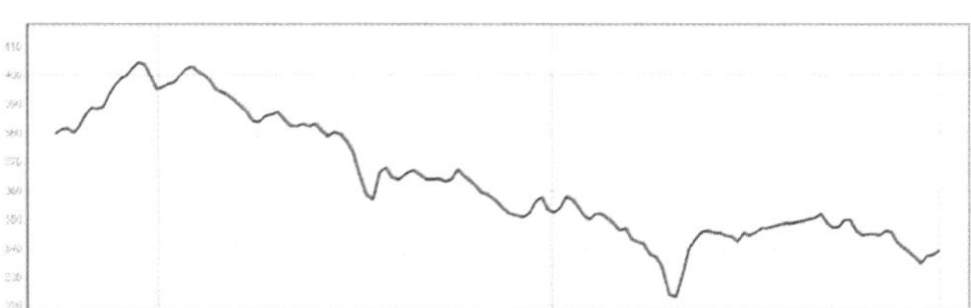

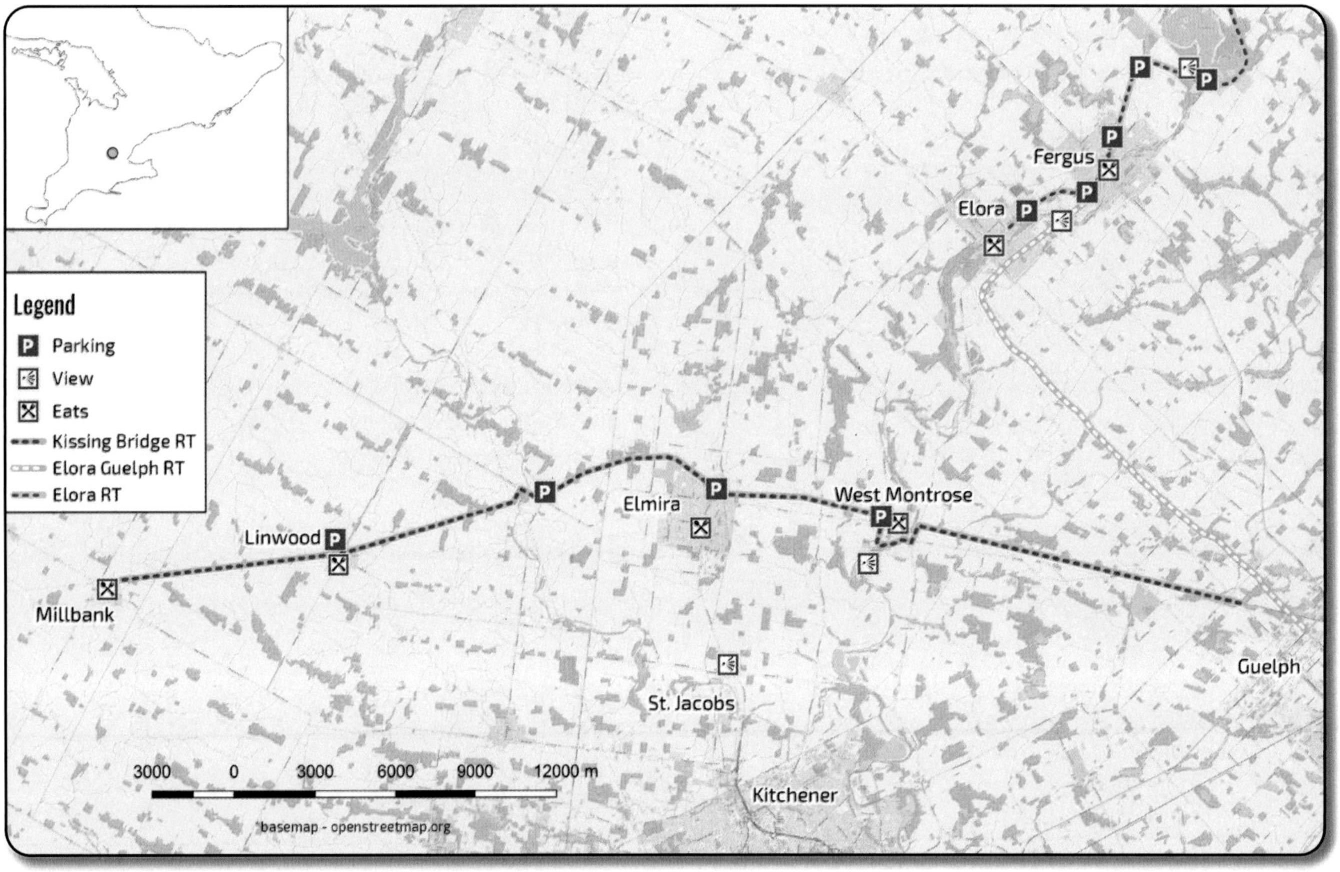

Legend
Parking
View
Eats
Kissing Bridge RT
Elora Guelph RT
Elora RT

Fergus
Elora
Elmira
West Montrose
Linwood
Millbank
St. Jacobs
Guelph
Kitchener

3000 0 3000 6000 9000 12000 m

basemap - openstreetmap.org

Review:

The **45 km Kissing Bridge Rail Trail** comprises the eastern segment of the **G2G Rail trail** route, running through the middle of prime Ontario farm country.

This is **big sky** country with large, wide-open agricultural fields that fade off to meet the clouds.

A rather straight-running rail line, this route starts at the east end just outside of **Guelph.** It is the most-used and redeveloped stretch of this **127 km** rail line, and leads to the shores of **Lake Huron** at **Goderich.**

As with most Rail trails, how much **manicuring** and **maintenance** local volunteers do (give them a hand and donate!) will dictate how the terrain goes.

I found the **east side,** out of **Guelph** and past **Elmira,** in great shape. The path was **wide and mostly crushed stone,** with some grassy patches.

In **West Montrose** the **covered bridge, aka "Kissing Bridge",** on the **Grand River** is the main attraction along this route. You will need to **detour for 2 km** south to get there, and to cross the river. (The railroad company took out the bridge, likely to sell it for scrap.)

Unfortunately, you will again have to detour along the road about forty-five minutes later while trying to cross the **Conestoga River.**

In the middle of the route, **Elmira** is nicely placed and is large enough to find lunch or a place to stay over. Just south of here, about 7 km, you could play tourist and visit the famous **St. Jacobs Market**.

You may also find a few amenities further on and into the towns of **Linwood** and **Millbank**.

As you progress to the west, close to **Millbank,** things start to get rough; the stones along the trail get larger and weeds get taller. Watch out for **gopher holes,** as they can be a nasty surprise!

A MTB would be a good choice for riding any farther, as this Rail trail does continue for another **79 km** to **Goderich.**

The trail has a few shady stretches, but most of the ride is **open** and **sunny** and **prone to wind.**

As this is **Mennonite** country, riders are likely to encounter them travelling on the side of the road, or in a horse and buggy.

By the size and condition of the farms one sees on the ride, the farmers look to be **prosperous in these parts.**

Great for a change of scenery, this is an outing for those who need some **country air** and **large vistas**.

History – Built in **1907** by the **Guelph & Goderich Railway (G2G),** this **127 km** trail spans the length between these two towns. The railway served rural communities and farms, bringing produce to markets and to the port on **Lake Huron.**

Grain was also hauled in from **Manitoba**, and up to **four passenger trains** a day travelled through here in the 1920s.

Decades later, increased auto and truck traffic reduced demand for train travel. The last passenger train passed through in **1955**. Moving freight continued until the 1980s.

By **1988, the CP Railway** had decommissioned the route and removed the tracks and bridges. This Rail trail was officially upgraded and reopened in **2015.**

LE & N – Rail Trail

Brantford to Port Dover

Length – 46 km (one way)

90% rail trail path
10% roads, crossings, detours

Elevation – Flat with a very gradual slope.

Terrain – Crushed stone dust with some gravel, asphalt (more than usual!)

Skill – Easy

Traffic – Bicyclists, hikers, and dog walkers; cross-country skiers in winter. Note no eBikes are permitted on Lynn Valley.

Maps – A map board is located at the trailhead gates.

Facilities – Parking and outhouses, benches and picnic tables, and lodging and food in Brantford, Waterford, Simcoe, and Port Dover.

Highlights – Railroad bridges (rather large in Waterford), shaded woodlots, and old farming communities worth a visit.

Trail Fee – Free

Phone – None

Website – Norfolk Pathways, Norfolk Tourism

Similar Trails – Kissing Bridge, Omemee

Local Clubs – Turkey Point MTB Club, Bike Fit Sunflowers, Short Hills Cycling Club

Access – Found at most side road crossings. A few parking suggestions:

- **Brantford**, at the end of **Beckett Dr.**
- **Waterford**, at the west end of **Nichol St.**
- **Simcoe**, at **Argyle St.**
- **Port Dover**, at **Silver Lake Lions Park**

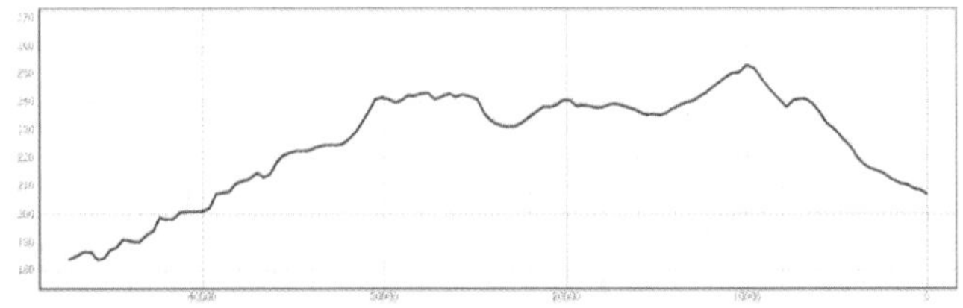

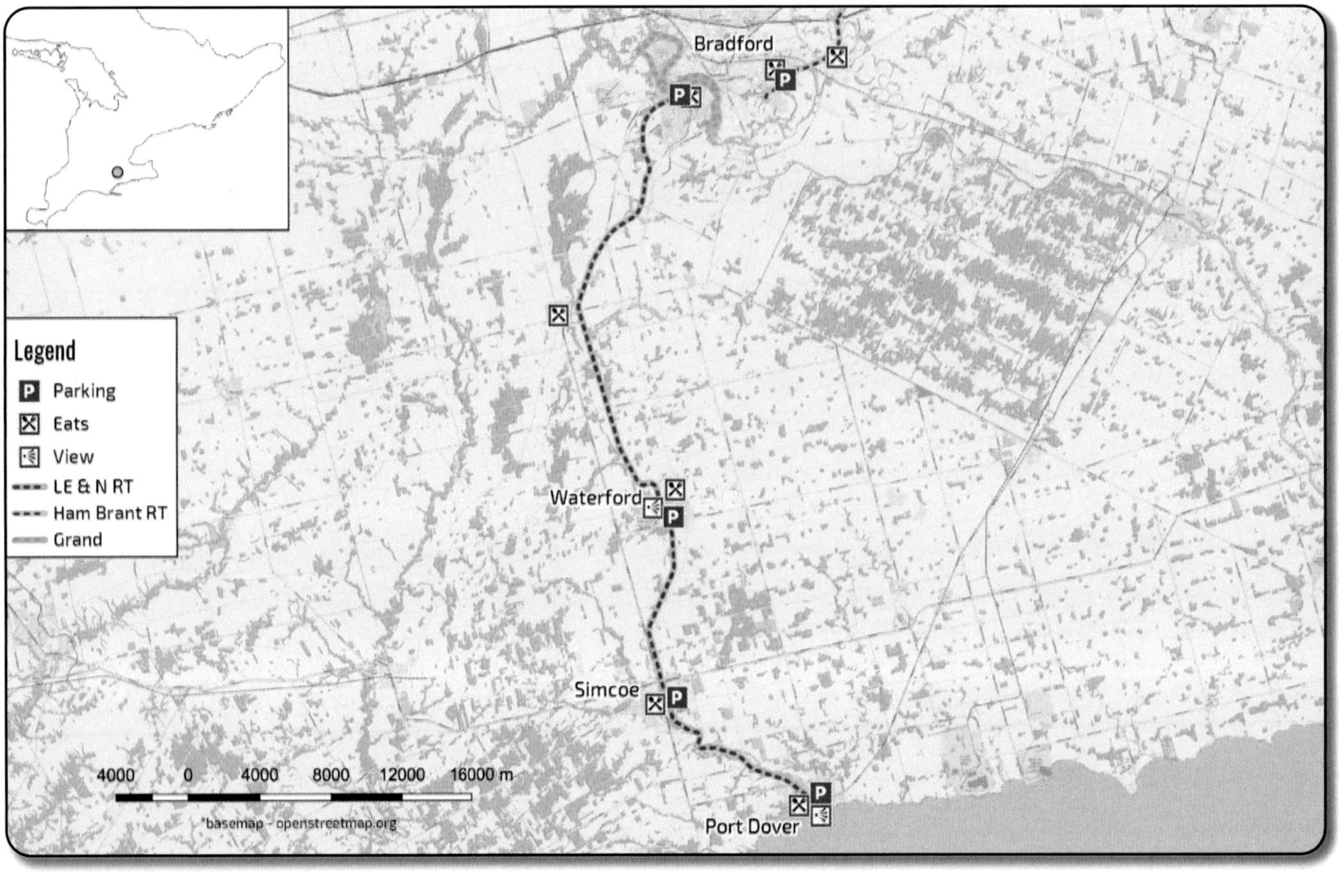

Bradford
Waterford
Simcoe
Port Dover

Legend
Parking
Eats
View
LE & N RT
Ham Brant RT
Grand

4000 0 4000 8000 12000 16000 m
*basemap - openstreetmap.org

Review:

The **LE & N Rail Trail** was once the **Lake Erie & Northern Electric Railway** before being repurposed as a recreational cycling trail. At **46 km**, this section runs from **Brantford** to **Port Dover.**

As a **popular and well-maintained Rail Trail**, it travels south to **Lake Erie** across farm fields, through many woodlots, and a few old towns that this line once served by transporting people and goods.

Local counties have taken parts of this route and given it their own names, but the riding path remains the same.

As it leaves **Brantford** from the **Veterans Memorial Pkwy**, the route is referred to as the **LE & N Trail.** For **14 km** it passes by neighbourhoods, curving gently out of town along a **shady, tree-lined path** to open farm fields.

Eventually, the trail meets up with another, the **Toronto, Hamilton, & Buffalo Railway (TH & B)**, which it joins and provides riders another way back.

Then, as it passes through **Waterford** for **18 km,** the route is called the **Waterford Heritage Trail.** After, it splits; take the left path to go over a **large iron bridge** and past grain silos. Look below to see the other rail lines (which you can ride) running through the valley.

As it enters the town of **Simcoe**, the name again changes briefly to the **Norfolk Sunrise Trail** for **4 km;** it finally becomes the **Lynn Valley Trail** for the last **10 km.**

I can't say there is much of a valley here, but there are **four old bridges** and it's almost all a **shady, tree-lined path**. Along the route is one small road detour that jogs around a corner, but then you're back on the trail again.

Reaching the trail's end in **Port Dover,** continue straight down the side streets to the **harbour.** Being a great town for tourism in the summer there are plenty of eats, and a beach to rest at, before you return.

Comparing this Rail Trail to most in Ontario I found it well-maintained; so much so that many parts were **paved in asphalt!** (Truly not necessary, but so they were.)

Plenty of signage helped along the route, and **historic placards** kept us informed. Much of the length is **shaded,** which is appreciated to avoid that baking sun.

It's **one of the best Rail Trails** I've encountered, and worth an overnight stay at any of the towns along the way. As a bonus, it is close to plenty of other attractions in **Southern Ontario**.

History – From **1916** to **1960**, this was an **electric railway** line until diesel engines replace it. Built to serve passengers and transport local agricultural goods such as tobacco, fruits, vegetables, and flowers from greenhouses in the south; fresh fish from **Port Dover** was also delivered.

The **Lake Erie and Northern Electric Rail Company (LE & N)** abandoned passenger service in **1955**, as road travel by bus coach was cheaper and more accessible.

Freight operations continued, however, and combined service with the **Grand River Railway** until **Canadian Pacific Rail** lifted the track in the **1980s.**

Sauble Falls – MTB/Park Trail

985 Sauble Falls, Parkway 13

Length – 18 km

80% park path
20% dirt road

Elevation – Flat with short, rolling hills and ancient sand dunes.

Terrain – The trail is smooth forest cover, with a few muddy and sandy areas.

Skill – Easy MTB trail; Moderate Park trail.

Traffic – Cyclists, hikers. Quite area never busy.

Maps – Located at entrance, as well as a few signposts along the trail.

Facilities – Parking is found by the ski club hut, as well as shelters and benches along the route.

Highlights – The picturesque Rankin River, as well as a dam, a pond, and sand dunes. Sauble Falls offers some good swimming.

Trail Fee – Free

Phone – None

Website – Ski Sauble

Similar Trails – Brant Tract, Bendor, Long Sault

Local Clubs – Owen Sound Cycling Club

Access – Found at the north end, about **1 km** from **Sauble Falls** on **Hwy 13**; will be on the east side at the entrance to the **Nordic Ski Club** at **985 Sauble Falls Pkwy.**

Another access point can be found further up the road as well.

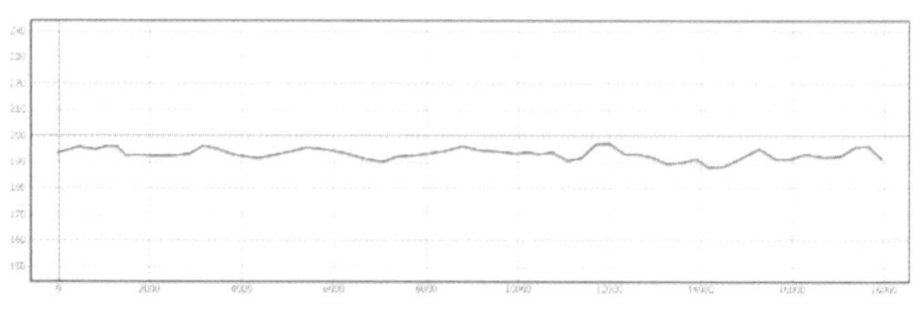

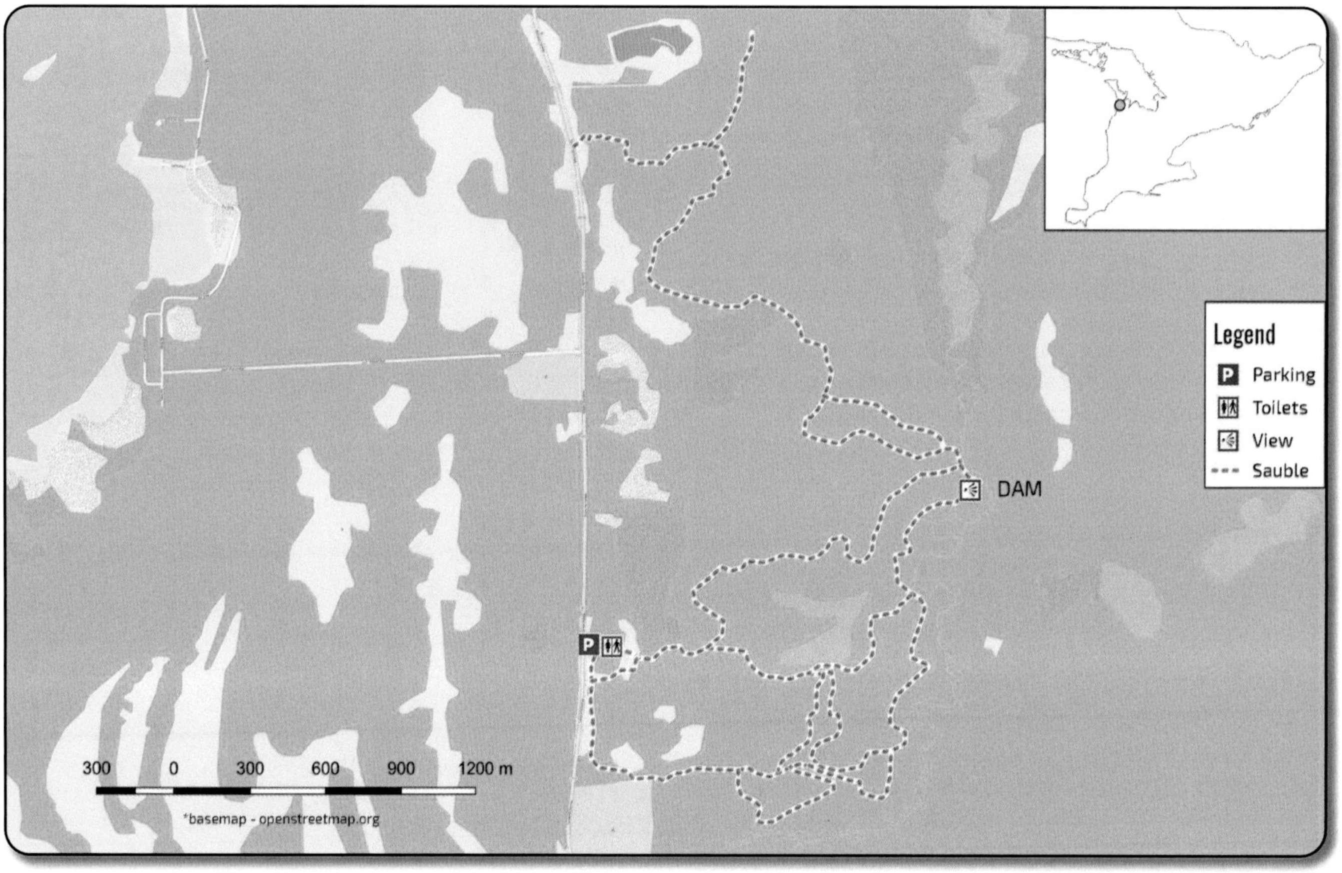

Legend
Parking
Toilets
View
Sauble

DAM

300 0 300 600 900 1200 m

*basemap - openstreetmap.org

Review:

These **18 km** of forest trails are part of the **Sauble Nordic Ski Club** network of loops, now open to cyclists in the summer.

As such, the ski paths are **wide with no tight turns** (though I find most Nordic ski trails are wider).

Now rather wild and grown-over, the area was mostly sand dunes many years ago so the terrain has **quick, up-and-down hills**.

How to categorize this ride? To some, it could be an **Advanced Park** ride, yet for a **mountain biker** it is rather easy, **Beginner-level** terrain.

Sauble is a **well-treed ride** with a sandy base, so **wide tires** are suggested. However, there is one open patch on the north side many may find **too sandy**. Calling all **Fatbikes**!

The south end is covered in forest and could have soft muddy patches if it has rained. (And then you can be sure to expect bugs 'n bites!)

Other than perhaps getting stuck in the sand, most of the **ride flows well**.

Make it to the **Rankin River** and riders will find a small, **picturesque pond** and **dam,** with a shelter and some benches that make this area ideal for a snack break.

This is **rarely a busy place,** although in the summer you may see a few locals riding horses or walking their dog.

Riders may also get lost if they don't pay attention to the **limited signage**. So be prepared, and pay attention.

If you want to **cool off,** a dip in **Sauble Falls** just south down the road is a must. Or, drive west for **4 km** to the famous **Sauble Beach** on **Lake Huron**—another favourite!

Also nearby is an area you can **camp,** or simply visit **Sauble Falls Provincial Park.**

Far from most larger cities, if you do happen to be in the area this trail is well worth considering for a bit of an adventure.

Speed River – Park/Rail Trail

Guelph

Length – 7 + 2 km (one way)

95% park path
5% roads, crossings, detours

Elevation – A gradual incline as the route follows the **Speed River**; road and bridge crossings.

Terrain – Mostly paved with some interlocking brick, but gets a bit rough and more natural at the north end.

Skill – Easy

Traffic – Not busy, with the typical path users.

Maps – Adequate signposts and maps throughout.

Facilities – Local amenities in town, as well as benches along the trail.

Highlights – A lovely forest setting with bridges spanning the river and a dam.

Trail Fee – Free

Phone – 519 822 1260

Website – City of Guelph

Similar Trails – Greenway, Beltline, Thames Valley

Local Clubs – Speed River Cycling Club

Access – Parking is found at **Riverside Park** (on both sides of the river), also near the **Guelph Lake** dam and by the **Guelph Youth Music Centre**.

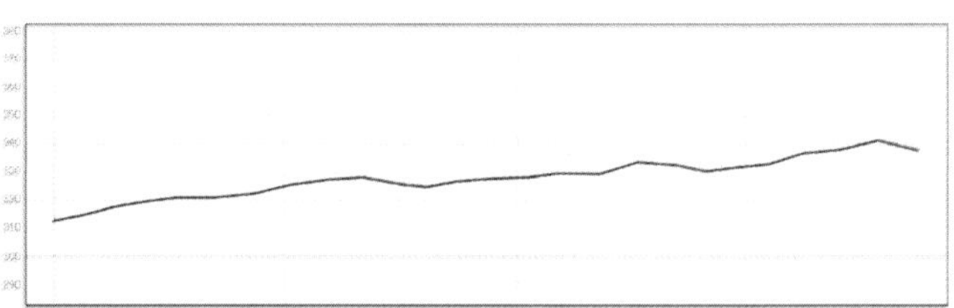

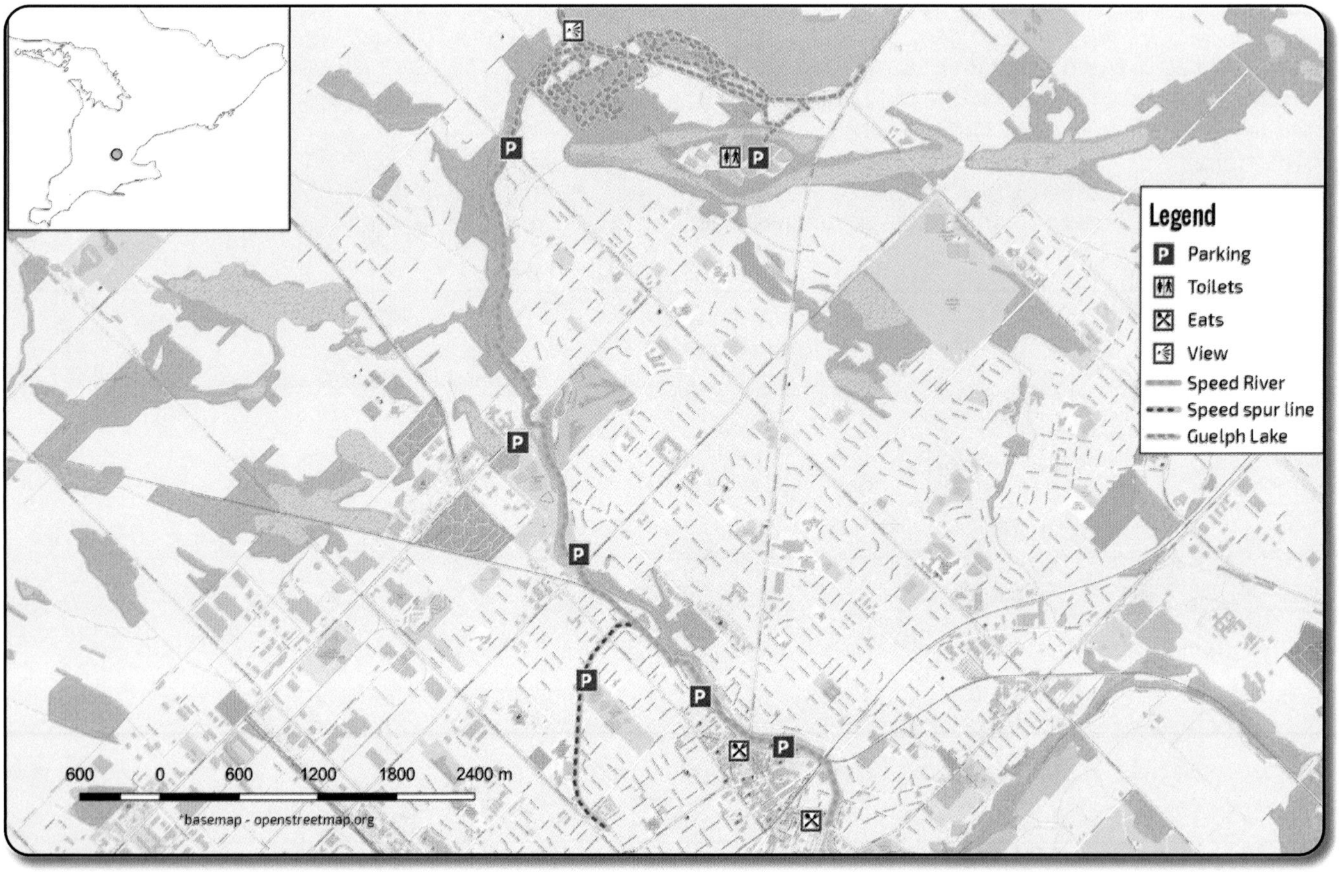

Legend
Parking
Toilets
Eats
View
Speed River
Speed spur line
Guelph Lake

600 0 600 1200 1800 2400 m
*basemap - openstreetmap.org

Review:

Right from the **heart of downtown Guelph** runs a **7 km** Park/Rail trail that leads all the way out to **Guelph Lake**. This is one of the **Royal Recreation Trail** routes, which follows the **Speed River** to the **dam** at the lake.

The route is a mix of **old rail line, parkland,** and **forest,** with five road and bridge crossings. Following the river makes this a comfortable and **flat, yet long, ride** if one does the full length and back (16 km).

The scenery is indeed **varied** and **enjoyable.** Starting from downtown, at **Wyndham St. S.** and **Wellington St. E.,** the **Downtown Trail** (as locals call it) works its way from there and up the riverbank.

The path passes by **old stone buildings** (some in ruins) and through parklands, providing glimpses of the slow-flowing river on the right.

One can see old homes and industries while travelling on behind the buildings.

As an **urban Rail Trail**, some of the route runs parallel to train tracks that I believe are still in use. After **George St.** a short **2 km** of the trail splits off west and into the neighbourhood, ending at **London Rd. W**.

This **CNR Spurline Trail** once had a track that connected to another line, which can be seen crossing this intersection.

Sticking to the main path, continue for **5 km** along the **Speed River Trail** to the dam. The trail goes from a paved route through open parkland to more of a **natural wooded and gravel/dirt terrain**.

At the fork stay on the left to get over **Victoria Rd. N.** to access the main trail going to the dam.

Once there, head up the east side for some fun MTB trails at Guelph Lake. Most require an Intermediate skill level and be sure you have a **MTB or a good hybrid**.

If you do visit **Guelph,** check out this enjoyable and short ride, as well as the **lively downtown** vibe. The route has a nice mix of city life and a back-to-nature feel.

There is also more to cycle on the city's **Royal** bike paths just south of here, following the **Eramosa River**.

Thames Valley – Park Trail

London, Ontario

Length – 5+8+8 = 21 km (one way)

90% park path
10% roads, crossing, detours

Elevation – Flat as it follows the river, with a few short hills.

Terrain – Mostly wide, paved path with some crushed stone and gravel.

Skill – Beginner; Intermediate for longer distances.

Traffic – Can be busy on weekends with typical path users, like walkers and bicyclists.

Maps – Maps are at trailheads, as well as signposts on the path.

Facilities – Plenty of parking and washrooms, as well as benches, picnic tables, restaurants, and hotels along the route.

Highlights – The Thames River, old bridges, the Storybook Gardens, a dam, a fountain, downtown London, and Western University.

Trail Fee – Free

Phone – 519 661 5575

Website – City of London

Similar Trails – Nokiiddaa, Ajax Waterfront, Humber River

Local Clubs – London Cycling Club

Access – Find parking lots at **Ivey Park, Springbank Park, Greenway Park, Medway Park**, and **Pottersburg Park.**

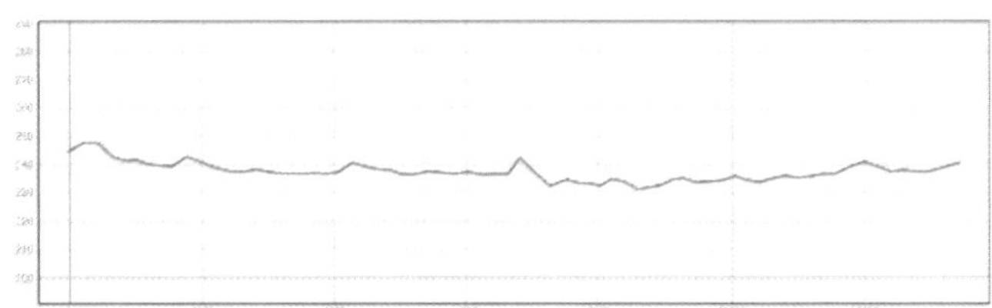

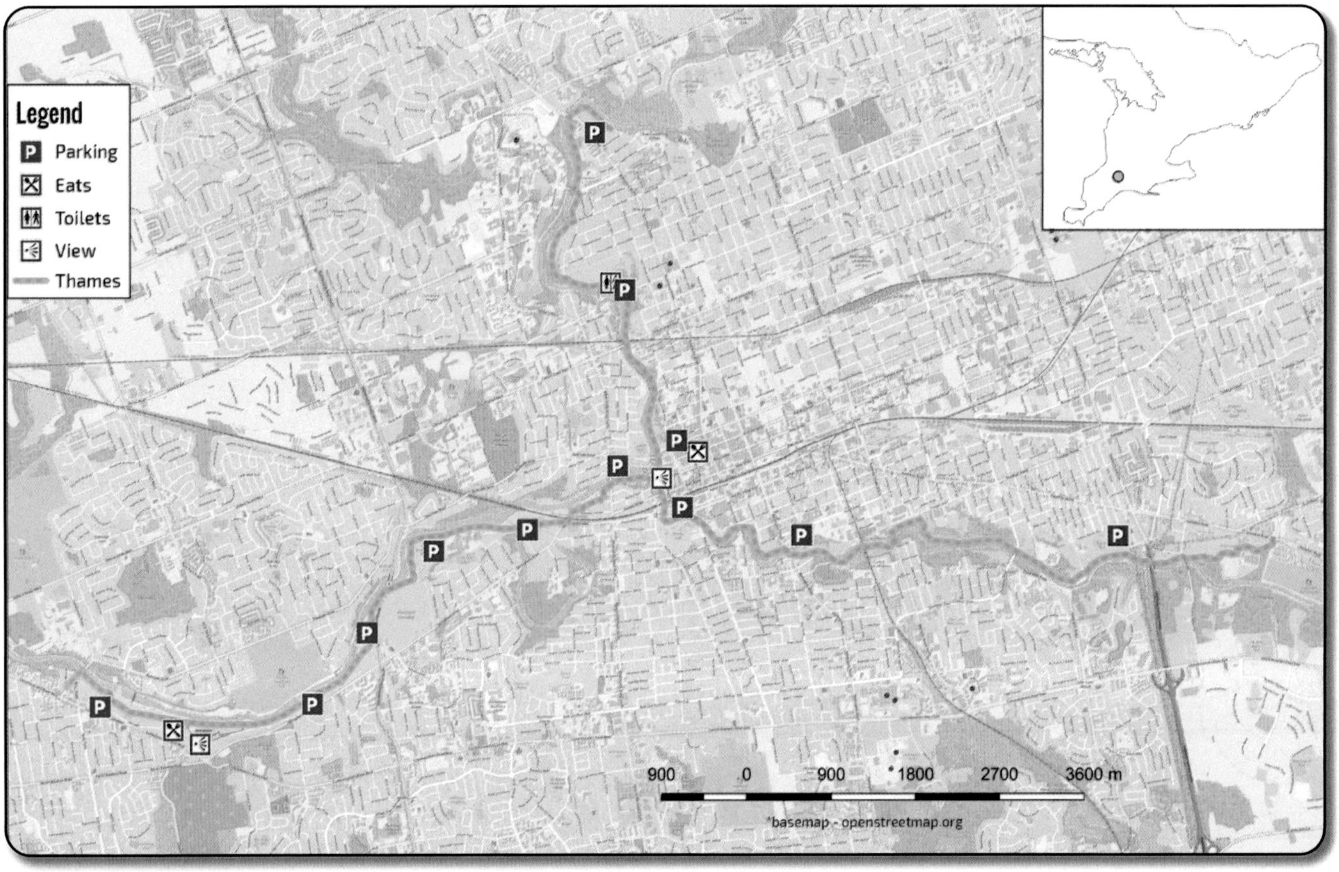

Review:

The **Thames Valley** Park trail network in downtown **London, Ontario** contains some of the **best bicycle paths in the province.**

This large city has **well-maintained** routes that head in **three directions** along the riverbank; expect **22 km** of great cycling!

These city park paths offer a continuous variety of **scenery** by the water's edge, over mainly paved and designated paths.

The north and west branches have **brief detours** through quiet neighbourhood streets that connect to further trails.

All **three paths** branch out from **downtown London** near the **Ivey Park** fountain, where the rivers meet. You

can start the ride on either side of the river, but the east side goes further.

Heading north **5 km** brings you to **Western University**. Heading west **8 km** along the south side of the **Thames River** leads to a dam and **Storybook Gardens**, a great destination for kids.

In the opposite direction, **8 km** along the east branch, the river offers more pleasant parkland riding, with two road bridges you may cross to continue on your ride.

Add another **4 km** if you leave the river path and head up to **Dundas St.**

All routes have **excellent signage** to keep riders on track and informed as to how far they have cycled.

As with any river route, the ride is flat and easy-going, with quick climbs to get around or under bridges. As the path meanders, there are numerous short side paths to explore.

It is well worth considering a visit to London for a weekend to take in a few of these trails, as it is **a bike-friendly city**.

May I also suggest, if you have a hybrid bike and want a more **Intermediate Park** ride through the woods, try **Fanshawe** just north of the city. (You can even **camp overnight**.)

The Pinery – Park Trail

9526 Lakeshore Rd., Grand Bend

Length – 13 km (loop)

50% park path
50% roads, bike lane, crossings

Elevation – A flat and wide path, with some small hills over dunes.

Terrain – Goes along an asphalt road (share the road!), as well as a crushed-stone path with sandy spots.

Skill – Easy

Traffic – Busy on weekends.

Maps – Found at trailhead, as well as signs along the trail.

Facilities – Find parking, washrooms, and a general store, as well as bike rentals and camping sites.

Highlights – Beaches along Lake Huron, the river, Savanna woods, and spectacular sunsets.

Trail Fee – $17.00+ for a park day pass or camp permit.

Phone – 519-243-2220

Website – Ontario Parks, Friends of Pinery

Similar Trails – Awenda, Wildwood, Fanshawe

Local Clubs – Lambton Outdoor Club

Access – This provincial park is located at **9526 Lakeshore Rd., Grand Bend**. Access the trail at many entry points.

The main starting point is at the park store, or from campgrounds or parking lots at the beaches.

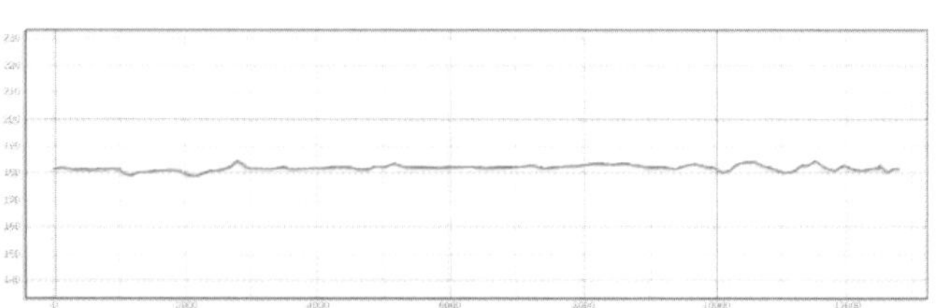

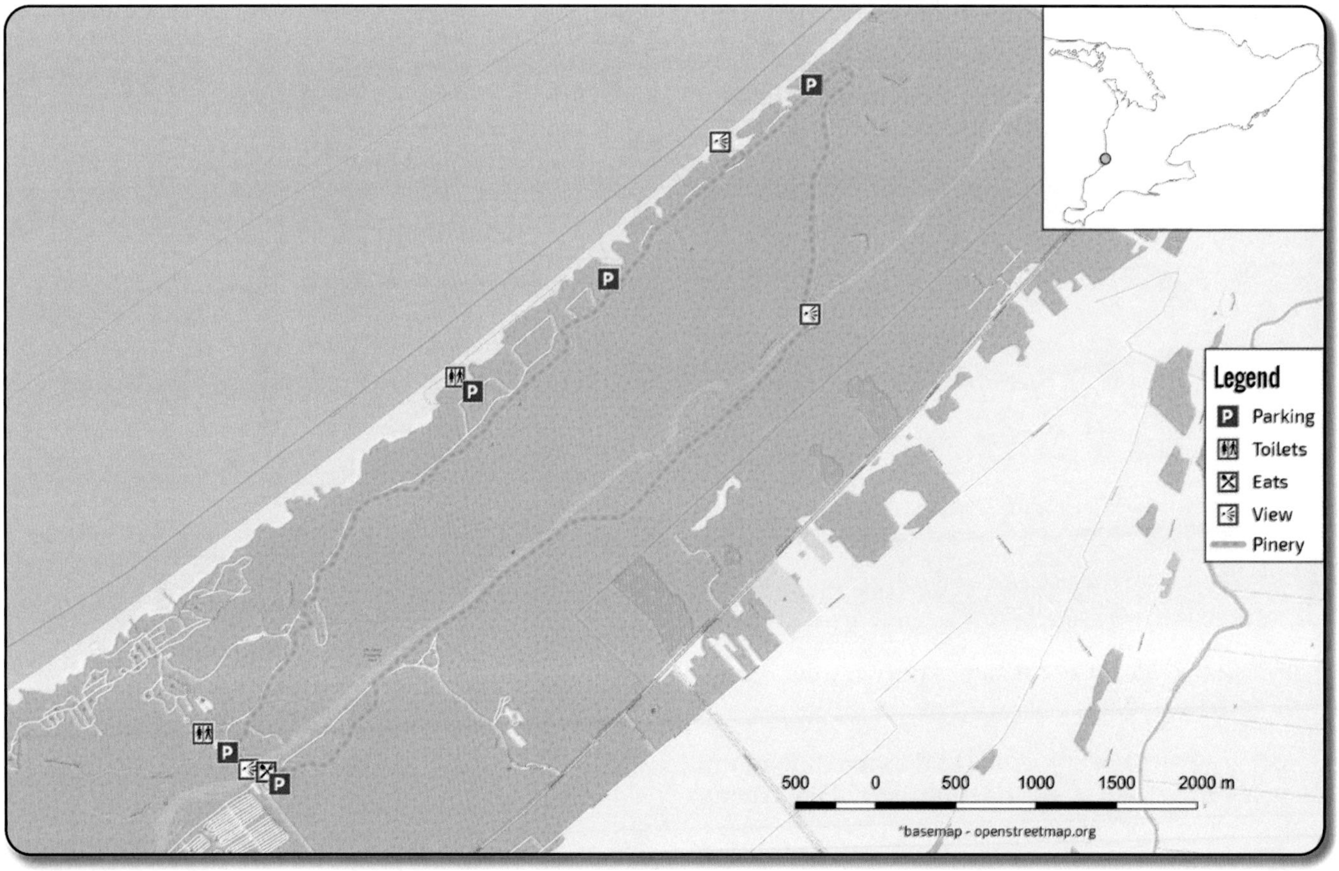

Legend
Parking
Toilets
Eats
View
Pinery

500 0 500 1000 1500 2000 m

°basemap - openstreetmap.org

Review:

On the shores of **Lake Huron, Pinery Provincial Park** has a **13 km** bicycle loop worthy of listing for its pleasant, quiet pace and its sheer popularity with campers.

The **Savanna Trail** is an effortless ride for most, with rolling mounds and flat road to traverse. That said, only about half is **good trail riding.**

The Park trail is a winding, crushed-stone path that meanders over small dunes through the open **Savanna forest of pine and oak trees**. Lovely indeed, but the other half of the loop shares the road with cars.

The wacky design of this section has riders go along a **bike lane on the left while cars going one way use the right lane**. So, picture a designated bike lane, on this paved country road, right next to a lane of cars.

I don't want to dissuade anyone from trying this ride, there are few cars on the loop, and they move rather

slowly. (I only wish the Ministry would cut the whole trail through the woods. There seems to be room, so do this one day please!) Still, I must quote my young son's remark: *"This is flat and boring."*

A nice feature about this loop is that riders never need to retrace their route for a return trip, as is often required on most recreational trails.

There is a **central canal** (the Old Ausable Channel) you see from the trail, where you could stop to relax and soak your toes while watching the canoes pass by. Lookout points at each end give you a chance to take some good pictures.

The scenic **Lake Huron** beach is long, and the **water is warm** by mid-summer. Getting there by bike is a little challenging, as you may have to push over a **sand dune** or two, but it's a must see.

There are a few road crossings to be aware of, as this **park is bustling on weekends.** Expect near the campgrounds more cyclists touring around.

All sorts of **bikes may be rented** at the park store, which is also a good starting point. Plus, a promise of ice cream awaits as a reward upon your return!

Wildwood – MTB/Park Trail

3995 Line 9, RR #2 St. Marys

Length – 25 km

30% MTB single track
50% hiking trail
20% double track access roads

Elevation – Some small hills, gradual climbs along the banks of the dam, and a few long descents.

Terrain – Mostly smooth soil, sandy spots, some gravel, roots, muddy areas; wood structures.

Skill – Intermediate Park trail. Easy MTB; Hardwood loop is Advanced.

Maps – At the trailhead by the gate; with numbered post markers on the trail.

Traffic – Cyclists and hikers. Note – On odd days please ride trail counter-clockwise.

Facilities – Include a parking lot, washrooms, bike rentals, bike repair station with bike wash, camping, swimming, and boat rentals.

Highlights – Varied scenery, lake views, camping by the trail.

Trail Fee – Day pass: Adult $8, Child $4, Vehicle $14

Hours – From Dawn to Dusk; no night riding.

Phone – 519 284 2292

Website – Wildwood Conservation Area

Similar Trails – Fanshawe, Minnesing, The Pinery

Local Clubs – Woodstock Cycling Club, London Cycling Club

Access – Wildwood Conservation is where **Hwy 9** meets **Hwy 7**; at the roundabout go to **3995 Line 9, RR #2 east of St. Marys.** The trail signs start at the highway underpass and dam by the gatehouse.

Helmets are mandatory on trails.

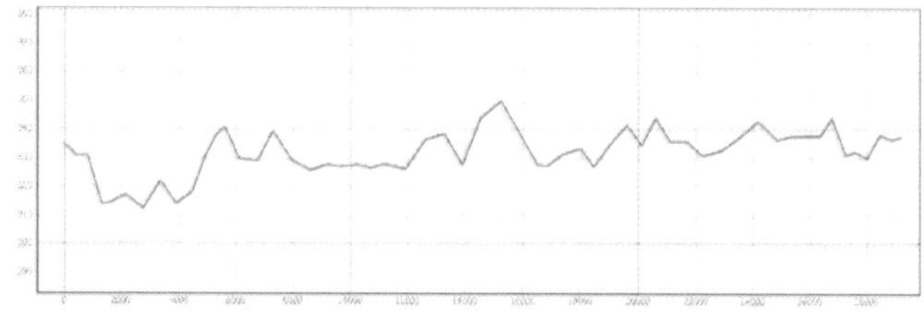

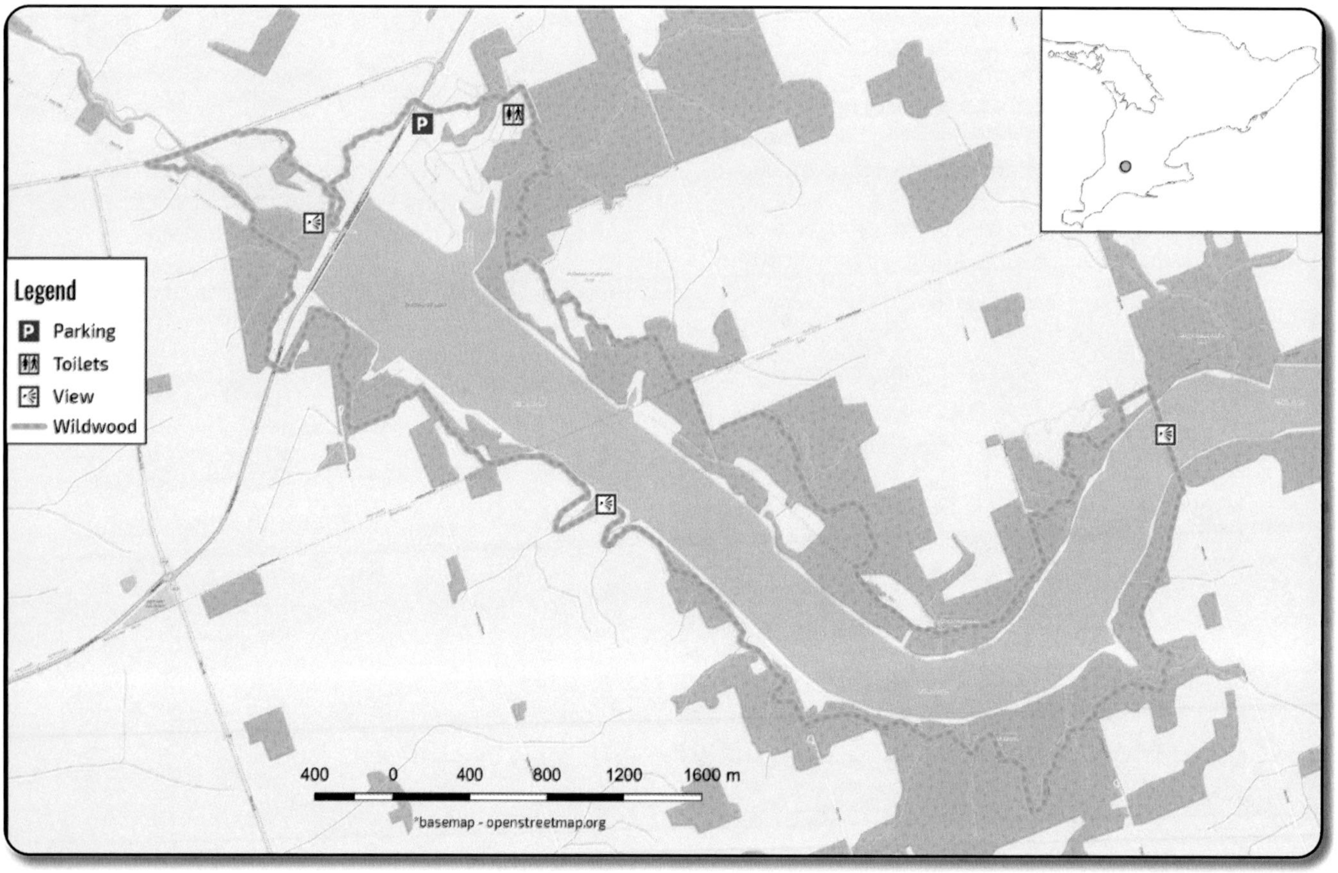

Legend
Parking
Toilets
View
Wildwood

400 0 400 800 1200 1600 m

°basemap - openstreetmap.org

Review:

Wildwood Conservation Area offers **25 km** of **cross-country** type cycling and two **MTB side loops**. This bike trail circles the reservoir offering a variety of terrain and scenery, and makes a good outing for the day or a weekend.

Situated in the middle of **Ontario** farm country, it lies north of **London,** and 10 minutes east of the town of **St. Marys.** Since there is not much other trail riding to be had in the area, I found this spot decent enough to try, even with the **family** on **hybrid bikes**.

The track **moves quickly**, and you can keep your pace going for most of it. However, there are opportunities to stop and take in the view, picnic or sit by the water on the way.

The terrain varies from a smooth soil or a gravel base to lumpy roots, muddy patches and even a tiny creek crossing. You will appreciate the scenery continually changing from open fields to mixed forest.

Glimpses of the lake can be seen, though some of the trail takes you far from the shore. On the way, you will encounter bridges, boardwalks, and the **large dam.**

On the **north side** of the lake, the path is wide **double track.** There are a few rather long hills (which are fun going down) with farm fields and cottages to see.

The **south side** is narrow **single track** that winds through a forest with some rooty sections. Here you will find the **Hardwood Trail** loop eventually; a must for the experienced MTB thrill seeker. Be forewarned that the other side loop, **Field of Burrs** is lame. The lack of trail wear tells me others think the same.

Unfortunately for some, this long loop has **no shortcut.** This means one has to commit to doing it all or doing a U-turn at some point.

The general flow of traffic **alternates direction** every day. (On odd days it is counter-clockwise) Plenty of signs keep you going so you can't get lost. Numbered posts help for map reference.

You can start the loop at any point, at the gatehouse, or from your campsite.

There are three sections on this loop that briefly meet up with **car traffic.** From the gatehouse, there is a highway underpass to get to the base of the dam. The trail then takes you to **Hwy 9**, where you cycle on the shoulder long enough to cross the road bridge, and then dodge back into the bush at the **13th Line**.

In a few minutes, you will need to cross **Hwy 7**, which seems to be busy. Beyond are happy trails for the next hour till you get to the far end. To cross the lake, there is a quiet gravel road at **29th Line** that also offers a panoramic view.

For the **Park** trail rider, this is rated as a harder **Intermediate** ride. Try the north side first, and then if you do well, try the south side. There are some good-sized hills, roots and the odd surprise, but it's not impossible to manage.

The length may be a bit much for young kids and the unfit. My son, who was 10 years old at the time, managed to do the entire 25 km loop with me, then slept quite well that night in the tent.

This long trail loop is very similar to Fanshawe in many ways. Both park areas are run by the same local conservation authority. I feel **Wildwood** is a bit better, but they both have their good points.

Consider **camping overnight**, as it's inexpensive and the trail is right by the campgrounds. A swim in the lake is a welcome idea after a hot day of riding too.

If you wish to practice some **Bikepacking**, there are 4 backcountry campsites on the loop. I would think you need to reserve ahead.

Bike rentals are offered at the gate for MTB and Fatbikes, and they looked decent.

1000 Islands – Park Trail

Gananoque to Butternut Bay

Length – 38 km (one way)

95 % park path
5 % road, detours

Elevation – Flat, gently rolling hills, 3 m-wide path.

Terrain – New asphalt (2014), some loose gravel.

Skill – Easy

Maps – A few maps, signs on the trail; once on the path, you won't get lost.

Facilities – Beaches, swimming, picnic areas, hiking trails, restrooms, restaurants, lodging, B&B, camping.

Highlights – Scenic views of the islands, swimming, marinas, and Gananoque.

Trail Fee – Free

Phone – 1-800-437-2233

Website – Great Lakes Waterfront Trail, St Lawrence Parks, Parks Canada

Similar Trails – Cornwall Waterfront, Ajax Waterfront, Hamilton Beach

Local Clubs – Kingston Velo Club

Access – Parking possible at:

- **Gananoque Harbour ,** Hwy. car pool lot
- **Mallorytown Landing** - Environmental Awareness Centre
- **Brockville** or **Brown's Bay** - St. Lawrence Parks Commission
- **1000 Islands Parkway** picnic and parking spots

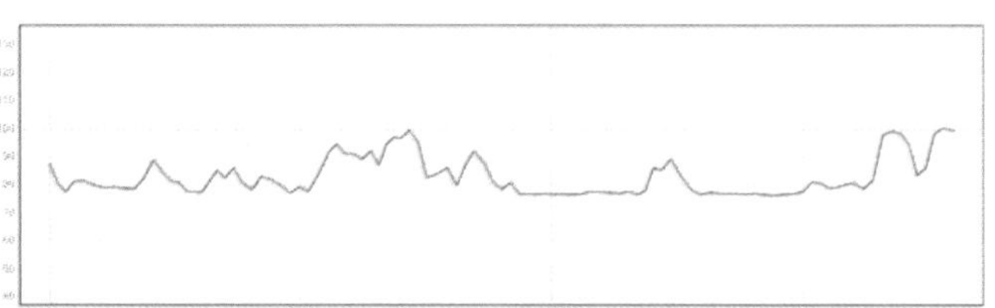

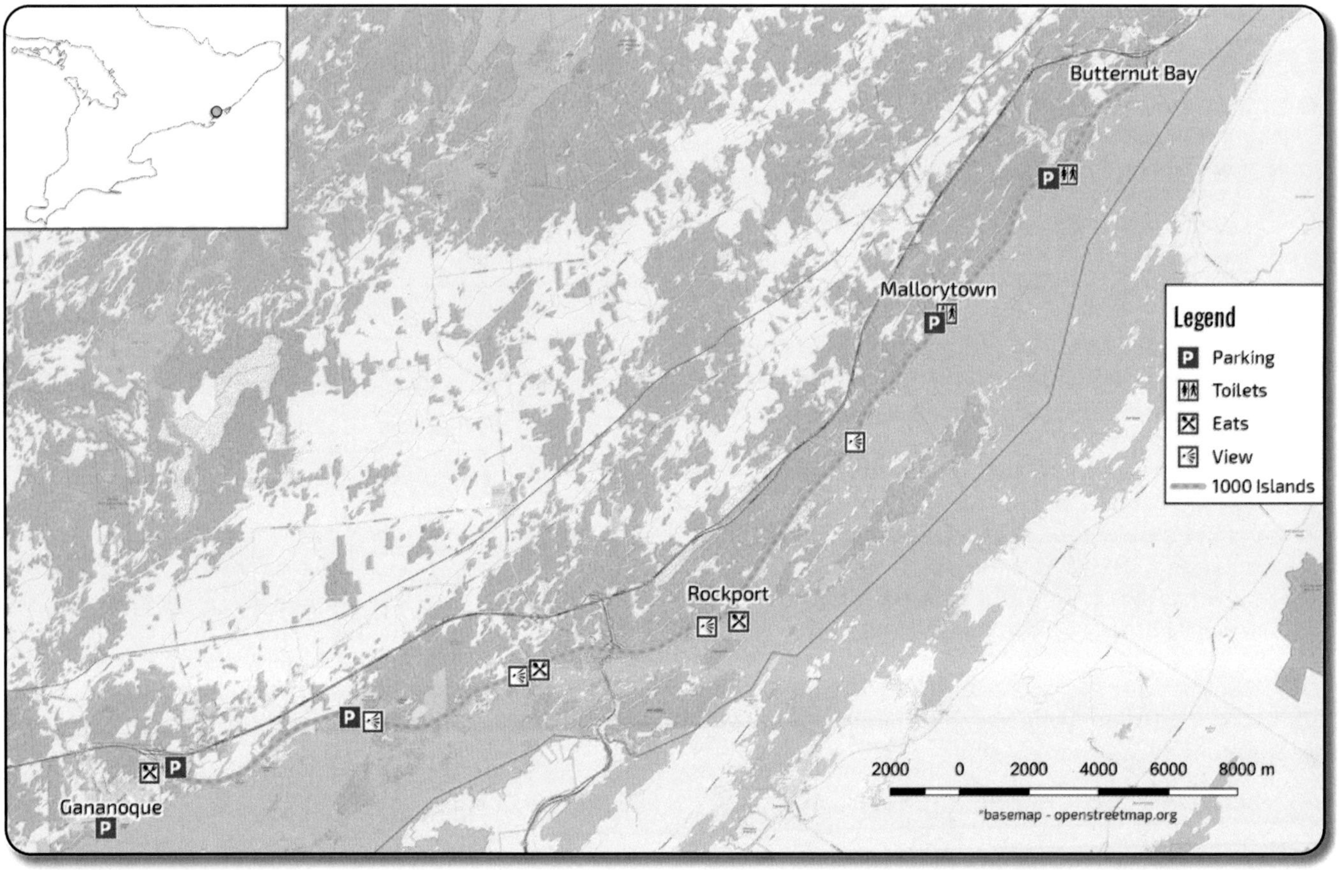

Review:

If you are looking for a weekend getaway, then this **38 km waterfront trail** along the **Thousand Island Parkway** might suit your fancy. Not only is it relaxing, **scenic bicycle ride**, there are also plenty of other things to see and do afterwards.

Starting just outside the town of **Gananoque,** the path meanders eastward along the **St. Lawrence River**, ending at **Butternut Bay**, just as the Parkway meets **Hwy 401** again near **Brockville.**

Listed as a **park ride** on this site, it has less of a park and more of a **road ride** feel to it, which has its own **dedicated path beside a road.**

There are trees on the sides and grass lawn medians on this relatively **straight, wide open** parkway. I found the lack of landscaping sterile and a little boring.

If **prevailing winds** are blowing from the **west**, they might slow you down on this open trail. That said, there is **not much shade** on this path, so put that sunscreen on.

This paved path follows the **Thousand Island Parkway** for all of its length on the **north side,** and at times it is **lower** than the highway. If it was on the south side, closer to the river, then you truly get a **Waterfront Trail**, as it has been called.

Sure, you can get the **occasional view of the water** on this ride, but not as the name implies. You may find yourself **crossing the road to lookouts** to take a picture or two. The good news is the highway is quiet and underutilized, as most cars are using **Hwy 401.**

You will encounter a **few rolling hills**, and mounts occur as you cross roads and driveways. So the route is not totally car free at those intersections.

However, recently new, dedicated lanes over the Hwy 137 bridge now make for **37 km of continuous off-road riding.** (Applause)

Along this route, one can find numerous appealing places to **eat, lodge, camp** or take a dip in the water. Explore **Gananoque**, a quiet tourist town, or **Ivy Lea** and **Rockport** (halfway points), which offer popular boat tours of the **1000 Islands**.

Further up, tiny **Mallorytown Landing** has a **visitors' centre**, and Brown's Bay Park makes for a **good picnic stop.** Or ride beyond to **Brockville** which is the largest town heading east, 8 km away on a side road.

Be sure to pack what you need, as **this highway is not busy** and you will not find countless convenience stores or diners. There are a few camping spots for those who like to **bike tour** and add this path to their route.

On a warm summer day, with the cool winds blowing, this makes for a great family outing or a date.

Brock – Rail/Park Trail

Brockville

Length - 7 km (one way)

85% park trail path
15% roads, detours

Elevation - Flat, with very little slopes.

Terrain - The main path, made of asphalt, crushed stone, and gravel, narrows at the top end. Also watch for road crossings and a detour around **Hwy 401**.

Skill - Easy

Maps - There are few maps and signs; needs improvement, but this will be done soon.

Traffic - Bicyclists, walkers, and dogs.

Facilities - Parking, picnic tables and benches, as well as toilets, lodging, and restaurants.

Highlights – There is a delightful train tunnel experience, some historic stone buildings, and the waterfront of course.

Trail Fee – Free

Phone – 613-342-4357

Website – Brock Trail, Brock Railway Tunnel

Similar Trails – Speed River, Greenway

Local Clubs – None

Access – The suggested best starting point is by the south tunnel entrance; **Water St. & Market St.**, parking is across the street, or near **Harding Park** by the water.

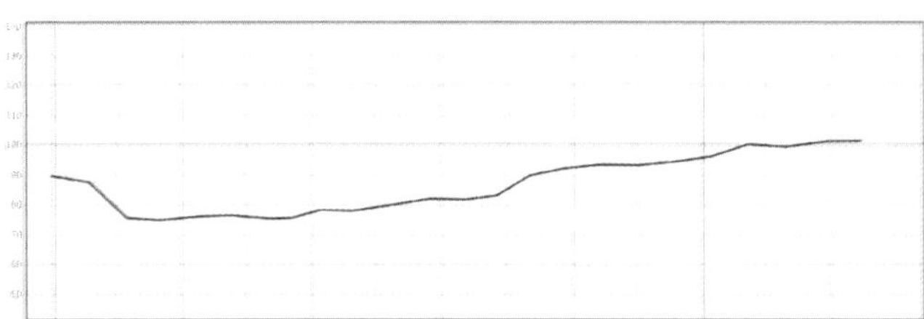

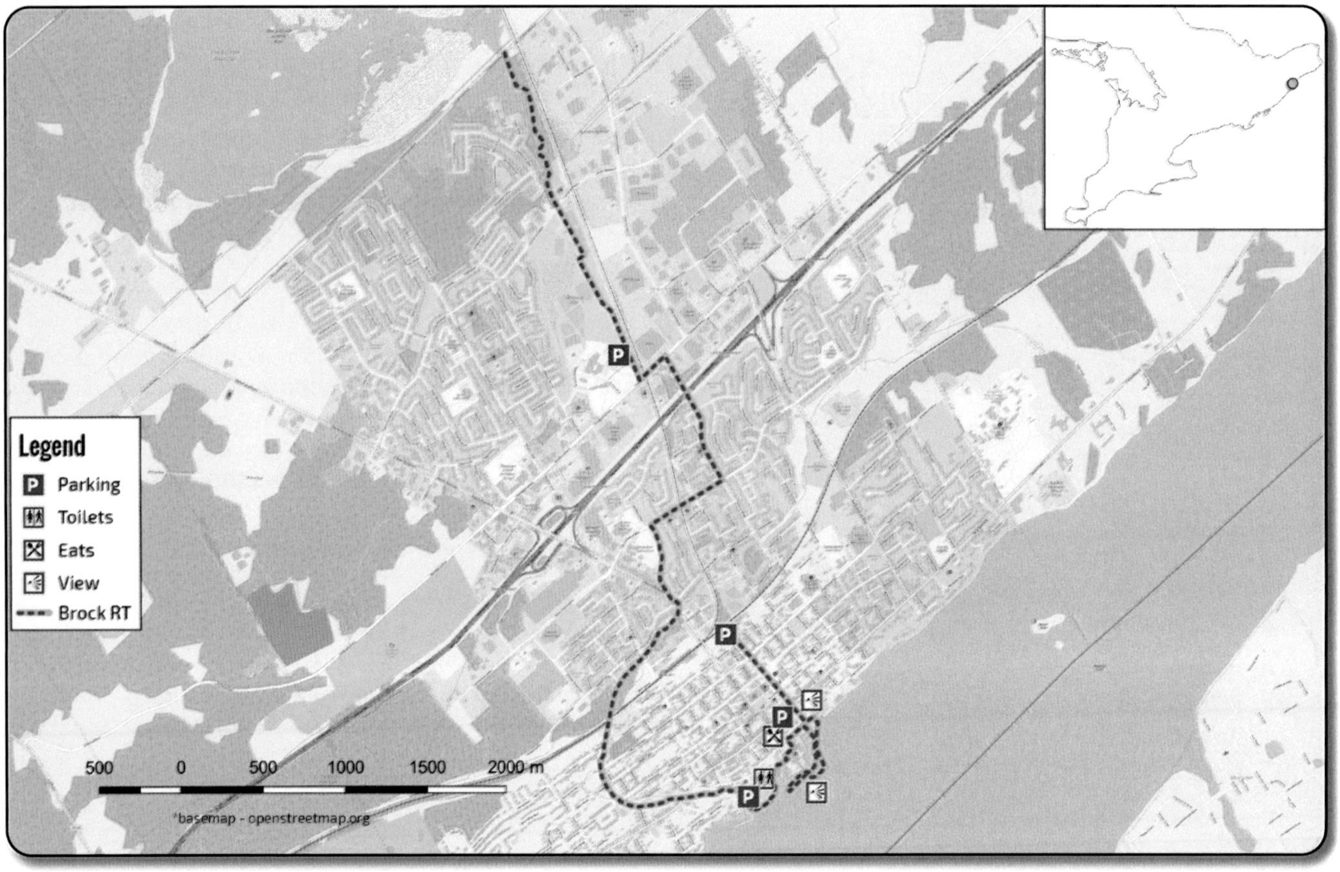

Review:

This one is an **odd bike-ride** destination. The paved Park route through town **has a train theme**, found everywhere you look. Part Park ride, part **train tunnel sound-and-light show.**

Travelling along Hwy **401,** I did a stop over and scouted a small park trail that was a mere **7 km long**. Though pleasant, it was a tad short to review —but then **we found the tunnel!**

The **historic train tunnel** runs **under the centre of town.** It's a delightful, yet bizarre, bit of **Canadian history** to stumble upon.

The tunnel was the **first built in Canada,** and has been **completely restored** and jazzed up. Free to enter, we proceeded up this dark, **half-kilometre long** tube, following the sound of rock tunes, watching a light show, and reading signs stating interesting facts; **well done!** The air was cool and damp, and water dripped down the walls in this **man-made cave.**

You can **walk your bike** through the tunnel to the north exit, where there is a short stretch you can ride either way **parallel to the main line. CN** has fenced off a **trail laid with gravel** behind the lots of buildings, where you are assured to see train traffic.

The actual trail ride? Starting from the tunnel's south entrance one can ride along the peninsula to **Blockhouse Island,** then out and back to view the **marina** and the **USA across the river.** Interestingly, this peninsula was made from the rubble made by excavating the tunnel.

The **main route** heads **west** along the back streets; it is a few blocks to **Hardy Park.** Old, **century stone homes** make up this area, and **historic plaques** mark what was once a busy waterfront town with warehouses, robust industry, and train traffic.

Riding the **trail along the creek,** there are sure signs this path was once an **old rail line**, with many **embankments** and an **underpass**. We could hear **train horns** and **locomotives chugging** in the distance.

As we rode up and around, I had to wonder if this was the cheaper **alternate route** suggested instead of the tunnel. The path is now mostly paved, but **varies greatly** in width and terrain.

As you skip through **parkettes** you can turn back when you get to the end at **Brookview,** or hit the road for a **1.5 km detour** to get around **Hwy 401**. The trail runs for **2 more kilometres** along the **CP train line,** heading north out of town to **Centennial Rd.**

So, at around **14 km (return ride),** there is not a lot of trail riding here, but it is more of an interesting travel destination for all the **train buffs** out there.

Also, if you do go, consider cycling around the side streets in **downtown Brockville** to gaze at the many stunning, **old stone buildings**. Traffic is light, and drivers are not in a rush and give you space.

History –Started in **1854**, the route took 6 years to dig and was not the easiest or cheapest for trains to take to the waterfront. But **who doesn't like a tunnel?** So, one was built.

Half made of brick, with the centre blasted out from the rock, the tunnel ran under the centre of town for **525 metres**. There was not even a full-sized opening; at just over 4 metres, smaller locomotives had to be used.

It was used for many years by the **B&O** (the Brockville & Ottawa Railway Company), who ran the line up to the **Ottawa** area. Eventually owned by **Canadian Pacific (CP),** the tunnel served the waterfront commerce until **CP** closed the doors to the tunnel in **1970.** With Canada's 150th birthday in **2017,** funding restored the tunnel extensively and it is now a **tourist attraction**.

Cataraqui – Rail Trail

Strathcona to Smiths Falls

Length – 103 km (one way)

90% rail trail path, double-track
10% roads, detours

Elevation – The gradual elevation changes as expected, and there is an optional Opinicon Road loopback with big hills.

Terrain – Consists of crushed stone, gravel, tall grasses, and puddles when wet; suitable for hybrid or mountain bikes.

Skill – Easy to Intermediate, as some terrain is rough.

Traffic – Bicyclists, hikers, horse riders, cross-country skiers and snowmobiles in winter.

Facilities – Street parking, a few outhouses, and some small towns with basic services.

Highlights – See the Iron Bridge and Chaffeys Lock, as well as multiple rock cuts, lake views, and marshes.

Trail Fee – Free

Maps – Maps are located at the main parking lots, and signposts are found every few kilometres.

Phone – None

Website – Cataraqui Trail, & Facebook page

Similar Trails – Algonquin, Seguin

Local Clubs – Kingston Velo Club

Access – There are many entry points, including **Chaffeys Lock** and the towns of **Smiths Falls, Portland**, **Sydenham, Harrowsmith, Yarker**, and **East Camden**.

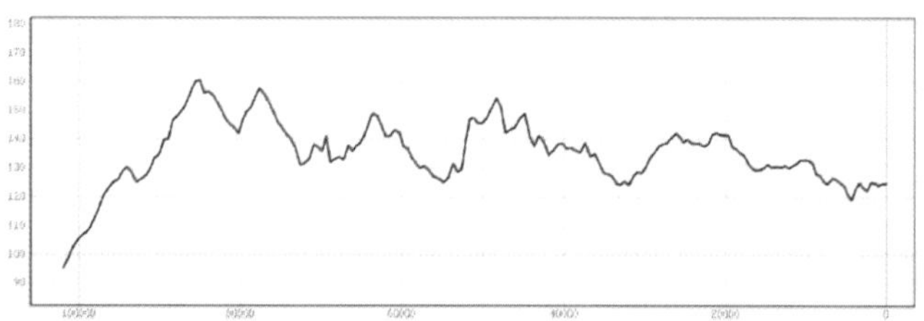

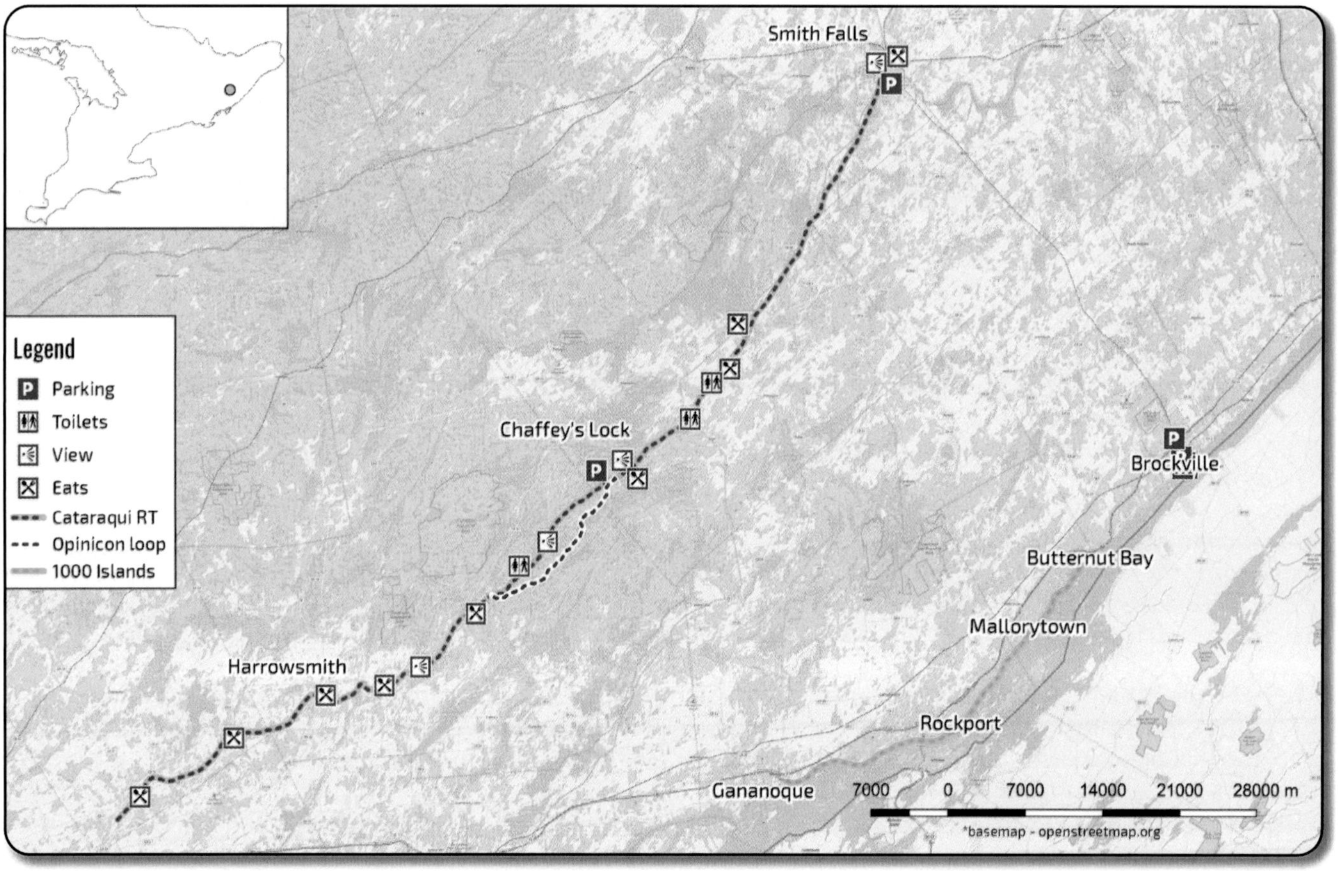

Smith Falls
Chaffey's Lock
Brockville
Butternut Bay
Mallorytown
Harrowsmith
Rockport
Gananoque
Legend
Parking
Toilets
View
Eats
Cataraqui RT
Opinicon loop
1000 Islands
7000 0 7000 14000 21000 28000 m
*basemap - openstreetmap.org

Review:

The **Cataraqui Rail Trail** is a popular route for bicyclists looking to get off busy roads and find some solitude. Situated in cottage and farm country **north of Kingston**, this **well-maintained** trail travels east to west. Starting in **Strathcona** it runs northeast to **Smiths Falls 104 km** away; the majority of it is also the **Trans Canada Trail**.

For most of the Rail Trail, the ride is a **mix of farm fields** and **forest**. The west end has more towns to stop by and explore, or to have lunch. (I recommend **East Camden, Yarker, Harrowsmith, or Sydenham.**)

In the middle of the ride the landscape changes to a **rockier terrain** as the **Canadian Shield** dips down a bit from **Perth Road** into the **Chaffey's Lock** area.

After, you are back on flat farm country with fewer towns to pass by (although there is **Portland**) until you finish in the large town centre, **Smiths Falls**.

We rode the section considered the most scenic, from **Chaffey's Lock** to **Perth Road** (about 16 km). Then, we cycled back to where we parked up the hill on **Indian Lake Rd.**, along the **Opinicon Road** for another **18 km.** At **33 km total,** the round trip was **a wonderful loop** I would recommend for any **fit cyclist.**

As most photos show, the trail runs west through **forested rock cuts and takes you up high vistas over marshes and lakes.**

With any rail trail there are no hills, but I felt a **gradual climb**. The paths were rocky in places, with tall grasses in others. A hybrid or mountain bike is a good choice for this route.

An odd sight on our ride was an enlarged **rock tunnel** for an underground stream just before we came to the

first of the farms—you can't miss it. This double-track path had a little **flooding** at the end, before meeting up with **Maple Leaf Rd.** and **Opinicon Rd.** So, if it has rained just be aware you might get your shoes wet!

If you choose the **paved road on the return,** expect more exercise on a few **steep but short hills .** The ever-changing scenery on this quiet road was welcome and a nice change from returning the same way.

Back at **Chaffey's Lock** there is an **old iron train bridge.** (No photo? How did I miss that!) By the locks find some good eats at the **Opinicon Resort Hotel.**

The **K&P Rail trail** also crosses at **Harrowsmith,** which is another great location to start a ride

History – Starting in the **1880s**, the Cataraqui rail line was built in various sections over a few decades by numerous rail companies.

It was eventually consolidated in **1918** by the **Canadian National Railway.** CN's service was discontinued by **1986** and the track was removed three years later.

For more train history, visit the fascinating **Smiths Falls Railway Museum**

Cornwall Waterfront – Park Trail

Cornwall to Upper Canada

Length – 10 to 22 km, with an optional 7 to 10 km road connection (one way)

75% park path
5% crossings, detours
20% road travel

Elevation – Mainly flat, with a few gradual inclines.

Terrain – Paved, with a dual lane; narrows to a gravel trail at the west end.

Skill – Easy to Intermediate

Traffic – Bikes, Hikers, not crowded

Maps – There is little signage, with no map boards, so follow the painted line for the waterfront trail.

Facilities – Parking lot, toilets, and other amenities, including campsites and beaches.

Highlights – An old canal and a bird sanctuary, as well as bridges, a power dam, and Upper Canada Village.

Trail Fee – Free

Phone – None

Website – St. Lawrence Parkway, Go Biking, City of Cornwall

Similar Trails – Rideau Canal, Welland Canal, 1,000 Islands

Local Clubs – Cornwall Cycling Club

Access – There is plenty of parking at the **Cornwall** waterfront, as well as **Long Sault, Ingleside**, and **Upper Canada Village.**

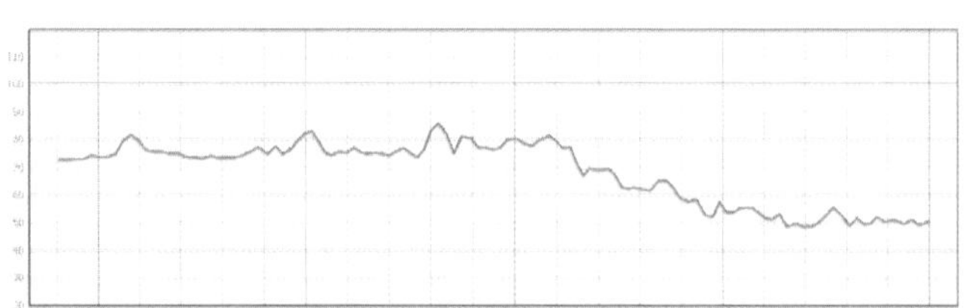

Legend
Parking
Toilets
Eats
View
Cornwall
Cornwall road

Long Sault
Cornwall
Ingleside
Upper Canada

2000 0 2000 4000 6000 8000 m
*basemap - openstreetmap.org

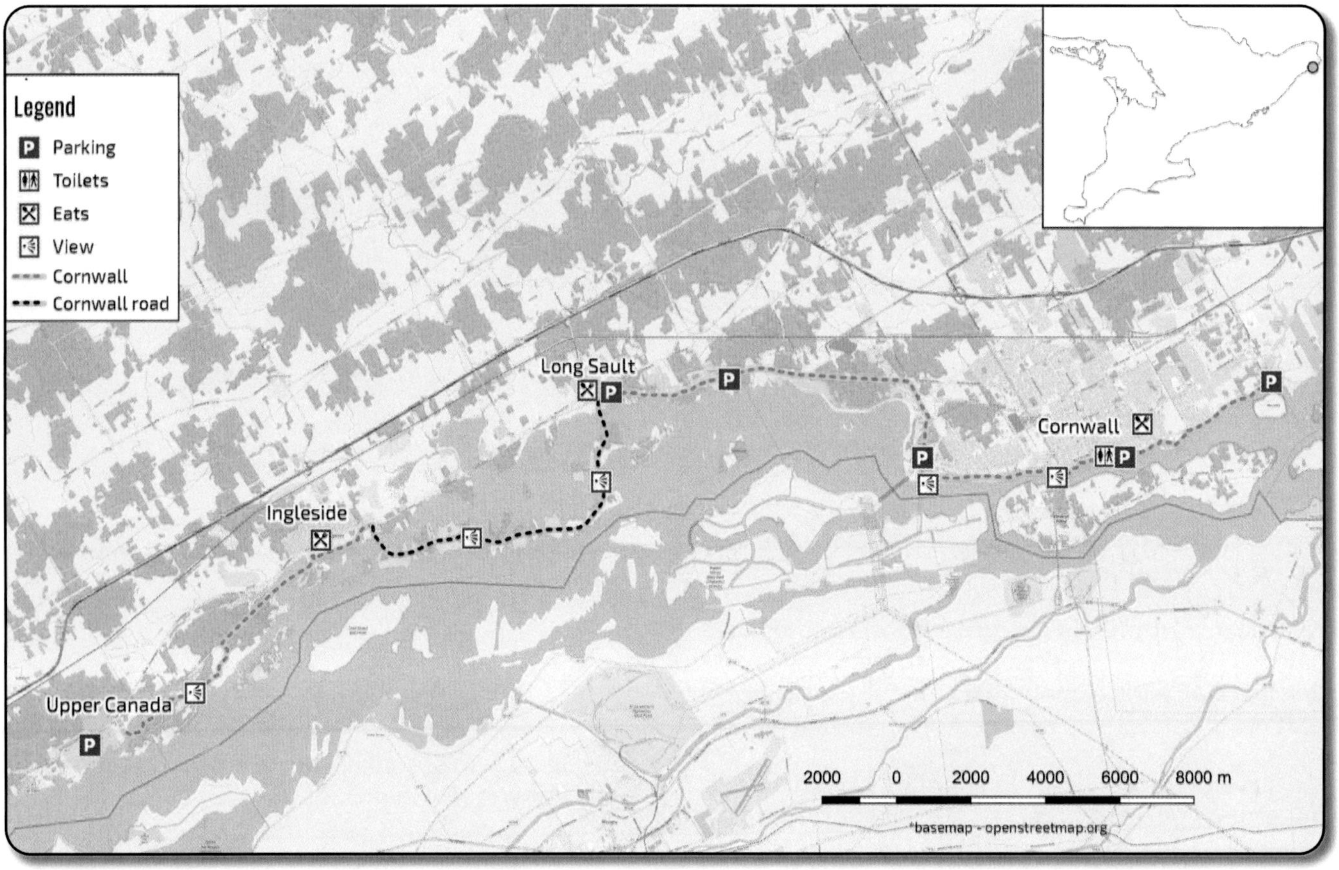

Review:

One of the **better park rides** in **Ontario** can be found along the **St. Lawrence River,** out by **Cornwall.** This **22+ km Waterfront Trail** has all the desired qualities that make it **a great Park ride:** long, scenic, and well-maintained.

Unlike the 1,000 Islands bike trail further up the river, this one actually does closely follow the waterfront for most of the journey. The path takes you along the **fast-flowing St. Lawrence River**, past **marinas, old shipping canals, and dams,** to the city's waterfront parkland.

I thoroughly enjoyed this trail when an old riding mate showed me the route last summer.

Mainly flat, you will encounter a few **long, gradual climbs** and, at the west end, some **narrower gravel trails;** all easily manageable, and never crowded.

This path had **few signs** and map boards, but we followed the **painted centre line** and that got us to where we wanted to go.

This long path can be divided up into a few stages, consisting of one **22 km** and **two 10 km trails**. Starting the route from the **east end**, it follows **Montreal Rd.** and hugs the shore from **Gray's Creek** on the eastern limit of **Cornwall.** As it reaches the city centre it opens up to the waterfront parkland.

Beyond this, after you pass under the **large bridge,** the path takes riders along what was once the **old canal** and **locks** the freighters used. What is odd, however, is that the view of the water on each side of your path is at different levels!

The route will turn **north** and then **inland** for a stretch through fields and woodlots. This part is **newly paved,** making the way enjoyable as it reveals **pretty views of the river.** The Lost Villages Museum is located on this section, and is a miniature version of the historic homes collected at Upper Canada Village.

Back in the 50's the **river was raised** and **dammed,** with new canals to allow larger ships to navigate. This ride shows evidence of the changes to the land, and the people, it made.

Eventually the path reaches the **Long Sault Parkway,** where there is a chance to get food at a nearby mall.

Here, you can make the choice to **turn back** the same way you came or take a long **road connection** to get **10 km** more of quiet wooded trail that passes through a bird sanctuary and leads to **Upper Canada Village.**

If you do want even more riding, I recommend skipping along the **scenic 11-island** chain by taking the **10 km Parkway Road.** It has no shoulders, but there is little traffic. For a shorter return, take the straight road at **Hwy 2** after **7 kilometres**.

The area offers many opportunities to expand your outing by visiting the **Upper Canada Museum, swimming** at a beach, **camping** overnight, or planning a nice **lunch in Cornwall.**

So, the choice is yours to ride the full **80 km** return route, or stick to certain sections. For my cycling friend Paul (who has ridden across Canada) this trail is no problem, but there are many choices for more casual riders.

My recommendation would be to first add the **old canal section** to your trek.

This trail was a nice find, and is **sure to be an enjoyable** stop for anyone coming (or going) to **Montreal** or are on a day trip from **Ottawa**.

Greenway – Rail/Park Trail

Peterborough to Lakefield

Length – 15 km (one way)

90% park path
10% roads, crossings, detours

Elevation – As flat as they come; follows the Otonabee River, with a few inclines to get over bridges.

Terrain – All asphalt, with some patches of gravel and sand.

Skill – Easy

Traffic – Cyclists, walkers, dogs, families.

Maps – Maps and distance markers can be found on the trail.

Facilities – Street parking, with washrooms at Nicholls Oval Park.

Highlights – Century homes, the varied architecture of Trent University, a charming downtown, old canals and bridges, a power dam, the lilacs in spring, and picturesque beaches.

Trail Fee – Free

Phone – None

Website – No official page.

Similar Trails – Speed River, Nokiidaa, Ajax Waterfront

Local Clubs – Peterborough Cycling Club, Northumberland Hills Cycling Club

Access – Enter this trail at many spots, and find lots of parking along **Auburn St., Peterborough**, in **Lakefield**, and inbetween at several dams along the river.

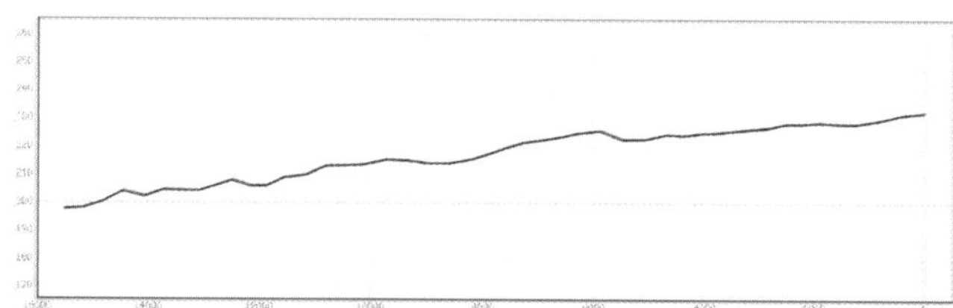

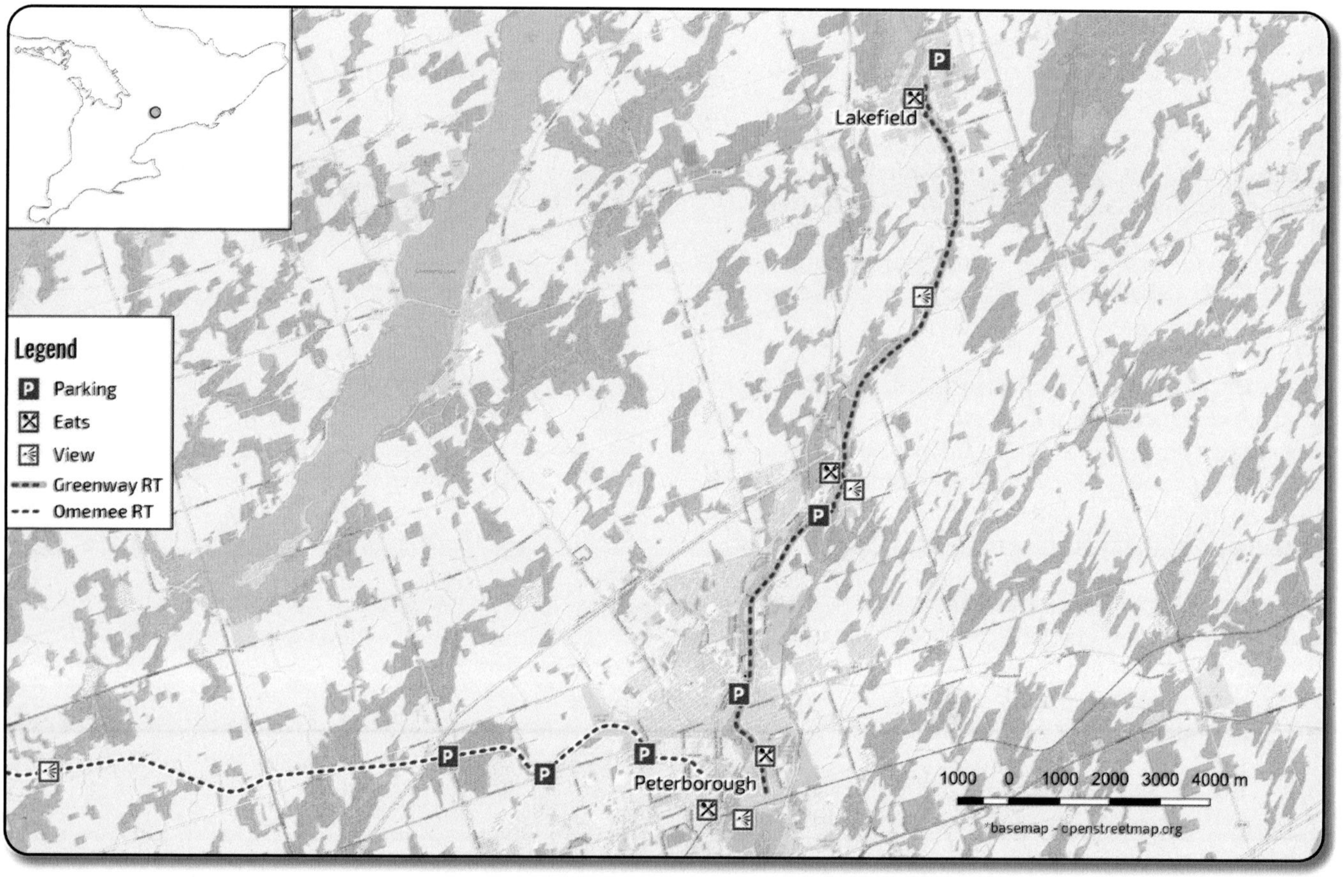

Legend
P Parking
Eats
View
Greenway RT
Omemee RT

Lakefield
Peterborough
1000 0 1000 2000 3000 4000 m
basemap - openstreetmap.org

Review:

For an easy path to cycle out of town, consider doing the **15 km** (one way) **Rotary Greenway Trail**. As a **Park** trail and a **Rail** trail, it's a bit of both and a great bike excursion.

Expect this bike path to be **flat** and **straight** with gradual bends, typical of a rail bed. This path between **Peterborough** and **Lakefield** is paved, with some areas having a crushed-stone base.

The very beginning of the trail, at either end, starts where the Rail line thins out to a dead end behind neighbourhood homes. With plenty of other entry points and parking, riders may wish to start the ride in either the city or somewhere along the route.

From **Peterborough,** the bike path makes its way through city parks, with an option to cross the bridge to get to **downtown.** (An excellent destination afterwards for a beer and a burger!)

The **Otonabee River,** which the trail follows, has been tamed with **locks** and is part of the **Trent-Severn Waterway.** Worth stopping at are any of the nine rapids, locks, and dams (some power-generating) along the way. The map notes where these are, otherwise you may unknowingly pass by.

Although the **Greenway** path follows the river, the views are not as frequent as one may wish as it does veer off inland and into the bush, often behind a treeline.

Still, riders can drop down to the water at many spots to rest, to soak their feet, or to swim.

There are a few **century-old homes** along the way if you look for them. **Historical, environmental,** and **ecological signage** posted along the route may also be of interest. **Lilac** bushes can be seen, which look and smell wonderful in the spring.

The path contains helpful **distance markers** to tell you how far you've gone, and how far you've yet to go. **Busy intersections** in town have crossing lights to manage your ride through these parts.

Just as the trail gets to **Trent University,** look for a new trail bridge that crosses the canal by the **old rail swing bridge**. This canal leads back **south** to the famous **Lift Locks**. (Definitely worth visiting!)

This newest section of the path skirts by the campus. Take a moment to check out **the beautiful architecture.**

Beyond and into **Lakefield**, this path becomes a mellow country Rail Trail, with farm fields on one side and the local road and river on the other.

Those who seek a more challenging trail can find a few stretches of **single-track MTB** trails closer to the river.

Now, that should be enough to get you making plans and give this a spin one day!

Completed in 2018 + 2019

Millennium – Rail Trail

Trenton to Picton

Length – 49 km (one way)

90% rail trail path
5% roads, crossings, detours

Elevation – Flat with a gradual slope, as with most Rail Trails.

Terrain – Consists of crushed stone, gravel, grass, and some sand; rougher toward the ends. (The route is currently being upgraded.)

Skill – Easy

Traffic – Bicyclists, hikers, horseback riders, ATVs, and dirt bikes; snowmobiles and cross-country skiers in winter.

Maps – Plenty of signposts and markers.

Facilities – Parking on the street, as well as outhouse and rain shelter.

Highlights – Wineries, vineyards, farm fields, lake views, and cottages.

Trail Fee – Free

Phone – None

Website – Prince Edward County

Similar Trails – Omemee, Oro – Medonte, Elora Cataract

Local Clubs – Bloomfield Bicycle Club

Access – Currently, north end of **West St.** in **Wellington.** Future start points planned for 2019:

- **Novotny Court (Carrying Place)**
- **Salem Road (Consecon)**
- **Station Road (Hillier)**
- **Stanley Street (Bloomfield)**
- **Lake Street (Picton)**
- **County Road 49 (Picton)**

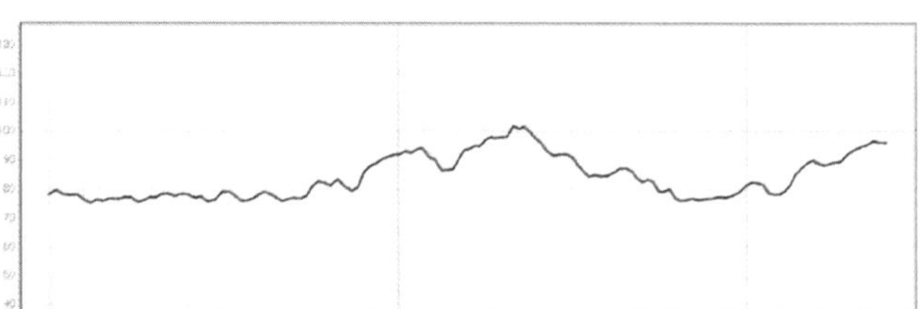

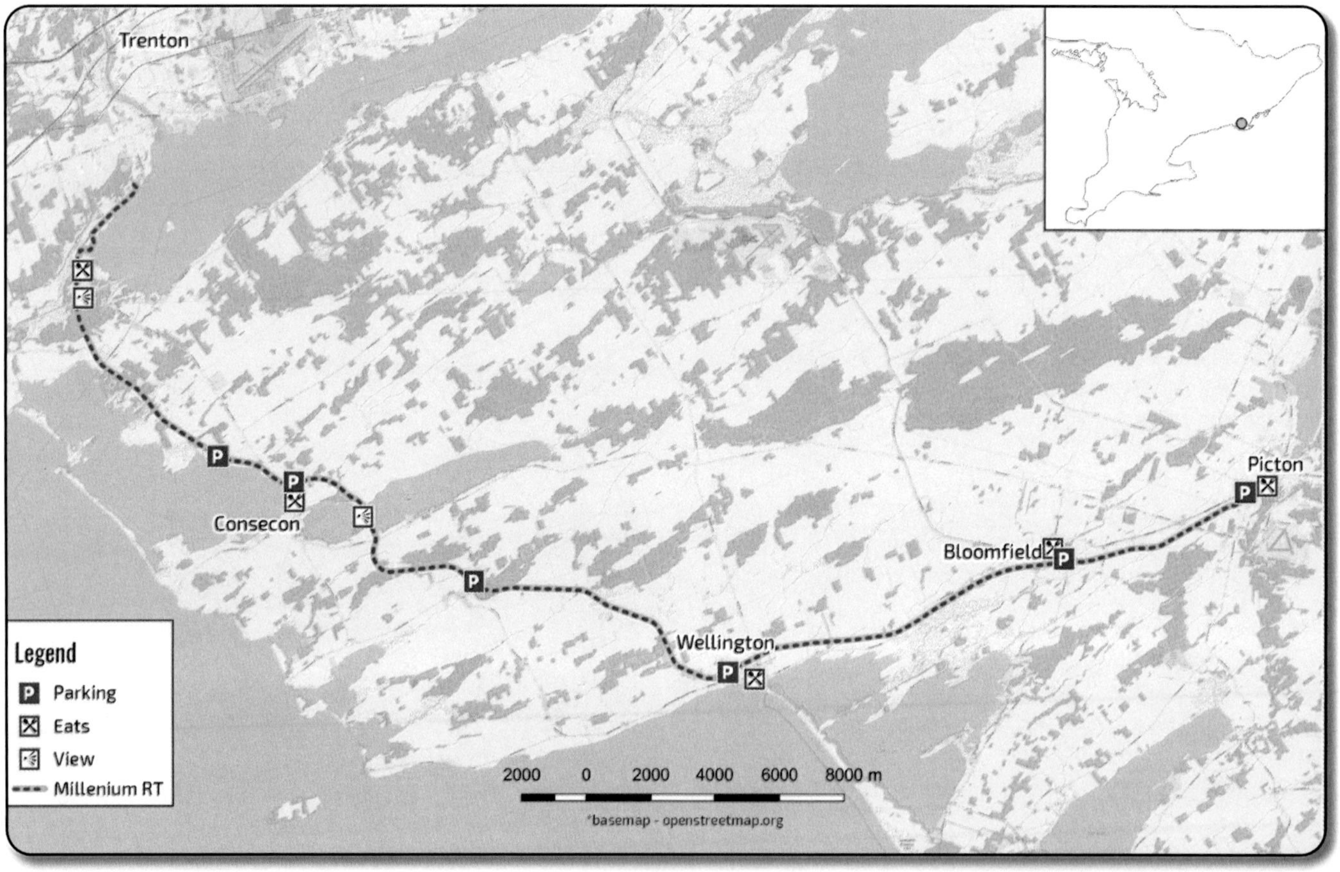

Trenton
Consecon
Wellington
Bloomfield
Picton
Legend
Parking
Eats
View
Millenium RT
2000 0 2000 4000 6000 8000 m
*basemap - openstreetmap.org

Review:

As a **new trail**, the **Millennium Rail Trail** holds much promise to serve as a recreational and scenic way to travel through **Prince Edward County**.

At **49 km,** it swings down from **Trenton** through **Wellington, Bloomfield,** and then on to **Picton**, the largest town on the peninsula.

This abandoned rail line is currently **being resurfaced** and upgraded, with a fine crushed-stone base, new signage, benches, and numerous side trails.

As of spring **2019**, the **middle section** around **Wellington** and **eastward** are done. The west section to **Trenton** should be finished by the summer I am told.

We rode a resurfaced stretch in the fall, heading out each way for about **5 km** from the **Wellington trailhead**.

Beyond this, the trail surface was a double track path with tall grasses and larger-stoned gravel. I would think that this has been graded and resurfaced by now.

We passed a few **side trails leading to wineries** you can visit. (Sounds like fun!) As you ride, one passes wetlands, farm fields, and country homes. There are plenty of **lake views** if you ride further.

I also noted a few ATVs, driven by seniors, buzzing around. (Don't worry! Nothing reckless to worry about.)

Wellington is a **quaint little village** that draws plenty of **tourists** and has some fine dining (with fine-dining prices, too). Do take a moment to stroll through town and down to the water's edge or the small beach.

Heading east to **Bloomfield,** or even on to **Picton,** makes for a day trip with plenty of opportunities to find **lunch, lodging,** or even a **bike shop** if you need one.

I saw others **renting bikes** from a local shop in **Wellington** to enjoy the countryside. After all, this route does make for a good summer weekend outing by the lake.

Finally, if you don't know about the famous **Sandbanks Provincial Park**, consider a side trip where you can do more biking, as well as swimming and camping.

Currently, there are plans for **six more trailhead starting points**. Yet a recent check found the funding has been delayed and progress is slow.

No matter, the trail is open almost finished and eventually will become a favourite country bike route for most.

History – This so-called **Prince Edward Rail Line** was built in **1879** for local transport needs.

It was then sold to the **Central Ontario Railway** to deliver iron ore from **Bancroft** to the port in **Picton**, destined for steel mills in **Cleveland, Ohio**. Unfortunately, the ore was of lower grade than expected and less than desired was shipped.

By **1919** the **CN Railroad** ran the line, serving local canneries, mills, and farms. On these tracks, soldiers went off to war and children off to school. Not ever a profitable route, the trains stopped rolling by **1996.**

Northumberland – MTB/Park Trail

101 Beagle Club Rd., North of Cobourg

Length – 40 + km

50% hiking trail

20% single-track MTB trail
20% double-track access roads

Elevation – Lots of gentle rolling hills, some quite large.

Terrain – Packed sandy and mixed soil, with a few tree roots and some gravel and rocks; watch for poison ivy.

Skill – Easy to Intermediate MTB trail; Intermediate Park ride.

Traffic – Quiet and rarely busy. Bikes, hikers, horseback riders, ATV, snowmobiles.

Maps – Found at trailhead, and the trail has signposts.

Facilities – A parking lot and outhouse, but no amenities for miles; Nordic skiing in winter.

Highlights – Plenty of solitude, provided by a wild, pine forest. (Smells piney fresh!)

Trail Pass – Free

Phone – None

Website – Northumberland County

Similar Trails – Ganaraska, Eldrid King, Long Sault

Local Clubs – Cobourg Cycling Club

Access – From **Cobourg**, head north on **Hwy 45**, then left on to **101 Beagle Club Rd**. There is a large parking lot, and map board at the trailhead that will get you started.

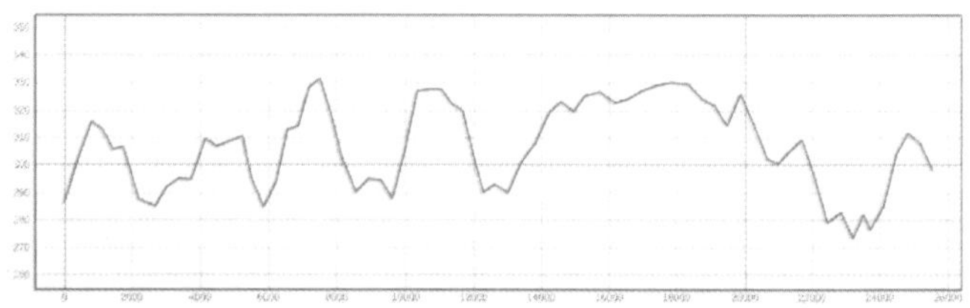

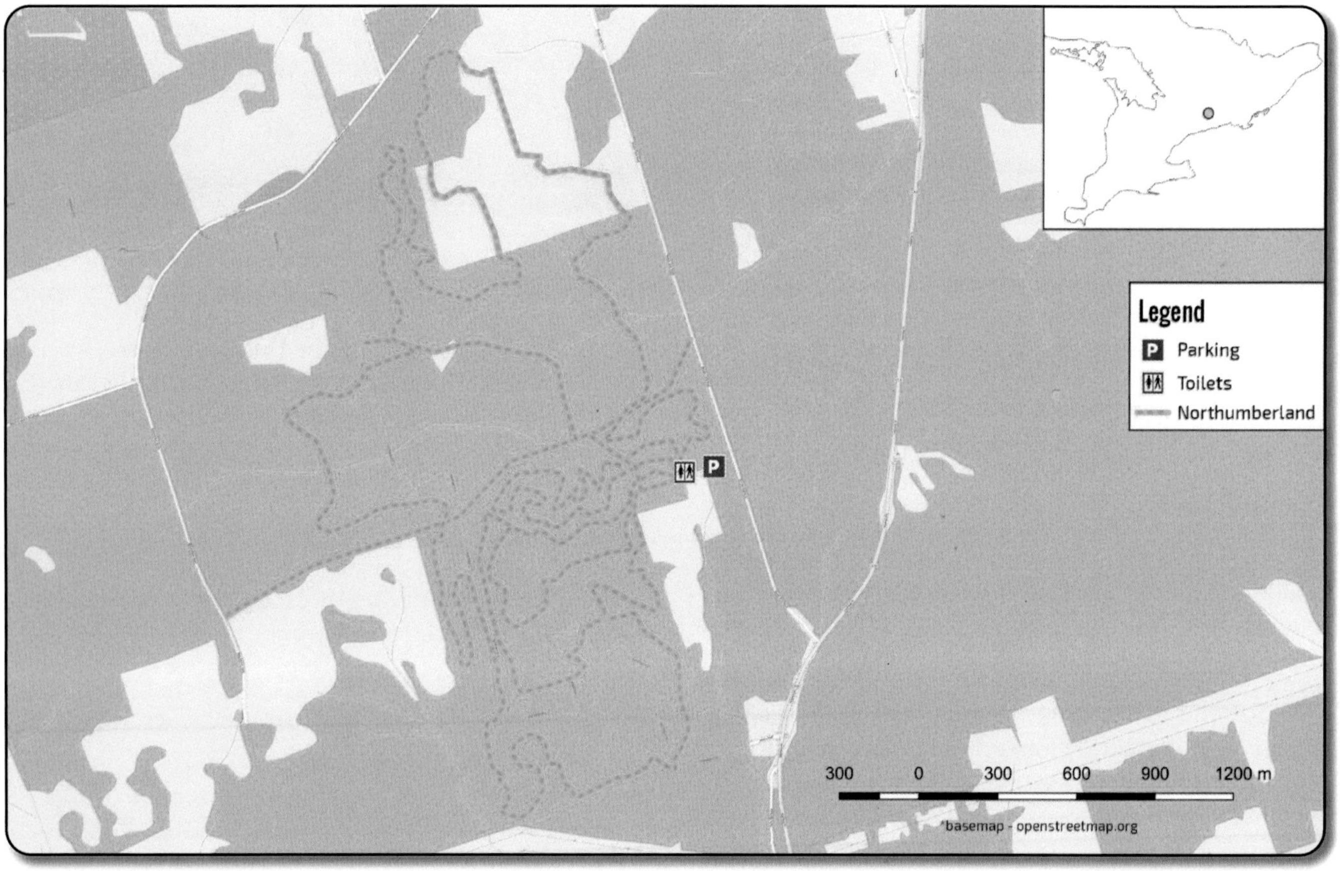

Legend
Parking
Toilets
Northumberland

300 0 300 600 900 1200 m

basemap - openstreetmap.org

Review:

This little-known **Northumberland County Forest** offers **MTB** riders plenty of choice to let loose.

With over **40 km** of track, riders get a **fast, hilly** set of cross-county style loops and roads. This area, part of the **Oak Ridges Moraine,** has a **sandy soil base**, with sections of root and the odd rocks. There are plenty of trails to discover.

The forest is large, mixed with **evergreen pines** and deciduous trees. As a result, it can feel **dry, dusty**, and a tad arid during the hot summer months.

Across the road, a local club cut the **4-km Dragonfly** MTB loop that leads further up the path to the **3-km Elderberry** and **2-km Stonewall** trail. This is where any **gnarly or twist stuff** is found.

Did I hear you say you like mean hills? Then ride **The Hogs Back,** if you dare.

Most of the other trails were made by **hikers** and are used by cross-country skiers in the winter, and are **tamer**. Numerous **dirty roads** and **ATV trails** also adds to the ride; I find it feels very similar to riding in **Ganaraska.**

For the **Intermediate Park** trail rider, I suggest taking these loops slower; it is a **pleasant outing** but has its rather challenging sections.

A **hybrid bike** will handle most of the trail, but watch for **deep sand patches.**

Sand is great for growing the itchy **poison ivy**. On less-travelled backwood trails, watch out. It doesn't seem to bother me, but the weed can be **waist high** by summers end.

Take a ride in the early spring, or in the fall after a frost, and you will see a lot less of it. Look for **raspberries,** too. Yum!

Also be aware that **black bears** wander these parts, so making some noise as you ride along could be a good thing.

This **rustic** location is **rarely busy,** so I suggest riding with a buddy. Being prepared and self-sufficient is also smart as there are no services anywhere close by.

This is an excellent spot for **Fatbikes!** Please stay off the Nordic ski trails in the winter.

For the curious or driven cyclist, more trail can be found **3 km** northwest at the **Woodland Trails**.

This **patch of wilderness** has much to discover. If you seek adventure or solitude, you'll surely find it here.

Rideau Canal – Park Trail

Ottawa

Length – 10 km (one way)

80% park path
20% roads, detours

Elevation – Flat as it follows the canal, then drops to the **Ottawa River** at the locks.

Terrain – A wide asphalt path with a centre line, as well as some sections of crushed stone and gravel.

Skill – Easy

Traffic – Mainly bike users

Maps – A map can be found at the trailhead, as well as signs along the trail.

Facilities – Parking on side streets, with washrooms at Patterson Creek, Lansdowne Park, and Dow's Lake Pavilion. Bike rentals are also available.

Highlights – The canal locks and bridges, Hog's Back Falls, Parliament Hill, and the Agricultural and Food Museum.

Trail Fee – Free

Phone – 613 580 2400

Website – Ottawa Tourism, Rideau Info, City of Ottawa

Similar Trails – Welland Canal

Local Clubs – Ottawa Bike Club, Kanata Bike Club

Access – There are numerous points to enter along the route and plenty of parking on side streets by the trail. It is likely easier to find a spot further from the downtown, or at **Dow's Lake Park**.

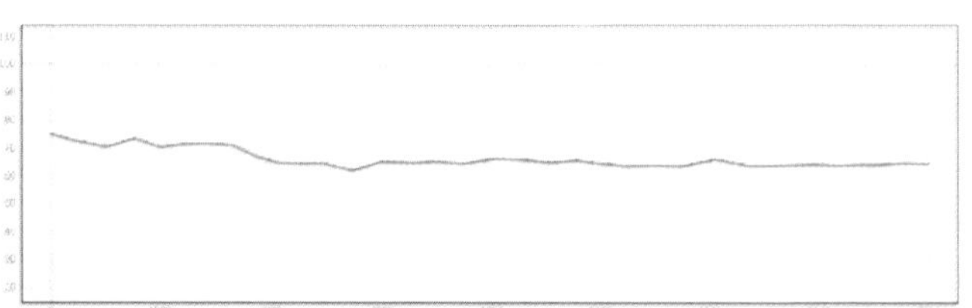

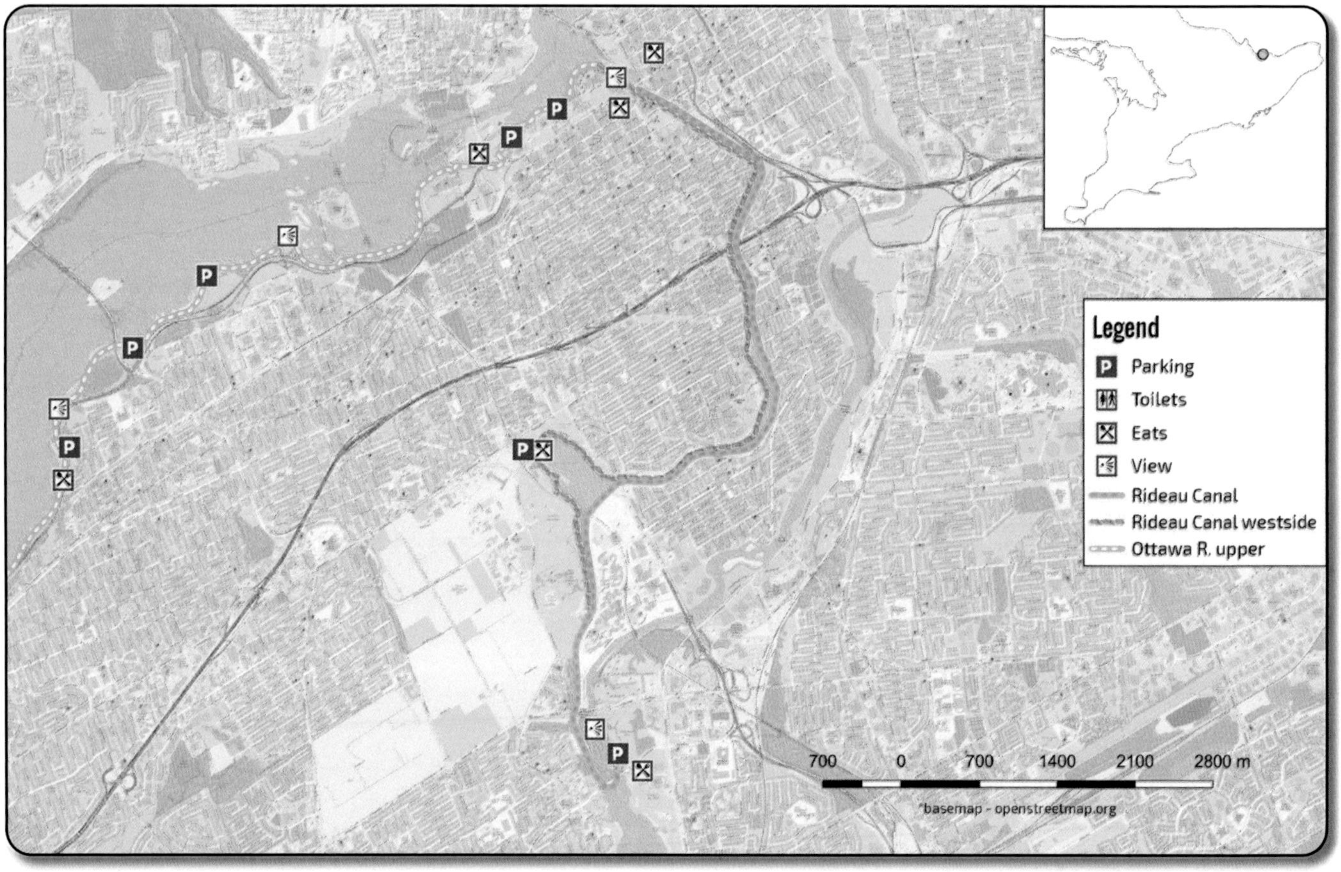

Legend
P Parking
Toilets
Eats
View
Rideau Canal
Rideau Canal westside
Ottawa R. upper

700 0 700 1400 2100 2800 m

*basemap - openstreetmap.org

Review:

A **popular Park trail** locals love to cruise, this route is on the **Rideau Canal**. As it winds from the **Hog's Back Locks** up to the **Ottawa River** (about **10 km**), the trail offers an ever-changing scenery of well-kept parklands and watercraft activity on the canal.

Well-maintained and **flat**, as trails along rivers tend to be, this is a **carefree ride** for the whole family.

One has even a choice of making it a loop, as there are paths on both sides of the canal for most of the way.

At the south end be sure to visit the **Hog's Back Falls**, as the rushing water is rather spectacular. (And now you know why there is a canal!)

Cruising north along the canal behind **Carleton University** and on to **Hartwell's Locks,** you then have a choice of continuing along on the east side or crossing the top of the narrow lock gates and heading up the other side.

If I were to recommend which side is better for bikers, it would be the **west side** as it is a little longer as it goes around **Dow's Lake** and also **more scenic, with fewer cars in sight**.

The east side is a bit more of a direct commuter path that winds along the road. (Although it is still enjoyable.)

On the west side, make time to stop at the **wildlife gardens** and the **Agriculture and Food Museum.**

Onward, the path curves around Dow's Lake and offers side trails to explore.

Both Park trails continue right into **downtown Ottawa** and **Parliament Hill,** where they join the **Ottawa River bike trail** going northwest.

Be sure to review your plans carefully, as there are only a few bridges to cross along the way. One of interest,

the **Corktown Footbridge,** has many padlocks decorating the rail, from lovers pledging their affection.

There and back, the total loop is about **19 km**; perhaps too much for the little ones in one go.

Another excellent option is a return loop along the **Rideau River** itself, which runs about the same distance back.

While here, why not visit the Hill, take a look at the locks by **Château Laurier,** or grab a bite at one of the many eateries.

As a bonus fact, **Colonel By Drive,** on the east bank of this canal, is closed to cars on Sundays 9 am to 1pm in the summer. A sure bet it brings everyone out on their two wheeler's.

Two Lakes – Rail Trail

Belleville to Madoc

Length – 38 km (one way)

95% rail trail
5% roads, crossings, detours

Elevation – A gradual slope northward.

Terrain – The trail is made of crushed stone and gravel, with some large stones and pothole hazards.

Skill – Intermediate

Traffic – Bicyclists, hikers, horseback riders, ATVs, and dirt bikes, as well as snowmobiles in winter.

Maps – Plenty of signage, much of it for ATV vehicles.

Facilities – Parking lots, food, and lodging can be found in Belleville and Madoc.

Highlights – Bridges, shaded forest, natural wetlands, as well as Moira Lake, and the town of Madoc.

Trail Fee – Free

Phone – 613 478 1444

Website – The Trail

Similar Trails – Cataraqui, Seguin

Local Clubs – Kingston Velo Club, Bloomfield Bicycle Club

Access – From side roads or two parking lots: one at the south trailhead where **River Rd.** and **Cannifton Rd. N.** meet, as well as on the other end of **Moira Lake**, at **Hwy 62** and **Watson Lane.**

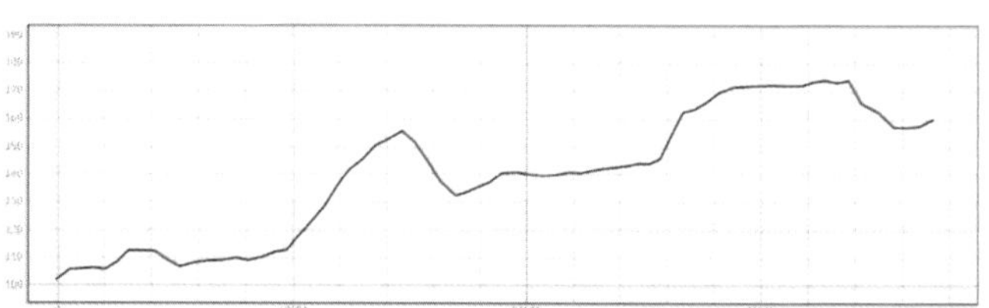

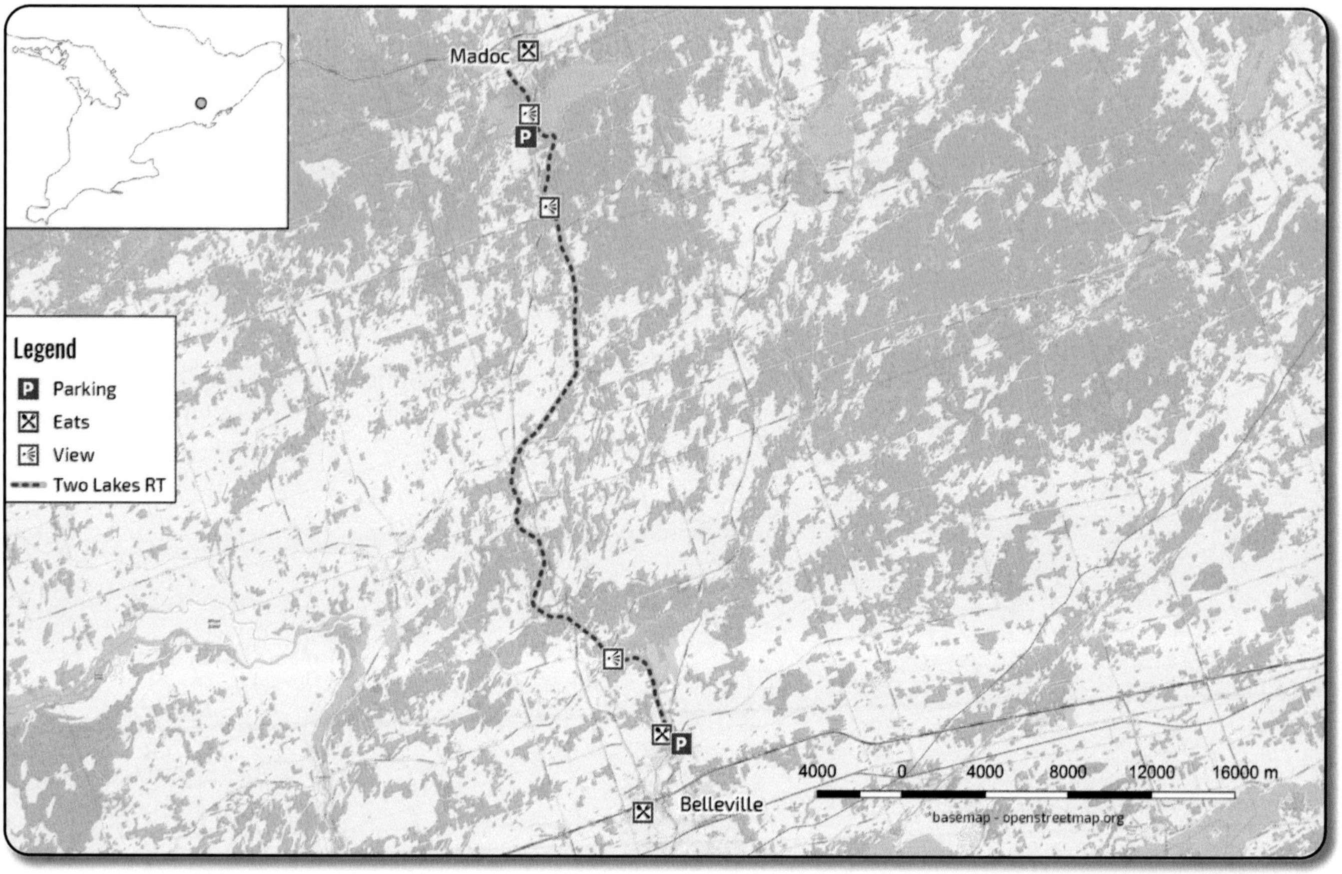

Madoc
Legend
Parking
Eats
View
Two Lakes RT
Belleville
4000 0 4000 8000 12000 16000 m
basemap - openstreetmap.org

Review:

The **Trail of Two Lakes** runs for **38 km** north from **Belleville** and up to **Madoc** along an old rail bed.

This Rail Trail is your typical, **multi-use repurposed** rail line and is more known (and used) by **ATVs** and **snowmobiles** than cyclists. As such, the surface terrain is coarse with the odd pothole and is better suited for **Intermediate** riders.

Since the path is unlike the fine crushed stone of other Rail Trails, a **good hybrid bike** with shocks or, better, **a mountain bike or Fatbike** is the ticket.

Bicyclists and hikers are welcome, just know that motorists are likely to pass on your ride. (We encountered perhaps eight ATVs on our trek, but they slowed down and were friendly folk.)

The rail bed continues along, with **gentle curves** and not too many straight sections that felt endless. Riders will come across many marshlands, giving open views and a break from the forest canopy.

One would think the bugs could be a problem in the spring, but I did not find this the case during my ride in the fall.

Along the way, crossing country roads reveals small communities with cottages and farmers' fields.

For the most part, this is a quiet, nature-filled bike ride. You may see turtles crossing the road, or songbirds in the marshes.

Just before **Mudcat Rd.** is the **largest bridge** on the trip; an old iron bridge spanning the **Moira River.**

I did note a long climb (harder for a train than you!) after **Smith Rd**. Listen for **Rawdon Creek** running alongside.

Right after **Tuffsville Rd**, the rail line **splits**; another trail branches left, heading **west for 28 km** to **Campbellford.**

Further north, about **15 km** and on the west side**,** the route passes **White Lake**. Just before this is an **underpass,** where the **Trans Canada Trail** (another Rail Trail) goes over.

The path now descends to **Moira Lake** and merges into **Watson Lane**. Crossing **Hwy 62** the trail travels over a wooden bridge, where (I would conclude) are **views of the two lakes**.

Go **3 km** more to reach the end at **Seymour St. W.** Taking this road east will bring you soon into the town of **Madoc,** with places to eat and refuel.

History – This route incorporates two old rail lines to make up the **Trail of Two Lakes.** The **Grand Junction Railway** opened a route in 1877 at the south end, running north from **Belleville** then west to **Campbellford, Hastings,** and **Peterborough.** The **Canadian National Railway (CNR)** abandoned the line in 1987.

In the north end, the line was built by the **Belleville & North Hastings Railway Company (B & NHR).** After two years of construction, it was connected in 1880 to a **9-km** east-west line, running past **Madoc** to service iron ore mining. By **1983** the **CNR** closed this section due to the costly repairs needed at the **Moira Lake** bridge.

Upper Ottawa R. – Park Trail

Ottawa

Length – 17 km (one way)

95% park path
5% roads, detours

Elevation – Flat, with rolling mounds.

Terrain – Mostly paved, with some gravel and sand, as well as bridges.

Skill – Easy

Traffic – Busy on summer weekends with bikers, people rollerblading, and walkers.

Maps – Plenty of map boards and trail markers; follow the centre line.

Facilities – Lots of parking , a few toilets, and a snack bar, as well as benches, picnic tables, and rain shelters.

Highlights – Scenic parks, river vistas, and beaches, as well as some interesting bridges.

Trail Fee – Free

Phone – 613 239 5000

Website – NCC – National Capital Commission

Similar Trails – Rideau Canal, Cornwall Waterfront, Ajax Waterfront

Local Clubs – Ottawa Bicycle Club, Kanata Bike Club

Access – Parking lots at: **Mill St. Pub, Westboro Beach, Deschenes Rapids, Britannia Beach,** and **Haydon Park.**

This trail connects from other bike paths along the **Rideau Canal and Pinecrest Creek.**

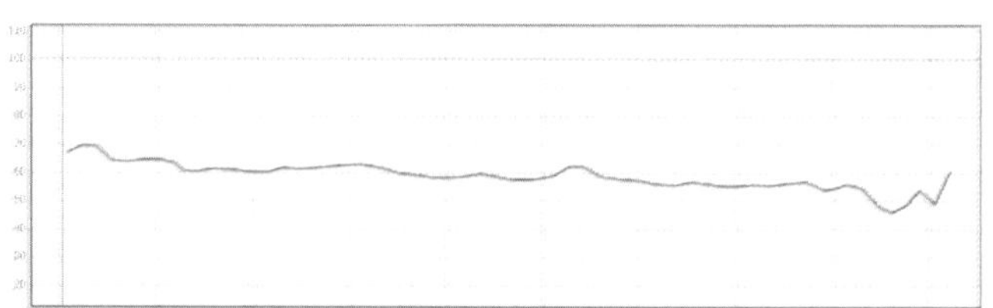

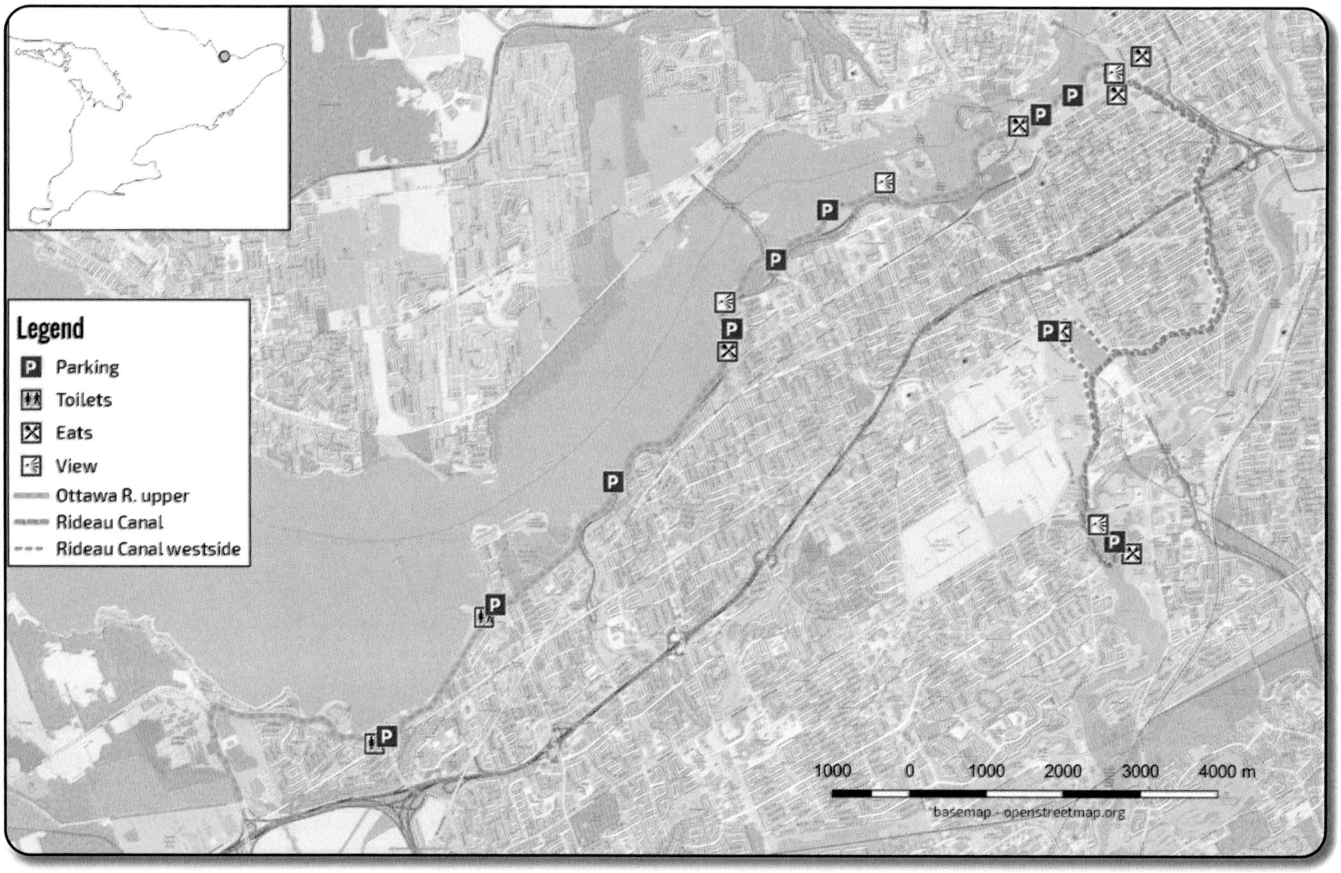

Legend

- Parking
- Toilets
- Eats
- View
- Ottawa R. upper
- Rideau Canal
- Rideau Canal westside

1000 0 1000 2000 3000 4000 m

basemap - openstreetmap.org

Review:

The **Ottawa River Pathway** is a favourite of many cyclists in town, either to ride recreationally or to commute. The pathway runs **30 km** along the river's south edge in **two sections.**

This review is for the upper **17 km section**, west of downtown, which starts at the **Rideau Canal Locks** and connects with the Rideau Canal bike path as well.

This Park trail is all **paved asphalt,** and meanders in a **continually curving path** that follows the river bank. No nasty hills here to strain yourself, just **easy cruising** over small mounds put in by landscapers to keep it interesting for bicyclists.

The trail goes through **manicured parkland,** with trees planted at random to give a little shade, although most is open to the sun and wind. (It was blowing hard the day I went!)

I may use the word too often, but **pleasant** it is, to describe this place.

The scenery seen along this mighty river is comprised of **islands, rapids, dams, bridges,** and **small beaches**. Citizens and tourists alike stroll and lay about, relaxing on the lawns. Numerous **lookouts** give riders the opportunity to stop and enjoy the view, with **plaques** to give historical context.

One negative aspect of the trail is you can never escape the **sight and sound of cars,** as you might in other city parks. With four lanes of traffic, the **Sir John A. MacDonald Parkway** also runs along the riverbank, and its presence is never far away.

Heading up the river from the canal at the east end, the bike path skirts around the cliff base, hugging the shoreline. Above is **Parliament Hill,** the **courthouse, the library,** and the **war memorial buildings**.

At **Portage Bridge** you may cross under and continue past **The Mill St. Pub;** an old grist mill and the only watering hole on the route. Further on, the sight of a closed, **rusty train bridge** makes me wonder when they will turn it into a bike route into **Quebec.**

More meandering, and daydreaming, leads you to **Champlain Bridge,** which is your chance to cross and ride back down the path on the other side.

If you choose to continue straight, in no time at all you will have arrived at the popular **Westboro Beach**, and a chance for a coffee and a nibble.

At about the **10 km** mark, many riders head inland on the **Pinecrest Pathway,** which loops around and back on the **Experimental Farm Pathway.**

If that's not to your liking, you can instead still head upriver, behind the **Britannia Conservation Area**, and on through more parkland to the picturesque ponds at **Haydon Park** and marina.

Officially, the path goes on to the **Carling Campus** and connects with other trails. However, I find this a rather boring paved shoulder to ride along **Carling Ave.**, so instead I recommend heading back.

If you do **return the same way,** the middle part of this route leads to an alternate yet similar path on the other side of the road.

On **Sunday mornings** in the summer, the westbound lanes are closed so you can ride on them —how cool is that!

In a future review, I will cover the **Lower Ottawa River Pathway**, which is a much different experience than riding this upper section.

Algonquin – Rail Trail

Rock Lake Rd., Algonquin Park

Length – 16 km (one way)

90% rail trail path
10% road, detours

Elevation – As with most rail trails, this one is flat.

Terrain – Wide path of crushed stone and gravel with some sand, as well as wooden bridges.

Skill – Easy (I find it family-friendly.)

Traffic – Good weather brings out the campers - Bicycles, Hikers, Fatbikes and Nordic skiers.

Maps – Well-marked, signs at gate and along path.

Facilities – Campground, amenities, and bike rentals at the Two Rivers Store can all be found on the trail.

Highlights – Beautiful views of the lakes and rock faces, old wooden bridges, and a dam— very peaceful.

Trail Fee – Park day pass is $11.25; Free for campers.

Phone – 705 633 5572

Website – Ontario Parks

Similar Trails – Seguin, Cataraqui

Local Clubs – None

Access – Enter from the east side of **Rock Lake** campgrounds, or use other campground side trails at **Pog Lake, Mew Lake, Coon Lake, and Kearney Lake.**

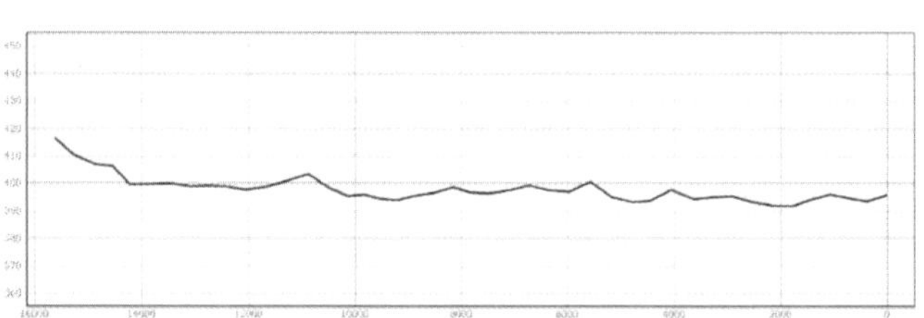

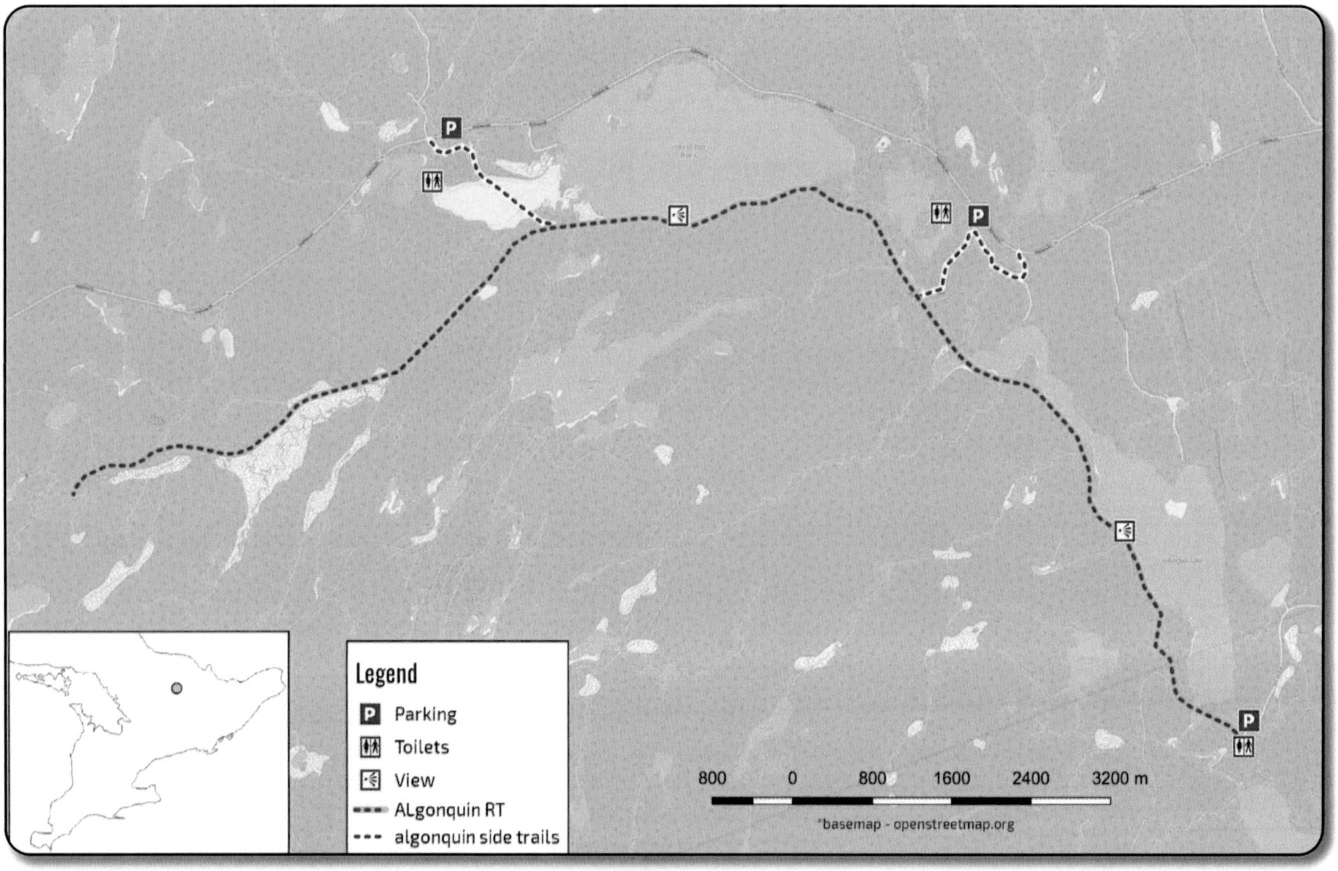

Legend
Parking
Toilets
View
ALgonquin RT
algonquin side trails

800 0 800 1600 2400 3200 m

*basemap - openstreetmap.org

Review:

In **Algonquin Park** the **16 km Old Railway Trail,** as they call it, is one of the more **scenic** and **popular** Rail Trails in Ontario. Used by **local** campers staying at campgrounds along the route, this makes it very convenient for families to set out for a recreational spin right from their sites. So, I would expect more cyclists on this trail than most Rail Trails, on which there is usually next to none.

When you ride the trail try and picture the hills bare of trees, as it once was when the forest was chopped down and hauled away. Thankfully, the track was removed 60 years ago and everything has since grown back.

Most of the trail terrain is **easy, crushed gravel** with the odd larger rock from the old rail bed poking through. There are **sandy sections** and **new bridges** over the original rotten spans. Look for the **rock cuts** blasted out on the sides of the path. Trains need **gradual slopes,** so that is what you have to ride on.

From the south end at **Rock Lake** campground, this rail trail runs along the west edge of **Whitefish Lake** to the **Pog, Kearney,** and **Whitefish** campgrounds. There are plenty of views of the lakes on this ride, so stop to get a few pictures.

Then, go beyond and along **Lake of Two Rivers** to the campground of the same name. Here is a short side trail that takes you to **Hwy 60** and the **Mew campgrounds**... and ice cream! After all, every hard-working cyclist desires something cool and the park store has what you need. You can also **rent bikes,** including **Fatbikes**.

Continue down this wide, flat trail to where (I believe) the **trestle bridge** was removed, marking the end of the line for trains and for your ride. If you wish, there is another trail close by, the **Track & Tower loop,** you can hike for a view.

A few sections open up to fields where there once stood **lumber-milling** operations; I saw a **small dam** and **interpretive panels** along the route explaining **Algonquin's history.**

By mid-July the bugs are fine if you keep moving. **Fall rides are certain to be beautiful** with the trees in full colour, and you can find **raspberry** and **blueberry bushes** on some of the open sections. Bonus—Yum!

You may even see wildlife on your trek, like **moose, bear, beaver, or loons** -- or make plenty of noise and see nothing.

In the winter, bring your **Fatbike** for a ride. There is plenty of snow here and you will be sharing the route with skiers.

History – Starting as the **Ottawa, Arnprior, and Parry Sound Railway**, trains started running in **1896.** At one time this line was the **busiest** railway in all of Canada! The track was built by lumber baron J.R. Booth to haul out timber to his mills (a large one in **Ottawa**) and to export abroad. Most of the prime **Algonquin Park** timber was cut to the ground to build sailing ships and homes.

Later, the line served to carrying grain and wood products from the west and wood products via the port in **Parry Sound, Georgian Bay.** This route also brought most of the **tourists** to the park inin the early days, to the park when roads were few and muddy.

The **Highland Inn** on **Cache Lake** was the main depot and focal point duringin the 1910s - 20's. With the widening of the **Welland Canal** and the closing of an unstable trestle bridge near **Cache Lake,** service decreased. Now split into two lines, the railway it operated until it closedr in **1959.**

Bracebridge RMC – Park/MTB Trail

Hwy 11, N. of Bracebridge

Length – 17 km (approx.)

90% double-track path
10% single-track

Elevation – Trails are level by the parking lot and descend to river. At the south end is a large hill to climb.

Terrain – A loamy, peaty path with a few gravel-and-stone mixed parts on hills.

Skill – Advanced for Park rides; Easy for the MTB crowd, for who new trails are coming.

Traffic – Light use by local hikers and a few cyclists. Active Nordic skiing area in winter.

Maps – Map at trailhead, as well as signposts.

Facilities – Parking lots, with outhouses and benches on trail.

Highlights – Plenty of bridges over both river and rapids; check where you may swim in the river.

Trail Fee – Free

Phone – None.

Website – Muskoka Trails Council, BRMC Facebook page

Similar Trails – Awenda, Sauble, Northumberland

Local Clubs – MORCA, a new MTB club.

Access – Take a quick right just off the Hwy, and watch for the entrance **2.5 km north of the Hwy 117 turnoff.** There is only one sign, posted mere seconds from the turnoff, so start hitting the brakes as soon as you see it—it comes up suddenly, and if the highway is busy I find this a tad dangerous.

There are 2 parking lots a minute or so into the park.

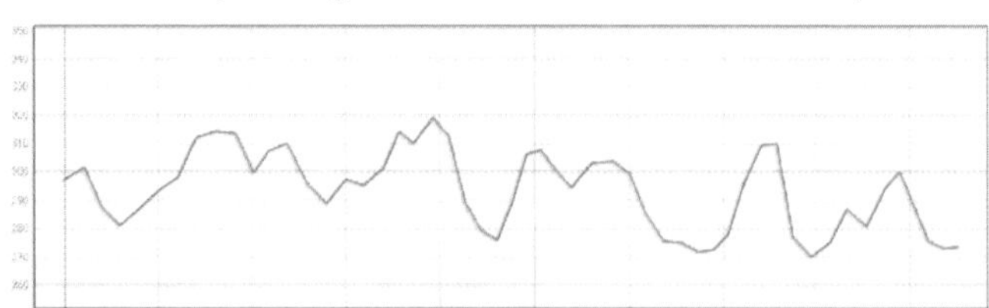

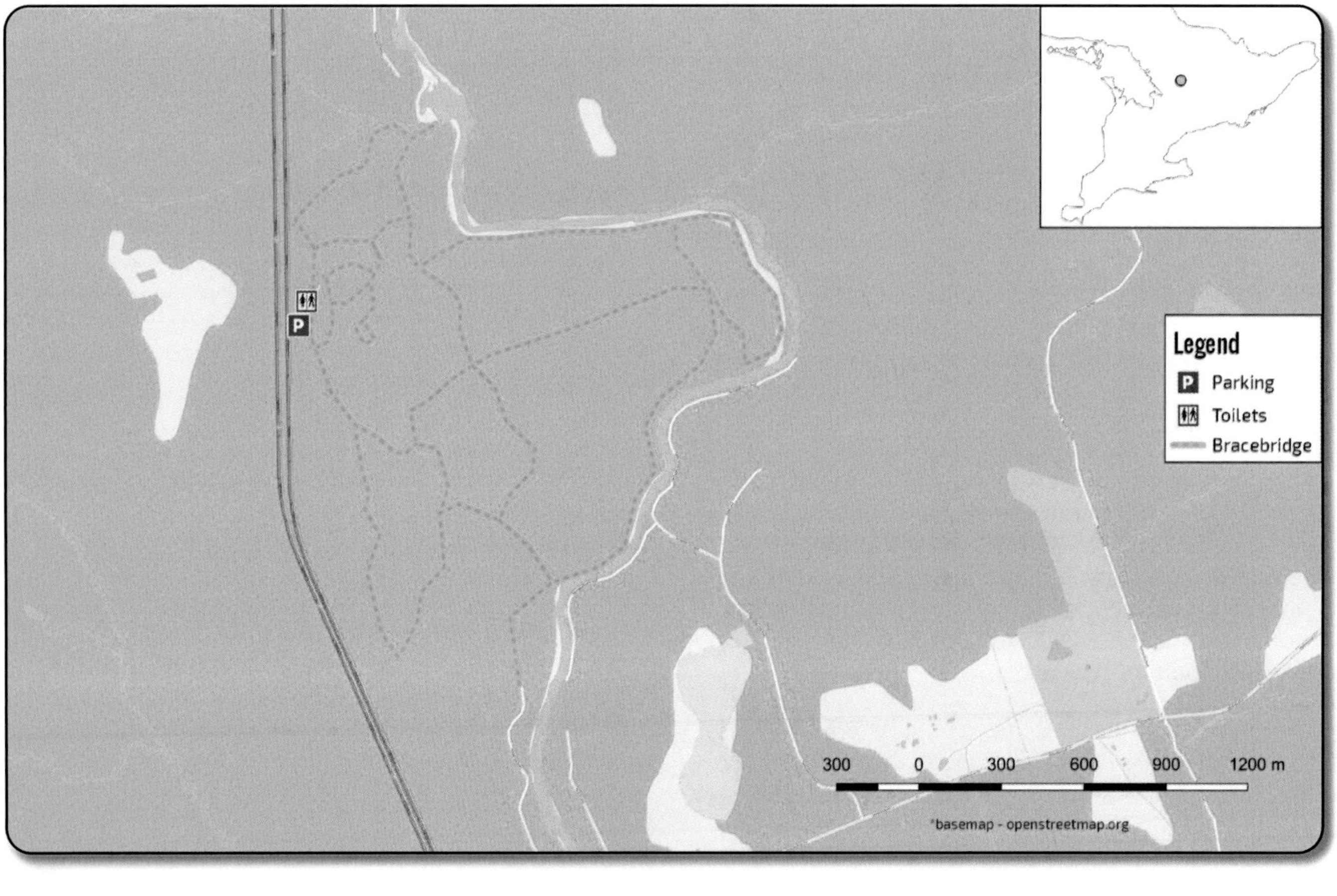

Legend
P Parking
Toilets
Bracebridge

300 0 300 600 900 1200 m

*basemap - openstreetmap.org

Review:

For those of you heading to cottage country, a stop at the **Bracebridge Resource Management Centre** for a quick spin with the family makes for a great outing.

These **17 km** of loops are basically **gently winding access roads** through the woods, making their way down to the **Muskoka River.**

The trail is rated between being an **Advanced Park Trail** and an **Easy Mountain Bike ride.** No tricky maneuvers or daring feats necessary, but **wider hybrid bike tires** are suggested. The trail is never crowded, with locals occasionally dropping by to hike or walk their dogs.

You will encounter a few **wooden bridges** and some **benches** to stop at by the river. There is a mix of gravel and stone in sections, with mainly peaty loam soil along which to navigate.

There are a few **soggy spots**, but I should think most of the ride drains well. As for the bugs, well, it depends; there were little on my visit late in the summer, but be ready!

Nothing too strenuous on this trail until you go up the **gravel hill** at the south end; most may walk it, or perhaps a **counter-clockwise** route may be the better ride direction.

It is well-signed and impossible to get too lost. Other than that I find it a fun little run right by the highway, but it should be noted the entrance is tricky to find.

Do not miss the entrance, or you are in for one long loop around with a rather large U-turn up and around and back down to the interchange.

Going back south requires you to drive up the highway to the crossover a few kilometres up the road.

Duck Chutes are small rapids that can be seen from afar on the northern loop.

It is worth mentioning that across the highway, when most head south, there is a picnic spot by **High Falls** at the **Hwy 117** turnoff. Here, you can see very **impressive waterfalls** any time of the year.

I am not sure if **Fatbikes** are allowed in the winter, as this is also a popular location to cross-country ski, but I should think the paths are wide enough for both. (Just stay off the tracks!)

Recently, **a new MTB club** has been formed, MORCA, and they are cutting a new mountain bike trail! I saw some photos of rocky fun stuff, and that's enough of an invitation for me to revisit. You?

(Also, can someone *please* give this place a more imaginative name than the Bracebridge Resource Management Centre?!)

Minnesing – MTB/Park Trail

Hwy 60, Algonquin Park

Length – 23 km

70% hiking trail
30% double-track access roads

Elevation – A wide path that ascends upwards, with a long run back down and large, rolling hills.

Terrain – Mostly smooth soil with rocky inclines, lots of muddy patches, and a few wooden bridges in need of repair; the back loop is less-used and overgrown.

Skill – Intermediate MTB; Advanced Park rider.

Traffic – Quiet with the occasional bike or hikers, as well as Nordic skiers and people snowshoeing in the winter. Wildlife? A bear bell might be a good thought.

Maps – Located at trailhead, with a few rather old signs at junctures on the trail.

Facilities – A large parking lot with outhouses, as well as a cabin with a wood stove at the trailhead, bike rentals in the summer on Hwy 60.

Highlights – Enjoy as much wilderness, and solitude, as you can handle.

Trail Fee – Park day passes, or overnight camping passes, are available.

Phone – 705 633 5572

Website – Ontario Parks, Algonquin Provincial Park

Similar Trails – Haliburton, Fanshawe, Wildwood

Local Clubs – None

Access – In **Algonquin Park** , near **Cache Lake** and **Canisbay Lake.** Take the dirt road north for a few minutes, until you reach the large parking lot and cabin. The trailhead is north of the parking lot, on the right side of the cabin.

(Note: The trail is used by skiers in the winter, and Fatbikes are welcome.)

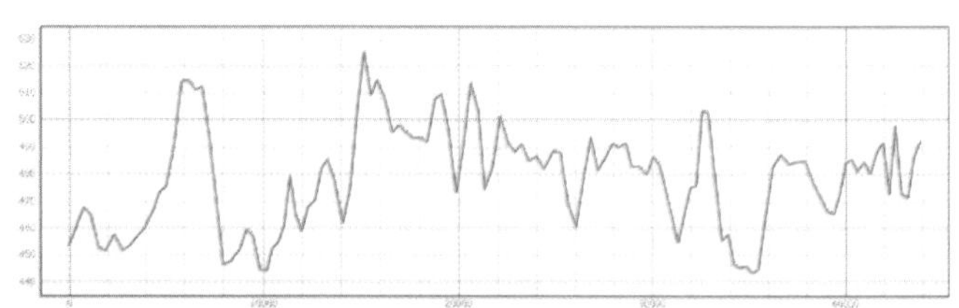

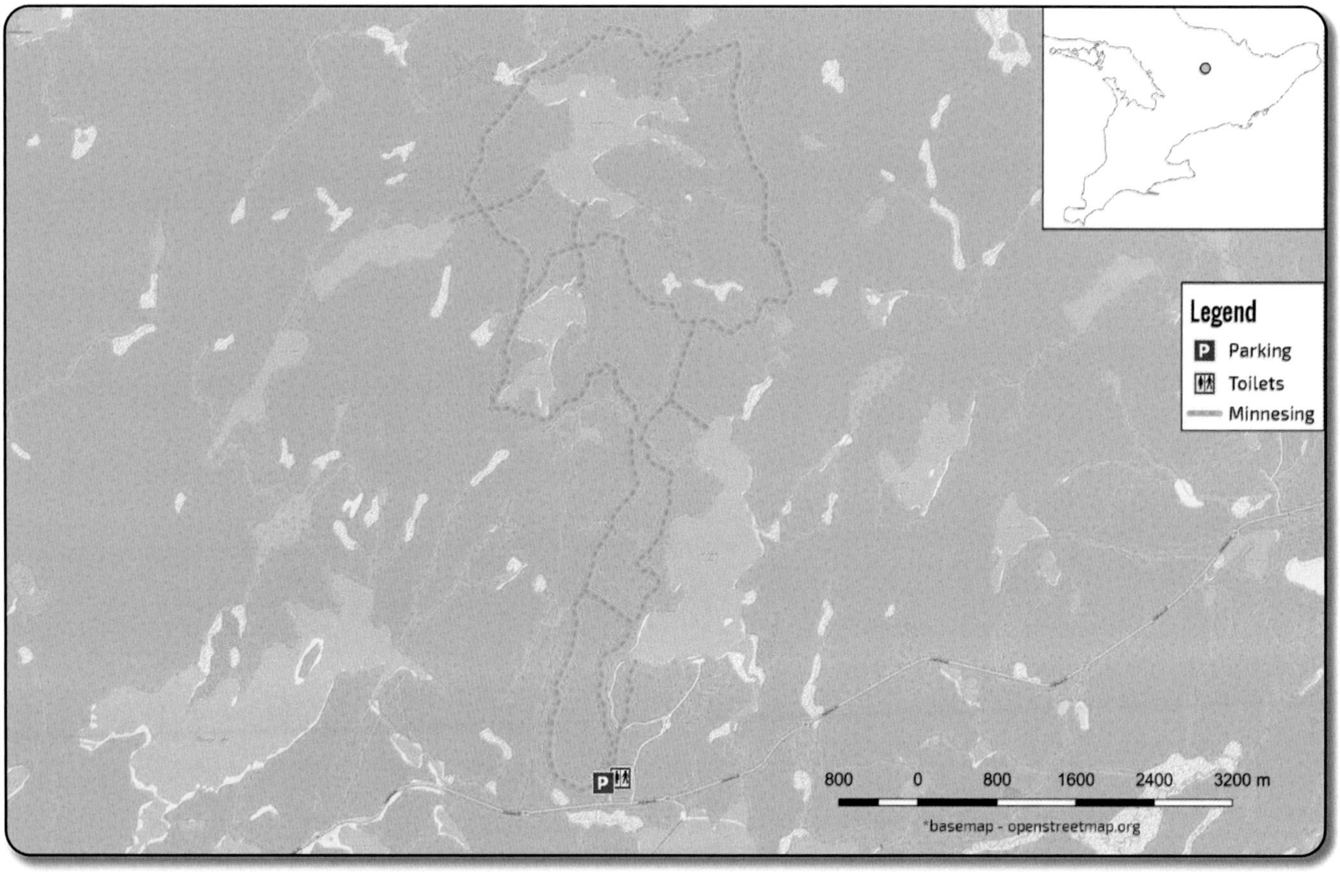

Review:

The **Minnesing** trail in **Algonquin Provincial Park** offers cyclists a challenging, **cross-country** style ride through the wilderness.

It has long consisted of **hiking loops** that are now officially also **MTB trails.** Bikers will experience a **long and fast forest** ride, mainly along single-track hiking paths.

There are four loops to choose from, each **5** to **23 km long** with shortcuts.

As with many hiking trails, **erosion is a problem** and over the years water has washed away the soil from the steeper inclines, revealing rounded **rocks and boulders.**

The flat sections remain a **fast, smooth ride on a black-soil base** with not too many roots. When you can **find a line** between the rocks and roots, **most hills are easy enough to climb**.

There are **many large muddy patches** at the **bottom of hills.** It would be nice if there were more boardwalks to cross the ooze in the future, but maybe it's all part of the experience.

There are a few small, old signs marking the trails, although I doubt you will come across any other side trails to get lost on.

By mid-July the bugs are tolerable—if you keep moving.

trails to get lost on. By mid-July the bugs are tolerable —if you keep moving.

We did find a **shortcut** on the second loop that was so overgrown we had to **hike-a-bike** up it. While it did bring us back, we took plenty of pounding as the trail is peppered with **large, round gravel** and **rocks.**

We exited the loop, on the **west side** of the parking lot by the cabin. This is **an old road** that, many years ago, took **tourists** to a **lodge** from the **train depot;** there is no sign of that lodge now.

Although it is fast on the way back, this is definitely no fun to climb, so I recommend taking the trail on the east side to head in.

I rate the skill level of this trail as **Intermediate MTB** and **Advanced Park ride.**

It's perfect for those who want **wilderness, adventure,** and **mileage.** This can be a fast, yet long journey, so be prepared and tell someone where you're heading. Frequented by few, you may not see anyone on you trek.

For those into **Bikepacking**, this is the place for you; pack your tent and make it a weekend!

I've only completed the first two loops, but have heard the outer **12 km** loop at **Callighen's Corners** is harder to manage as it is less frequented and likely you will be

doing a bit of bush wack'n. Certainly, it's a ride to **prove yourself** if you are motivated enough!

The last few years this large back loop has been **closed**, so call the gatehouse and check beforehand if you are planning to include this on your ride.

Sadly, it seems a lack of trail management (and imagination) has led to little ridership. **Algonquin Park** is such a huge area with so much potential, yet there is very little choice for the MTB crowd. Why?

In the winter, the **Minnesing Trail** can easily get a metre of snow, but a few Nordic skiers and snowshoe tracks help pack it down. There is no grooming, so hope they visit or otherwise your **Fatbike** will get stuck.

Seguin – Rail/MTB Trail

Parry Sound to Kearney

Length – 80+ km (one way)

95% rail trail
5% roads, crossings, detours

Elevation – This route is not as flat as most rail lines, and it dips down to cross smaller bridges.

Terrain – A crushed-stone base with larger rail bedding rocks, it is rather sandy in areas with large puddles after a rain; rock cuts for the MTB rider.

Skill – Advanced for Rail Trail riders, Easy for the MTB crowd.

Traffic – Busy on summer weekends, with bicyclists, hikers, horseback riders, and ATVs (main users), as well as snowmobiles in winter.

Maps – Adequate signage at gates, and the post markers along the trail have been improved.

Facilities – Parking, food, and washrooms can be found in the towns of Parry Sound, Sprucedale, and Kearney, as well as at Hwy 400 and Oastler Park.

Highlights – A scenic, hillier ride with rock cuts and wooden bridges. Enjoy the falls and the ghost town of Seguin Falls, as well as wetlands, many creeks, and farmland.

Trail Fee – Free for non-motorized use.

Phone – 888 587 3762

Website – Park to Park

Similar Trail – Algonquin, North Simcoe, Two Lakes

Local Clubs – Bike Muskoka

Access – A few good access points may be found at:

- **Parry Sound Harbour** at **Glen Burney Rd.**
- **Hwy 400**, approximately 10 km south of **Parry Sound** at **Horseshoe Lake Rd.**
- **Orville** community centre; trail starts 400 m east.
- **Seguin Falls** at **Hwy 518 N** and **Nipissing Rd. E**; roadside parking **Nipissing Rd.**
- **Sprucedale** at **Hwy 518 N** & **Stisted Rd.** S; street parking

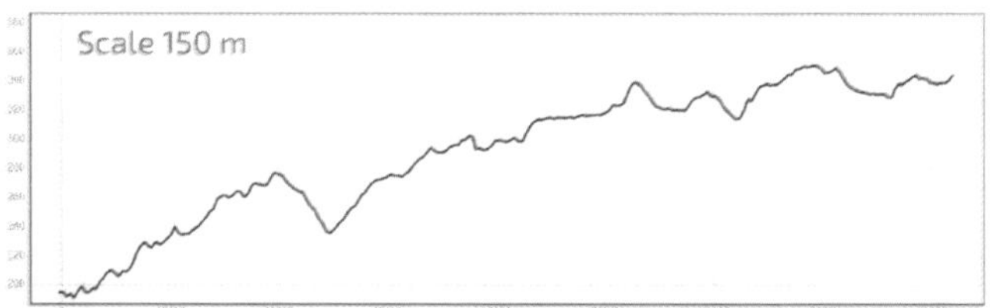

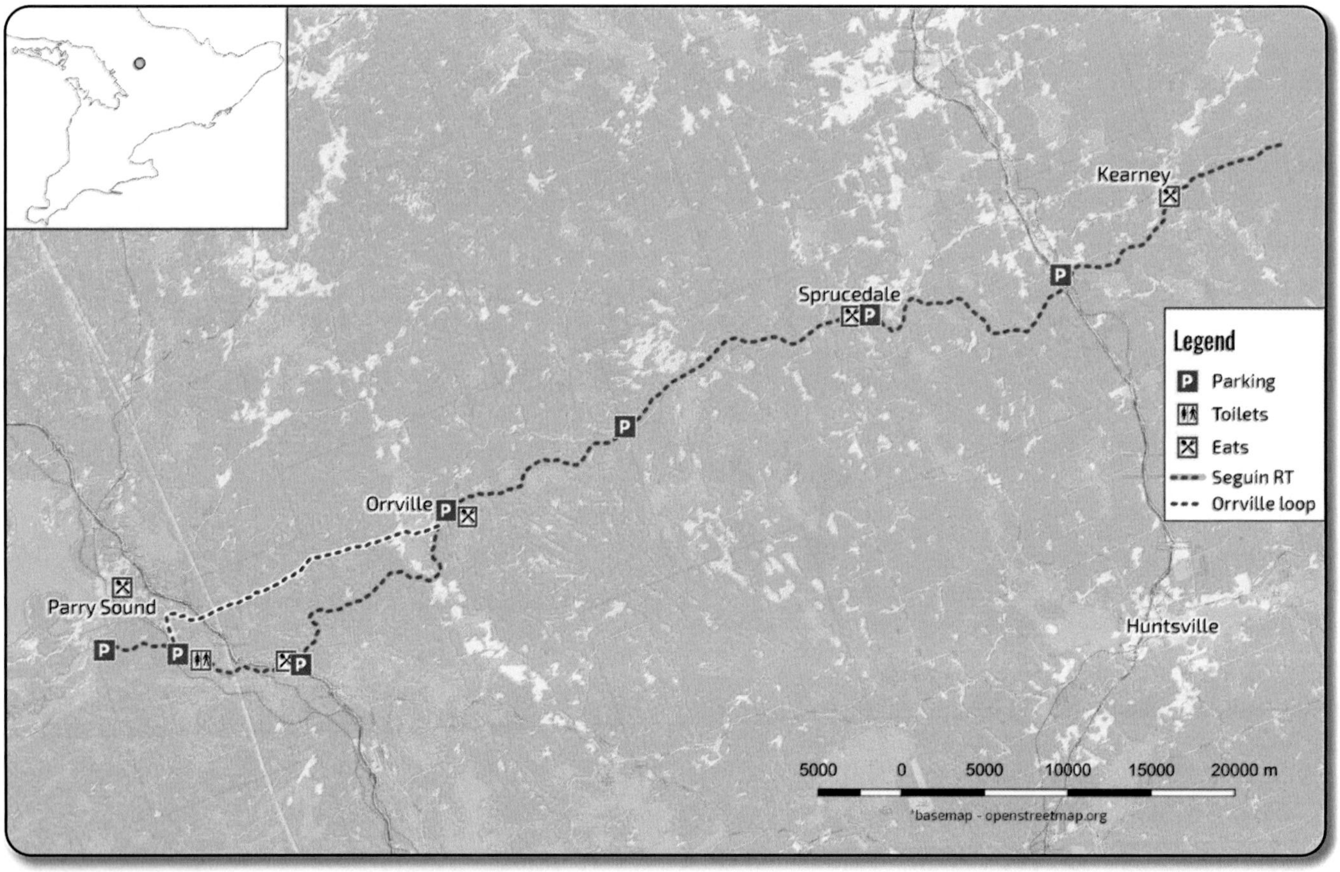

Kearney
Sprucedale
Orrville
Parry Sound
Huntsville

Legend
Parking
Toilets
Eats
Seguin RT
Orrville loop

5000 0 5000 10000 15000 20000 m

*basemap - openstreetmap.org

Review:

Starting at **Georgian Bay,** at the **Parry Sound** harbour, this Rail Trail passes over **Hwy 400** and crosses **Hwy 518** many times, leading to **Hwy 11** and eventually fading into the bush somewhere past **Kearney**.

This is not your average **Rail Trail**, although it is well-maintained and gets plenty of use by **ATVs and snowmobiles.** However, this causes the terrain to get chewed up and dusty, with large rocks and loose gravel everywhere.

Different sections have **large puddles** (more like ponds) that are wide and deep, and you have no choice but to ride through. Expect flooding in the spring.

This is not to say all of the route is challenging. Other sections appear to be smoother, but not for long. I did encounter **large sandy sections** that skinny tires could not manage. The terrain is best suited for **MTBs, Fatbikes,** or a good **hybrid bike**.

Therefore, I would rate this as an **Advanced Rail Trail** ride compared to the mellow routes in the south.

Most Rail Trails are rather flat except for here, where the original bridges were replaced with small wooden ones at a lower grade. This gives riders a **short hill** down in order to cross and head back up the other side.

At **80+ km one way**, this is a long trail, and you need to choose just a section of it for a day's ride.

I suggest a **43 km** loop I have done a few times. Head out from **Hwy 400** to **Orville,** then back on **Hwy 518**. At **Oastler Park Dr.** ride south to meet up with the trail before again crossing the **400**. I found the road traffic not busy on the return, and the paved shoulders on **Oastler** were surprisingly spacious.

Another good starting point is at the south end of **Parry Sound**, with an option to make a loop using **Oastler Park Dr.**, but this time head the other way through town for a short but hilly loop.

On the east side is an excellent place to pick up the trail, in the town of **Sprucedale.** Unfortunately, I am not so sure about **Kearney;** it could be over-grown and swampy.

For the more **adventurous MTB rider**, this can be a great **Bikepacking** trip. Take your tent, pack some food, and make it a three to four-day trek from end to end. (I saw signs of scenic, rustic campsites along the route.)

Oastler Lake Provincial Park is on the trail, providing a few more comforts and a good base for completing the loops mentioned.

Consider going in the autumn when there is less traffic and bugs, and the fall colours are out. Either way, enjoy this wild, rugged part of northern Ontario—start planning!

History – The railway was built by the former **Ottawa, Arnprior and Parry Sound Railway** in **1891**, funded by lumber baron **J.R. Booth**.

Trains carried timber from **Ottawa** to **Georgian Bay** for ship-building, and grain was sent eastward until **1933** when the **Cache Two-Rivers** bridge needed repair.

Being too expensive to fix, rails west of the bridge were abandoned and removed by the **1950s** to sell as scrap.

What is a Bicycle Park Path?

I think we can all envision what cycling a Park path is like, although I will not just be stating the obvious here. I want to mention how I personally **define the category,** as well as the **finer points** of Park trail riding for the reviews included in this guide.

I hope this will be informative for anyone new to cycling, as well as for any tourists visiting Canada.

I interchange the terms **trail** and **path** when talking about Park bike routes. They essentially mean the same thing, although I view a **"path" as wider**, about the width of a car.

Speaking of cars, they are seldom seen on these paths or trails (except for the odd detour), so that is **one less concern**. For my reviews, routes need to be more than **85% off-road, and most are 100% car-free.**

Park-type rides are split into **two sub-types: City Park** and **Forest Park** bike riding.

City Park riding is easy, with simple, beginner routes through a city park locals will all know.

Forest Park riding is for more experienced Park cyclists who want to go out of town and perhaps try a woodlot with rougher terrain, on a path that has few amenities.

Most trails do not loop back. This is important to note, so doing a shorter ride often requires returning down the same path. You can sometimes connect with other trails while working your way back, making it a longer route. Note that almost all routes have **two-way traffic**, so be aware of who may be around the bend.

What is it Like to Cycle a Park Path in Ontario?

A path running through a **City Park** usually has gentle turns to keep you interested (roads are so straight!). Sometimes, paths share old roads or rail beds that are no longer in use—you are usually able to tell.

Many Park trails follow alongside a creek or a river. This makes for a gentle incline, with few hills of any length.

These rides are typically in **well-manicured parklands**, with cut grass, flowerbeds, open fields, and a few random trees planted here and there.

You may pass by benches, picnic tables, baseball diamonds, and soccer, football, or cricket fields. Play sets offer places to stop for the little ones to go wild, and watch for exercise stations to get a total work out for yourself.

Some more popular paths now also have bike-repair stations. A nice touch if you have to tighten something or put some air in the tires.

I would have to say there are overall never too many washrooms on any given route. So, if you think you need to take a pit stop, do so. (The same goes for water fountains and snack bars.) I am, however, starting to see new water-bottle filling stations, which is a great idea.

A few other observations I have made is that Park trails can be busy on sunny weekends with not just other cyclists, but other challenging obstacles namely people, kids, and dogs. Some can be quite oblivious to cyclists coming up from behind, so ringing a small bell is a good idea or call out "on your left" as you pass (on the left).

In my experience, if you see someone roller blading, give them **lots of space**. If you hear a dog running after you, stop and stand behind your bike and use it as a barrier until they settle down.

The terrain of a Park path through the city will usually be all **smooth, paved asphalt**. Sometimes, especially at the ends where it peters out, trails turn to **finely crushed stone** or smooth soil.

Bridges take riders over waterways to keep them connected to trails beyond. Some are rather pretty and well worth the time to take a picture.

Not all city rides are manicured or landscaped, as some have a more wilderness feel with small woodlots and ravines to pass through.

The other type of trail is a **Forest Park path** that goes through even more of a **natural wooded setting.**

The terrain of these paths will be mainly **smooth soil** or **stone dust,** with sections of **sand and gravel.** There may also be **leaves, woodchips, and the odd rock, patch of mud, puddle, or animal burrow holes** to negotiate.

Some locations have hills which are not as steep as MTB hills, but they can be fair-sized inclines. None should take more than a minute to climb, however, as Ontario is not a mountainous province.

This kind of Park trail ride may also be at a **mountain bike (MTB) location,** as there is overlap between more **advanced Park riding** routes and **beginner MTB riding**.

Who knows? You may eventually take to it and start riding the basic MTB side trails. These are called **single-track trails** that loop in and out from the **main, wider access paths** you ride.

If you choose to ride beyond these Park trails, I would recommend using a **mountain bike** to navigate the twisty loops safely. You will better enjoy the experience, as well as be on a more solid bike with **fatter tires, shocks, better brakes, and lower gears for climbing.**

Who is Suited for a Park Trail Ride?

Well, *everyone* is the quick answer, but let's divide the masses into two camps:

#1 City Park

- Bike owners who are fair-weather riders and cycle a few times a year
- Beginners of all ages who are learning new skills and do not want to encounter road vehicles
- Commuters going to work or to shop
- Citizens and tourists exploring the city

#2 Forest Park

- Riders with an Intermediate skill level as a Park cyclist
- Cyclists wishing to improve bike skills and endurance
- Naturalists seeking a peaceful environment with some adventure
- Day-trippers from out of town, as well as vacation riders
- Advanced Park riders trying out the MTB world

City Park cyclists have few challenges, an **easy journey,** and plenty of time to unwind. They enjoy the weather and like to see the scenery drift by, far away from the office and dirty dishes.

This is a recreational pastime to meet up with friends, or to get the kids out of the house—NOT a race.

It is also a rather safe route to cycle, with no cars and easy terrain to negotiate. Yet, do **watch out** for kids and dogs zipping across your path.

One of the main **causes of accidents** are **riders chatting to each other** and not paying attention to what is ahead. (Yes, this has happened to me.) Also, when the leaves fall, they can hide nasty potholes and crevasses that will send you flying, and may be slippery after a rain.

Riders may also encounter **stairs** in order to cross bridges or to get up and out of a valley, but otherwise little biking skills beyond the basics are needed to stay the course.

A **Forest Park** ride, on the other hand, gets into what I rate as an **Intermediate Park ride.** It is good for seasoned road/path cyclists, where added skill and leg power are needed.

A forest setting is also good for those who want some **adventure** in a **peaceful environment**. You might even see some wildlife, like a deer, a hawk or a rabbit.

For wooded lots out of the city, it is a good idea to plan a day or weekend trip to discover Ontario. The paths also offer an excellent reason to stop and stretch those legs after sitting in the car while on a road trip.

As recreational cycling grows in popularity in Ontario, many paved paths can be ridden in the **winter** as long as you dress for it and have the right bike I love that many cities are starting to clear the snow!

What do I Need to Bring?

While riding in the city, one need not be totally **self-sufficient.** (Although it's better if you are.) The routes are usually within walking distance of a means of getting your bike repaired or for taking transit or a taxi back home. In the city, you can find many **places to eat** with a quick search on your phone.

If getting out of the city for a **Forest Park** ride, one needs to pack for the occasion and have a plan. Few forest rides have anything more than a **parking lot** and an **outhouse**.

Bring plenty of **water, snacks, a rain jacket, a bike tool kit, a pump,** and a **spare tube.**

On most trails, maps and signage are adequate, but reviewing your chosen location on your phone will help. I also recommend saving an **offline map** on your phone, or to print out a **paper map** as **cell reception can be limited** in rural areas. **GPS** will always work, if the clouds are not too thick.

Up north in the bush, having a **bear bell** might be smart as they do not like to be surprised! Or, keep talking, singing, or reciting Shakespeare to warn them you are coming.

Being visible is never a bad thing while on a bike. After all, you are a **thin object moving quickly.** Cars and people (or hunters) cannot easily see you if **dressed in black** and on a **black bike**. I know black is the trend, but it's not helping. (Why do you think road workers wear safety vests?)

Wear some **bright colours** folks! Do you have **lights** and **reflectors** on your bike for when it gets dark?

Riding local park paths with our parents or friends is how many of us started cycling. Why not carry on and **explore other trail areas** in your own neighbourhood, town, and province.

It's a great way to be a **local tourist,** and bicycling is perfect as you can see plenty at a leisurely pace. It's not too fast, like a speeding car, or too slow, like walking. There are no hassles with parking, gas, or traffic jams—I love it!

Consider combining your planned route with public transit routes to connect. Find the **local subway stops, GO Train stations,** or other forms of public transit to keep it simple and **make the ride stress free.**

And isn't that the way your day of cycling should be? Totally stress free!

If you enjoyed your ride we'd love to hear about it back on the OBT site! Go there and **leave a ride review.**

What is a Rail Trail?

What were once railway lines, many are now **public recreational trails.** As railroads abandoned many of their extra routes, local governments and outdoor groups took over the redevelopment of these transportation corridors.

With the tracks removed, railway beds are then often **re-paved with crushed stone** and marked with **signage** along the way.

The more popular Rail Trails are **well-maintained, drain well,** and have an even grade. Others are **more wild** and **overgrown** with little signage, larger gravel, and tall grasses. They could be missing a bridge or have fallen trees blocking your path.

Rail trails are **free to use, easy to cycle, and long in length**, but best of all are far removed from the chaos of the city.

As multi-use paths, you will share these routes with **hikers, joggers, horseback riders,** and **cross-country skiers.** Some Rail Trails **ban motorized vehicles,** while others allow **ATV** and **snowmobile traffic.**

What is it Like to Cycle a Rail Trail?

Cycling a Rail Trail is a **unique** and **different** experience than other forms of trail riding. Because trains needed **gradual slopes** to climb hills, and it was always cheaper to lay straight tracks, your path will be similar throughout its length.

This makes for an **easy cycle** along **flat, wide,** and **straight paths.** Any turns along the route will be an even, wide arc since trains need broad curves to stay on the tracks at higher speeds.

With this level ground, there is **little shifting to do**, so find your groove and start cruising.

What you will find are **quiet, car-free routes** that take you through **woodlots, across farm fields,** and behind **homes and cottages**.

You are also riding a strip of history and may see signs of long-forgotten industries, farms, and machinery along the way.

Nature is nearby as you ride through forests, cross open **wetlands,** and pass through **rock cuts.** You may even see a bear, a deer, or a beaver dam.

Some Rail Trails also offer opportunities for some good fishing or a place to pitch a tent.

Most trails are overgrown, with trees casting lots of shade. However, there are still times the **hot sun** and **blowing wind** will be present along the stretches of open farm fields.

Often, **old train bridges** and **underpasses** are still in place—which is pretty cool. Some sections of old rail line may have been sold off to farmers or land developers before the trail was created.

This, unfortunately, will create a small **detour down side roads,** and at other times a bridge could be missing or be replaced with a smaller wooden version. Railroads often tore up the track and removed the iron bridges, to sell as scrap.

Rail Trails are never crowded so there is plenty of privacy and elbow room for your bicycle. You might see one rider every fifteen minutes or so, coming the other way.

Some trails are barely used, **undiscovered** relics that are use more by the local ATV and snowmobile crowd.

Who is Suited for a Bicycle Rail Trail Ride?

There are two types of bike riders that would typically enjoy Rail Trails.

#1 Casual Cyclist

Those who ride easy park paths on a **hybrid bicycle.** They want no hills, and nothing tricky to navigate. These bike riders simply want to **cruise with friends** or family on a car-free route, maybe do **10 to 15 km,** then turn around and head back.

#2 Mountain Bike Rider

The cross-country rider who wishes to cover **40 to 80 km** in a day at a **faster pace** and is looking for an adventure on a car-free route. This could be a multi-day **Bikepacking** outing, where riders can connect with other trails or dirt roads to do a loop. They would carry supplies, similar to **Bike Touring** on a road trip.

I find Rail Trails are good for a **relaxing, effortless pedal to ponder** and **reflect** on things, or to think of nothing at all. To some this can be boring as it is nothing like mountain biking, which need your **full attention.**

They are also a great way to just cruise and **get away from your troubles,** and all your tasks back home. Thoughts can wander to plans of future projects, trips, ice cream and so on....

What do I Need to Bring on a Rail Trail Bike Ride?

Since most Rail Trails pass few towns that have amenities or bike shops, **you need to be somewhat self-sufficient.** As always, have your **repair kit** with you for flats or mechanical fixes.

It is possible to use a **road bike** to ride well-maintained routes with a **crushed-stone base,** but you may **get a flat** or **lose control** with those **skinny tires.**

A better choice is a **hybrid bike** or **MTB** that has **fatter tires** to manage the **large, pointy rocks** and **sand;** a must on trails like the Seguin. If **ATVs** use the trail, expect larger rocks and ruts where MTB bike shocks can dampen the pounding.

Pack lots of water and snacks. Some routes have **towns with small diners** and variety stores. Do check on this beforehand, because Ontario is a large place and these spots are far between with varying open hours.

Bring **layered clothing,** as the weather could change quickly with no rain shelter nearby. **Bugs are sometimes a problem** in the spring or during wet summers, especially when travelling through wetlands.

Since **Rail Trails are pretty wide**, picking up an itch from **poison ivy** or a **tick** is reduced if you stick to the centre of the path and avoid tall grasses. That said, lesser- used routes may be grown in.

Getting lost is not easy to do on this wide path, but a detour is sometimes not obvious as it cuts behind a silo, warehouse or temporarily turns into part of a side road.

Using **your phones GPS** can help tell you how far you have gone and how far you have to go. As some of these old railways go **straight on forever** you can start to wonder if you will ever reach your destination!

Rail Trail Bicycle Routes in Ontario

Having been here first, railway lines cut across Ontario in all directions. Many go straight **into town along waterfronts** and through now-populated neighbourhoods. These trains once carried people from town to town, and goods to port and to local enterprises.

Tracks also passed by **farms** in order to ship their produce, or at **mines** for their ore and **sawmills** for loads of timber.

Although much of this is now history, while riding a trail you can often **figure out what transpired** and why they laid the track as they did.

Often, railways had to **contend with costs** and trains need mellow grades and wide turns. I find it interesting on rides to note where they did put the track; what choices were made to get around the water or go over it, or to blast through the rock versus take the long way round.

The challenges of the rocky **Canadian Shield** were many, with **hilly terrain** dotted by **numerous lakes**. At times this required **switchbacks**, **bridges** to span valleys and rivers, or filling in **soggy wetlands** to pass straight through.

If a farm got there first, surveyors might have found a cheaper route then paid for rights to access the land. Placing track along a **marsh** or through **ravines** that could not be farmed was possible, although more costly to lay track.

But trains were a business, and in its glory days, before cars and trucks, they served the country well. Ships lost business to new rail networks, but eventually trains lost out to roads.

Now, we can cycle and enjoy the same routes while reflecting on the past.

Have a great ride, and give yourself LOTS of time

Cycling: Plan to Have Fun, as Fun is the Plan

10 Ways to Enjoy a Better Bike Ride

Enjoying your next bike adventure could be a spontaneous, pleasant endeavour—or maybe not.

To really better the odds of FUN all around, a bit of planning is suggested.

*If you are better prepared, the outcome of your next bike ride becomes more **predictable** and the way **you** want it—and not left to chance.*

Because cycling is an outdoor sport, and at times a solo recreational activity, some preparation also offers rewards.

A little research, regular bike maintenance, proper packing, and picking the right trail on the right day is a good start.

*Simply rushing out the door, eager to hit the trail, may set you back. A little **front-end prep** avoids an enjoyable bike ride potentially becoming a miserable, **short-lived outing.***

So, here is a handy list of ten things every rider should review before heading out on their next bike trek.

***Mentally check** them off every time you go out, and the odds are good you will be boasting about it over a beer—rather than crying into it!*

#1 Weather

Do not overlook this, which is the **most essential part** of your adventure. Without knowing the **local weather** for the next few hours, you risk everything as **weather is a deal-breaker** if things get ugly.

Find a **reliable weather service** and be able to interpret the forecast correctly. This sets up your trip by knowing what kind of clothes to wear, as well as what food and water requirements are needed.

Knowing the weather allows you to decide if it is better to ride early to avoid the **afternoon heat** or a coming storm. In the colder months, you may wish to wait for the day to warm up before setting out.

Cycling outside while the weather is fine is a great experience. But if the need for a ride is in you on a questionable day, knowing what you are up against helps you manage the nastier elements.

Blocking the wind, sun, rain, or snow, as well as keeping warm/cool, and dry are all good objectives. Failing in this can shorten your ride and put you off, or worse, endanger your health.

On any bad-weather day, having a mechanical or personal problem can amplify the situation.

So, always check first to see if the weather is worth the packing and the two-hour drive. (Simply looking out your living-room window is not weather forecasting!)

I can't tell you how often I've set out on a scheduled club ride thinking, as I drove there, that it would be cancelled. Yet, upon arrival, the sun came out and the riding was awesome!

#2 Clothing & Shoes

Next, we need to be **comfortable** on the ride. By knowing what weather to expect, riders can dress accordingly.

Nothing is worse than **over-** or **underdressing.** Overdressing causes you to sweat, and although removing layers will help, storing them is annoying as you ride. Where do you put your jacket?

Getting too cold or too wet is even worse. Now you'll be looking for a shortcut back, if there is one, to end the misery.

Wear thin layers to regulate your body temperature. A combination of a windbreaker, fleece jacket, and undershirt of synthetic, breathable material that wicks sweat is ideal. Proper bike shorts also help in many ways, so be sure to get some.

When it gets cool, long underwear and sports pants with narrow cuffs (to avoid the chain) is suggested. Polyester socks keep your toes happy, and wool stays warm even when it gets wet.

A cotton T-shirt is okay for only the most leisurely of rides, as cotton gets heavy and feels cold when damp.

Also consider **wearing bright, colourful gear** to prevent collisions on the trail, as well as ensure hunters can see you.

Shoes should be a bit stiff, and worn with socks. For those wishing to go further and faster, buy riding shoes that clip in.

I recommend starting the ride feeling a little chilled and **underdressed**. The exercise will warm you up, especially once you hit a few hills. If it might rain bring a waterproof rain jacket; you will thank me when it pours and you still have an hour to go.

Let's add optional **bug spray** and **sunscreen** to the list. Expect those pesky, biting blackflies by June anywhere there is running water. Then in July, mosquitoes take over where there is standing water. This usually calms down from August and into the fall. Weather plays a big part in what the bug action may be like on any given day.

I refrain from coating myself in chemicals like DEET, so I apply it to my clothing first—if at all. Most of the time, I find you can outride the little critters but if you stop too long or get a flat you had better pull out the emergency bug juice!

Anyway, when in doubt bring optional attire, including a **change of clothes** that you leave in the car. After the ride, peel off the sweaty or muddy parts and enjoy more comfortable fabric for the drive back or when stopping to eat. Who knows, you may even fall in the creek and need dry clothing.

#3 Food & Water

Do not forget **fuel for the body!** Lack of food or water on the ride will slow you down and shorten your ride.

Running out of water midway through a ride on a sweltering day, or having little energy when it is cold with no "power bars" left, is going to make the rest of the ride a struggle.

Sure, you can depend on fountains and snack bars along a city Park trail, but it is not a certainty they are open at any time of the year. A ride through the woods or down a country Rail Trail has nowhere to purchase supplies, so be prepared.

Try to keep your load light, and bring water in a refillable container . Also, it's a good idea to have a reserve bottle of water or two in the car. Drink lots of water **before** you get thirsty to avoid cramps.

The warmer the weather, the more water you need. Adding electrolyte tablets to your water, or drinking Gatorade-type beverages to keep your body balanced on long trips, is also suggested.

Bring **snacks or power bars** that fare well, as heat melts chocolate and things can get awfully messy on a snack break.

Dry snack food, such as granola, cookies, power bars, and trail mix, are light and give you some quick energy. Leave the heavy fruit (apples, pears, bananas, and ice cream; I'm kidding) back at the car for your return.

Keep in mind any needs of your friends or kids, as I have too often had to ration when my son drinks all his water thirty minutes in.

So, bring extra, more than you might need. Who knows, if you get so lost or hurt it may become dinner too.

#4 Bike Maintenance

Is your bicycle fit for the coming task? You depend on your bike to get there and back efficiently and safely. If in doubt, your day trip could be in jeopardy. Either take that gamble or be prepared and better the odds of trouble-free riding.

No one wishes for a flat, or worse, a broken chain, shifter, or seat post. All these have happened to me, repeatedly. But I was ready, had a recovery plan and, for the most part, solved my problem without too much misery.

Owning a **good-quality, dependable bicycle** is the best prevention. Spend a few extra dollars for better components and lighter parts, as it leads to a more enjoyable outing.

When bike parts fit better mechanically, roll with less friction, and weigh less, riders can then go further with less effort.

Hills are a part of any ride, and some are mean and relentless. Having climbing gears and a light frame helps to overcome the climbs.

Gears that shift well are a joy, but not so much when they skip and the chain keeps dropping. Brakes need to do their job without inflicting injury.

A happy cyclist has a bicycle that fits both their body size and their weight. If you are getting aches and pains, you may need to make adjustments. The most common issue I see is too low a saddle, bring it up!

Complete a mental checklist before pulling your steed out of the shed. Do the gears shift well, are the wheels true (not warped), is there enough air in the tires? Does the **chain need cleaning**? And regularly give them a bit of lube before you head out.

Also **pack a tool kit.** And definitely ride with a spare tube, a tire-patch kit, a pump, a multi-tool, a chain-link tool, extra chain links, and zip ties. Knowing how to use them also helps.

#5 Time

Give yourself **enough time** to not rush what is supposed to be an enjoyable outing. The ride should be fun, not a race; running short on time turns it into one. Know the time the sun sets if you go late in the day.

Factor in the time needed to drive there and back, plus the city traffic. (Uggh!) Then add the additional time to change, pack, and put the bikes on the car rack.

Once at your destination, consider the time you need to get ready for the ride, the actual ride, as well as the same packing needed for the return home.

Allow for extra time as you may find more trails and stop often, or your friend is late, or the tire blows, or you're out of shape, or a bear chases you ... Ha, stuff can happen!

Now can you see how you need a large block of the day to enjoy this pastime and not rush it? If you have a family to coordinate, then extend your time even further.

May I also remind you that nothing completes the day better than an après beer and burger with the buds. Good stories from the trail abound and this takes, you got it...more time.

So, for a good time, give it lots of time!

#6 Company

If you ride solo then your own thoughts will keep you company, no issues.

Cycling with others is a **sociable** and **enjoyable experience**. It's a great way to meet up with people who share our pastime. Ride with cyclists that have the **same level of skill, endurance,** and **temperament.** When the riding group is in sync, the route and the pace flow well.

Once members start to question the route, go too fast, go too slow, stop often or never want to stop at all, the fun is over.

Who brings what, how much, when or where to stop, and for how long all need answers from the group. I do not want to make this sound too structured an activity, so call it as you see it.

Group dynamics are always at play, so you have to let everyone know what they are getting into. Avoid **surprises**, and **overdoing it**.

Casually review the route with others, and discuss expectations and timelines. Feel out the cyclists and tailor the ride to their abilities and fitness level, so everyone can stay happy to the end.

Be aware that more accidents tend to happen in groups, either among other riders or due to distractions they cause. When you get chatty on the route, **pay attention** to where you are going.

Good company on a bike ride can be the best part of the whole experience.

#7 Location

Finding the right spot to ride has to be the right fit for you, and for everyone else. You want a good experience, after all. Enough to feel satisfied, but not as though a ride will break you.

I certainly realized this after having written all these trail reviews. Doing your research and knowing what you are getting into leads to less disappointment. Expectations can be met with fewer surprises.

Are you looking for a mellow ride with the significant other or with family members?

Or are you looking for a **scenic, historic,** or **urban experience?** Do you wish for the serenity of a forest ride, or the bustling paths in the city?

Pick a location with enough **distance to suit** you and your companions, and **do not overdo it**. Kids tend to get tired and bored quickly, so make these rides short and find a playground along the way.

In the spring it is much more common to **ride too far** after hiding indoors for so long. This results in "bike butt", sore limbs, blisters, and perhaps too much sun.

Always check current conditions at trail locations before you go. Since many may take an hour or more to reach, it's wise to know of any issues like floods, special events, races, road closures or detours.

#8 Terrain

What kind of terrain do you seek? Is your **stamina,** and your bike, up to the challenge?

Getting the right mix of **distance, hills, and technical skills** is your personal preference, but the better prepared you are the more **enjoyable the outcome.**

A few steeper hills and rougher terrain can push you and improve your riding skills. Yet too much or too hard of anything will make the ride slow, and will be more of a struggle to finish.

Do not overdo it or you will take the fun out of it.

Use the right bike for the right task. Asking a delicate race bike to ride over a rough path will not only cause a flat, but expect to break it. It also would not have good control, or traction, causing you to fall often.

Avoid accidents and delays, and make sure **both the riders** and **bikes** in your group are capable.

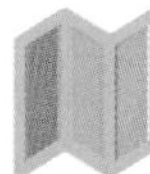

#9 Maps

Sometimes, a ride without a map is an adventure, discovering where a new trail leads. But getting lost, wasting time backtracking, and taking mystery shortcuts to "Nowheresville" can be unnerving.

Most Park rides in the city offer no problems; you are not going to feel lost for long as signposts are everywhere, and there may be other people around to confirm directions.

Country rides may need more planning and maps if you have never visited a location before.

Using a paper **map as a backup** is a good plan that does not require batteries. Also, taking a photo of the map board at the parking lot as a reference is good in a pinch.

In today's world, a cell phone with a simple mapping app can keep you on track. GPS is a free satellite signal that can be received anywhere. Note that when the weather closes in with heavy clouds or there is a dense tree canopy, it may cause a weak signal.

#10 Emergency Plan

Nothing is worse than an unexpected incident to dampen your fun.

Not that anything should happen, (and may never happen), but **considering the possibilities** of hitting your head and not remembering how to return home, or breaking a chain or leg (or both) 15 km into a ride and having to walk back helps, should the worse occur.

Telling someone where you are going and **when you should be back** is not only smart but helpful if something does go wrong. Riding with a **buddy** or in a **group** also gives better odds to recover from mishaps.

Carrying a **cell phone** has reduced the small risk of getting stuck, and waiting and wondering when someone else will pass by.

Having just read my list, I hope you can see that planning wisely and for maximum enjoyment reduces the chance for accidents. The ultimate buzz kill is not being able to ride at all, for **months**, as you recover.

Now, you are all set! As with most things, a well laid-out plan promises much success. You be the judge of how much you want to structure your ride and how much to leave to chance.

A little element of discovery and adventure always needs to be in the mix. (But I think you will get that, regardless.)

Enjoy your well-earned recreational time doing one of the things you love—cycling. I am sure you already have some of these tips on your mental prep list, so enough reading.

Keep the FUN in cycling... off you go!

About the Author

Dan Roitner has been riding red bicycles since he was a kid. In search of unknown trails, he bought his first mountain bike in 1985.

By 2000 he formed a MTB riding group for the Toronto Bicycling Network and lead rides for over ten years.

Those trail rides took him to new places, and eventually led him to share his knowledge with the cycling community on **Ontario Bike Trails.com,** a website he both produces and manages.

Dan's curiosity for finding new trails, combined with a love of cycling, map-making, photography, and a background as a multimedia artist, helps bring it all together—and keeps him busy.

He also produces a sister site, for winter Nordic ski and snowshoe trails called **Ontario Ski Trails.com**.

Based near the Beaches on the east side of Toronto, Dan can always find a reason to get out, leave town, and find a trail to enjoy.

This is the second edition of his first book, and others are sure to follow....

Contact Dan at *staff@ontariobiketrails.com*

Acknowledgements

The whole process of publishing this book has been a long one. I need to thank many people along this journey, and the most important are as follows.

First, my parents, who bought my first red bike and helped me stay upright.

I have greatly appreciated the company of all the friends I have met over the years, while riding with cycling clubs and those who joined me in search of new trails.

A big thanks to the staff and many volunteers, whose vision to create and maintain the bicycle trails in Ontario makes all this possible and keeps things enjoyable for everyone.

I wish to also thank the open-source community for creating Wordpress, Qgis, and Xnview, and to creativecommons.org, openstreetmap.org, and opentopomap.org for giving access to free tools and content to aid in creating this book. Free, (but not bug-free), I eventually managed to get the job done!

Thanks go to my sister, and to Jennifer Dinsmore Editorial, for copy-editing my text; it was definitely required.

Most importantly, many thanks to my son Trevor and my wife Teresa for their support and patience on the home front. They followed me down many a trail, scouting all over Ontario, with faith I could find our way back.

BONUS eBOOK OFFER

As a supplement to the printed book, I am offering you a **free extra bonus** download of the **PDF eBook** version as well. Go to a private page on the OBT site at **https://ontariobiketrails.com/sdm_downloads/bonus-ebook/**

Once there, to get the password, you will be asked a question that refers to this book. Enter the secret password to download the 15 MB PDF file.

Since the paperback book has no means of using hyperlinks to get you quickly to websites, you can then use links in the eBook to go directly to them. Or through my OBT website **ontariobiketrails.com** you can stay current and connect online with other resources.

Made in the USA
Lexington, KY
04 September 2019